gray horses

Amsterdam Park
Montpelier Ave.
83
Montpelier
Rarebit Rd.
Chestnut St.
7B
X17
Oxford St.
22
Grove Cemetery
Evelyn Ave.
101
Evelyn

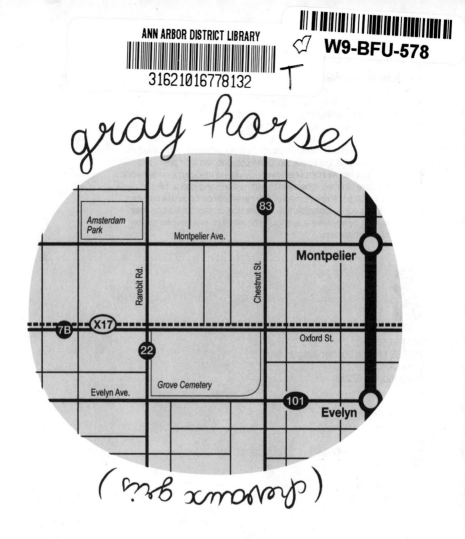

(chevaux gris)

Written + drawn by Hope Larson.
French translation by Rodolphe Guenoden + Laurent Orseau.

Published by Oni Press, Inc.

Joe Nozemack, publisher
James Lucas Jones, editor in chief
Randal C. Jarrell, managing editor
Maryanne Snell, marketing sales director
Douglas E. Sherwood, editorial intern

ONI PRESS, INC.
1305 SE Martin Luther King Jr. Blvd.
Suite A
Portland, OR 97214
USA

www.onipress.com
www.hopelarson.com

First edition: February 2006
ISBN 1-932664-36-X

1 3 5 7 9 10 8 6 4 2
PRINTED IN CANADA.

For everyone who rode on the El with me.

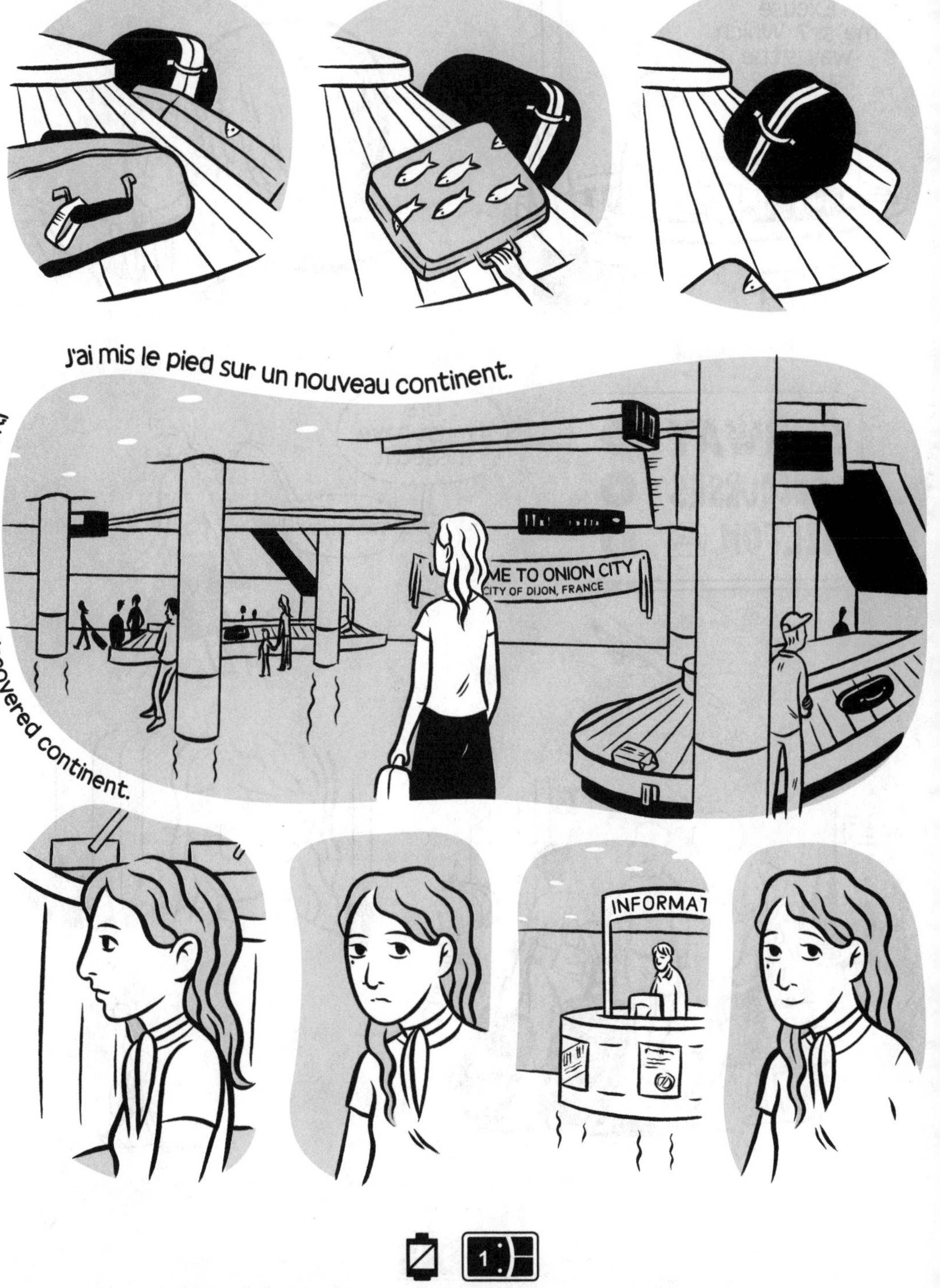
J'ai mis le pied sur un nouveau continent.
I've set foot on an undiscovered continent.
ME TO ONION CITY
CITY OF DIJON, FRANCE
INFORMAT

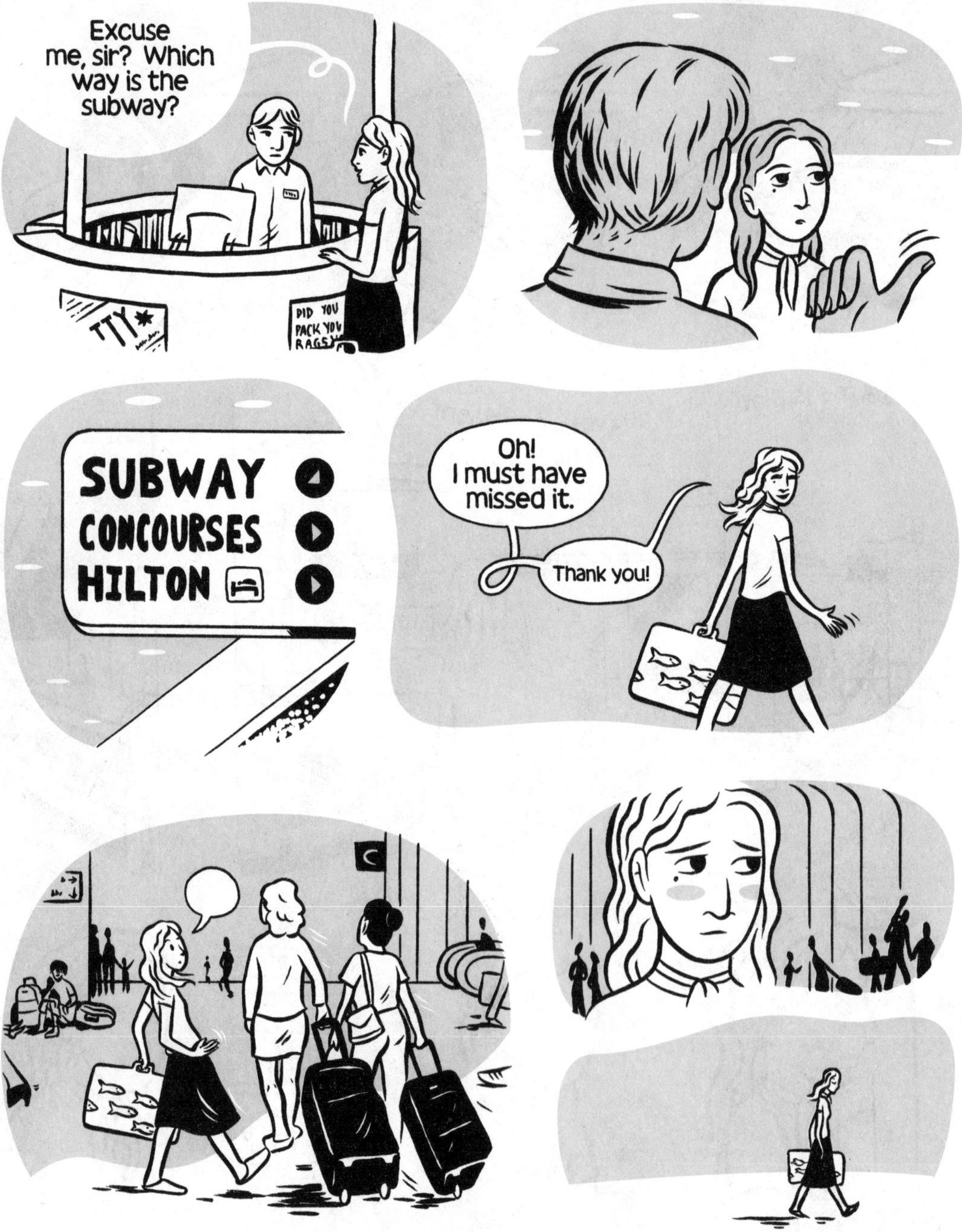
Excuse me, sir? Which way is the subway?
TTY
SUBWAY
CONCOURSES
HILTON
Oh! I must have missed it.
Thank you!

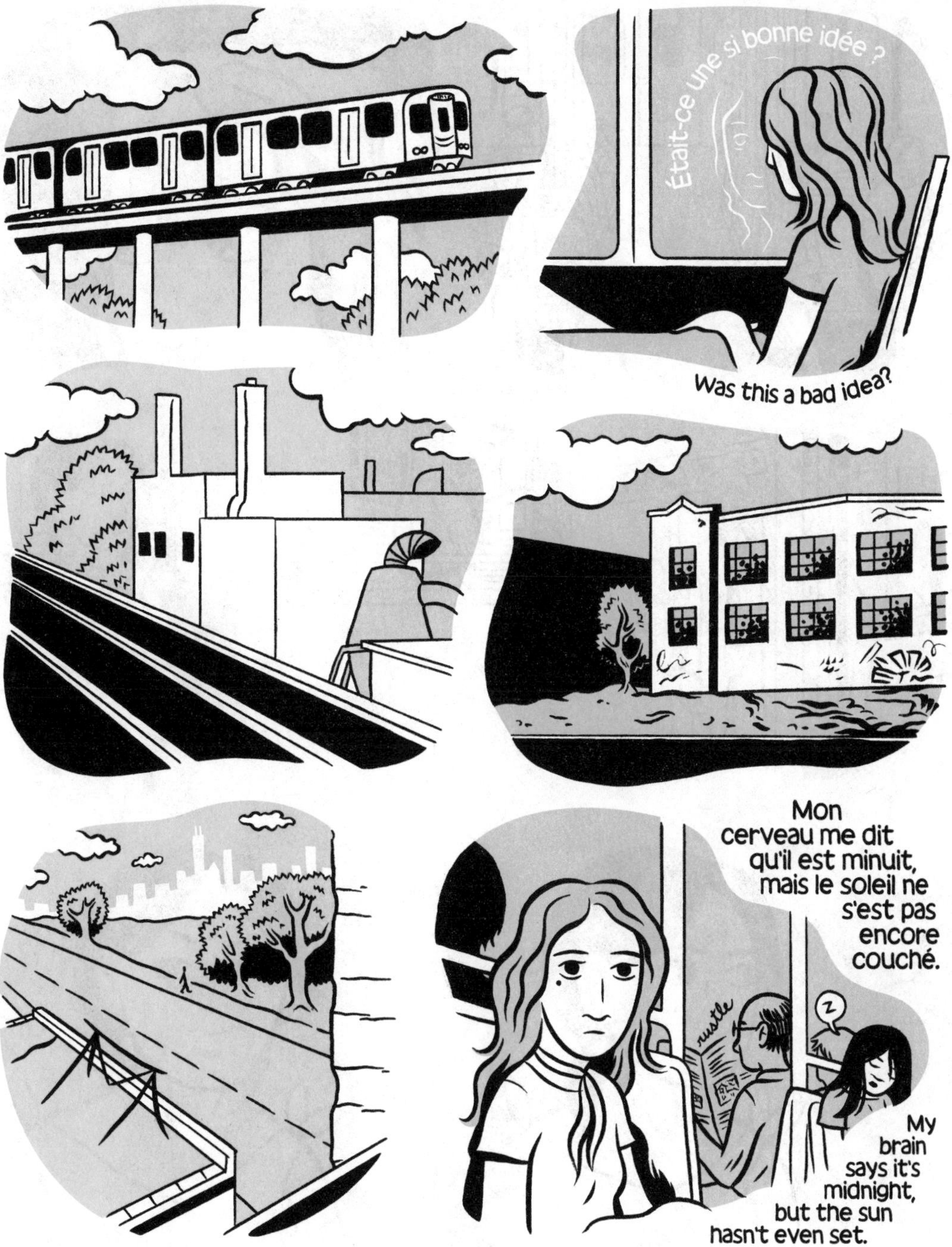
Était-ce une si bonne idée ?
Was this a bad idea?
Mon cerveau me dit qu'il est minuit, mais le soleil ne s'est pas encore couché.
rustle
Z
My brain says it's midnight, but the sun hasn't even set.

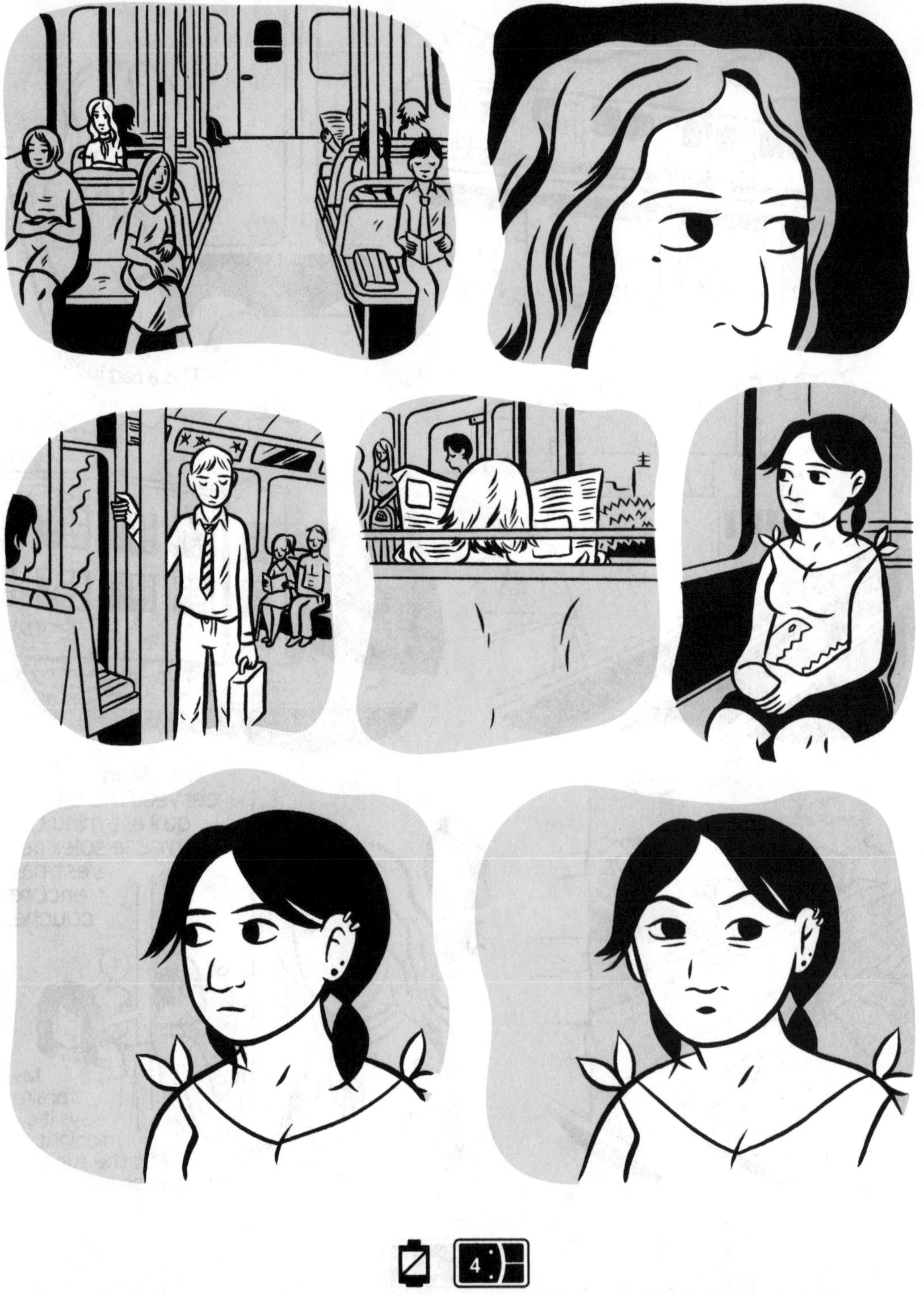

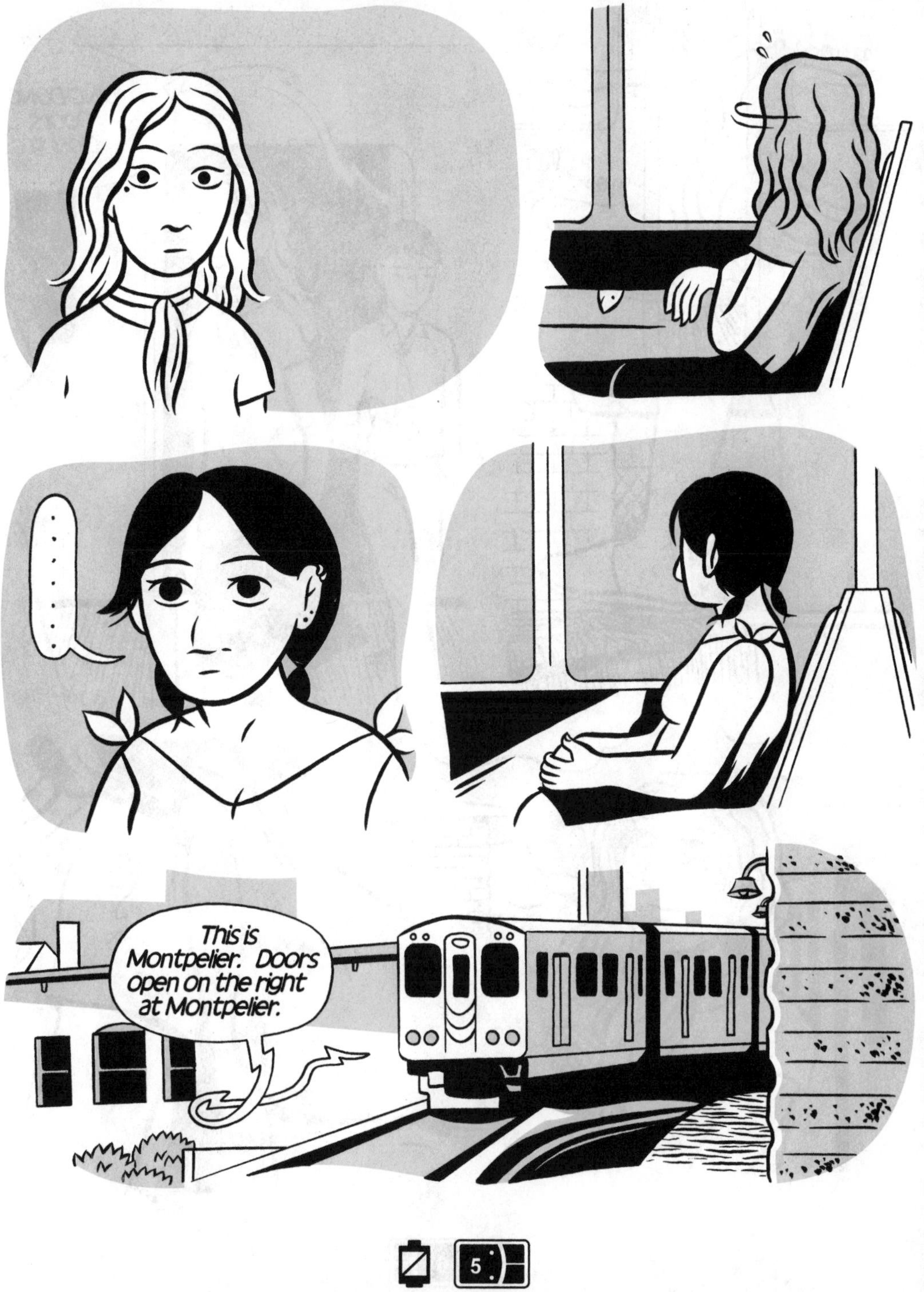
. . . . . .
This is Montpelier. Doors open on the right at Montpelier.
5

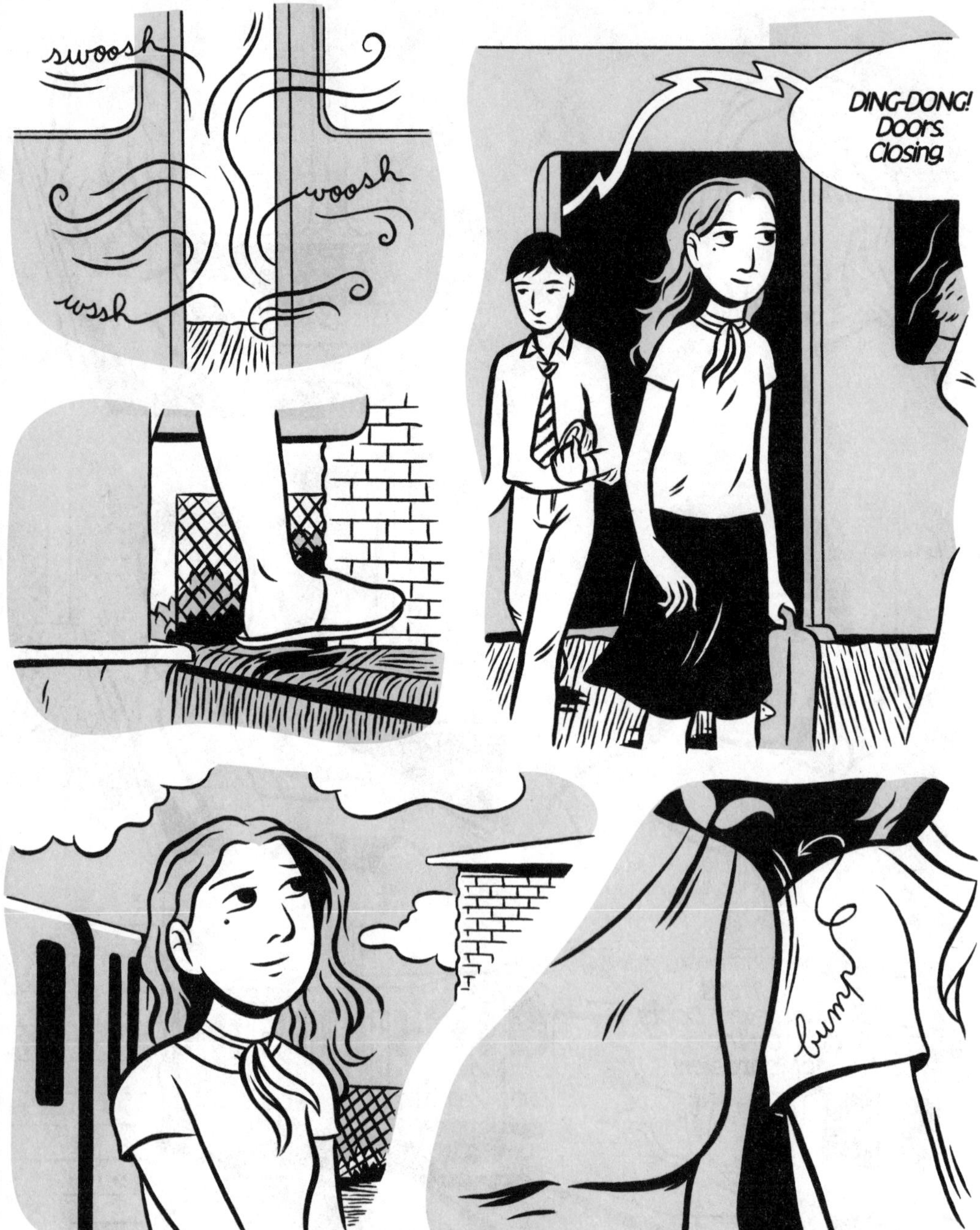
swoosh
woosh
wssh
DING-DONG! Doors. Closing.
bump

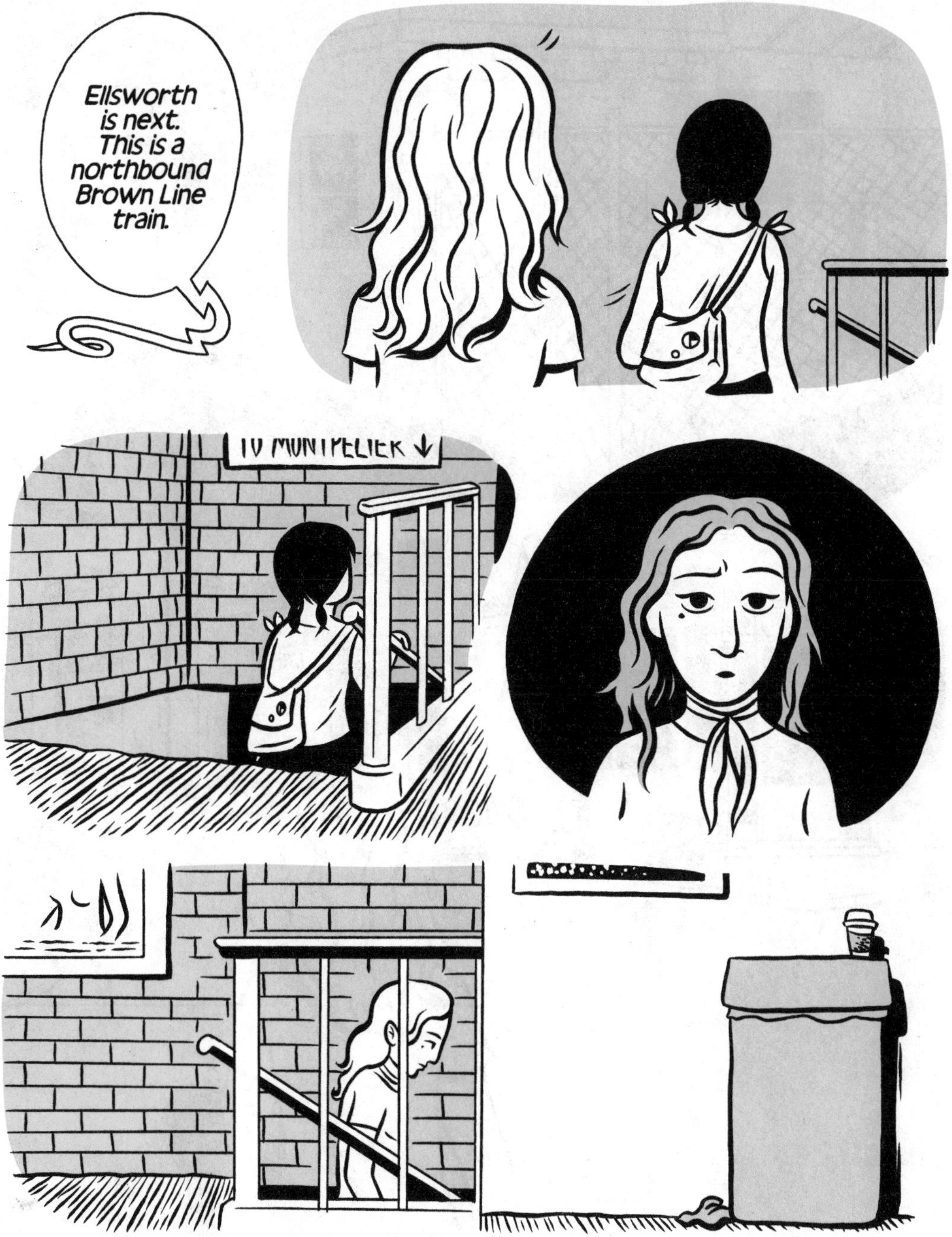
Ellsworth is next. This is a northbound Brown Line train.
TO MONTPELIER ↓

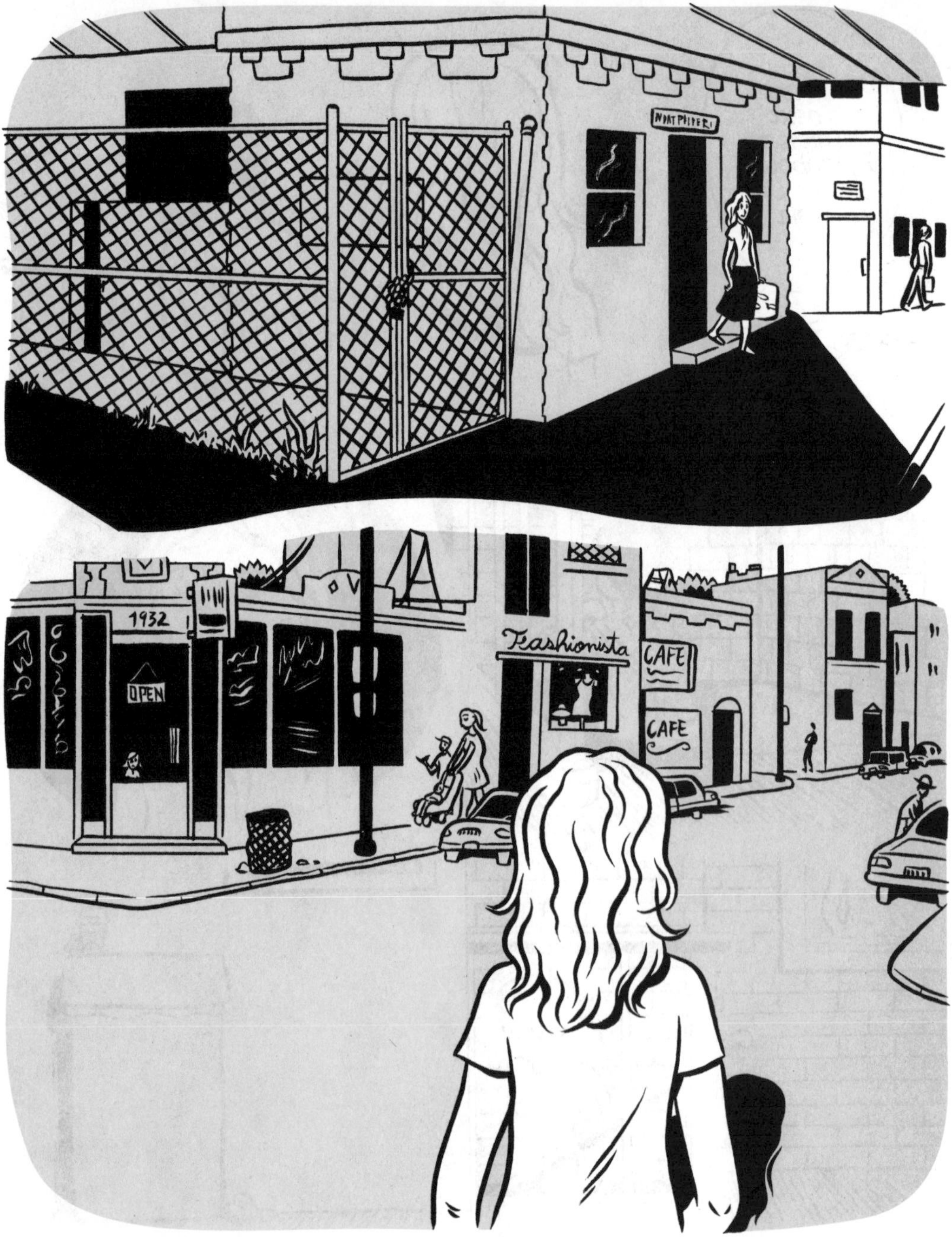
1932
OPEN
Fashionista
CAFE
CAFE

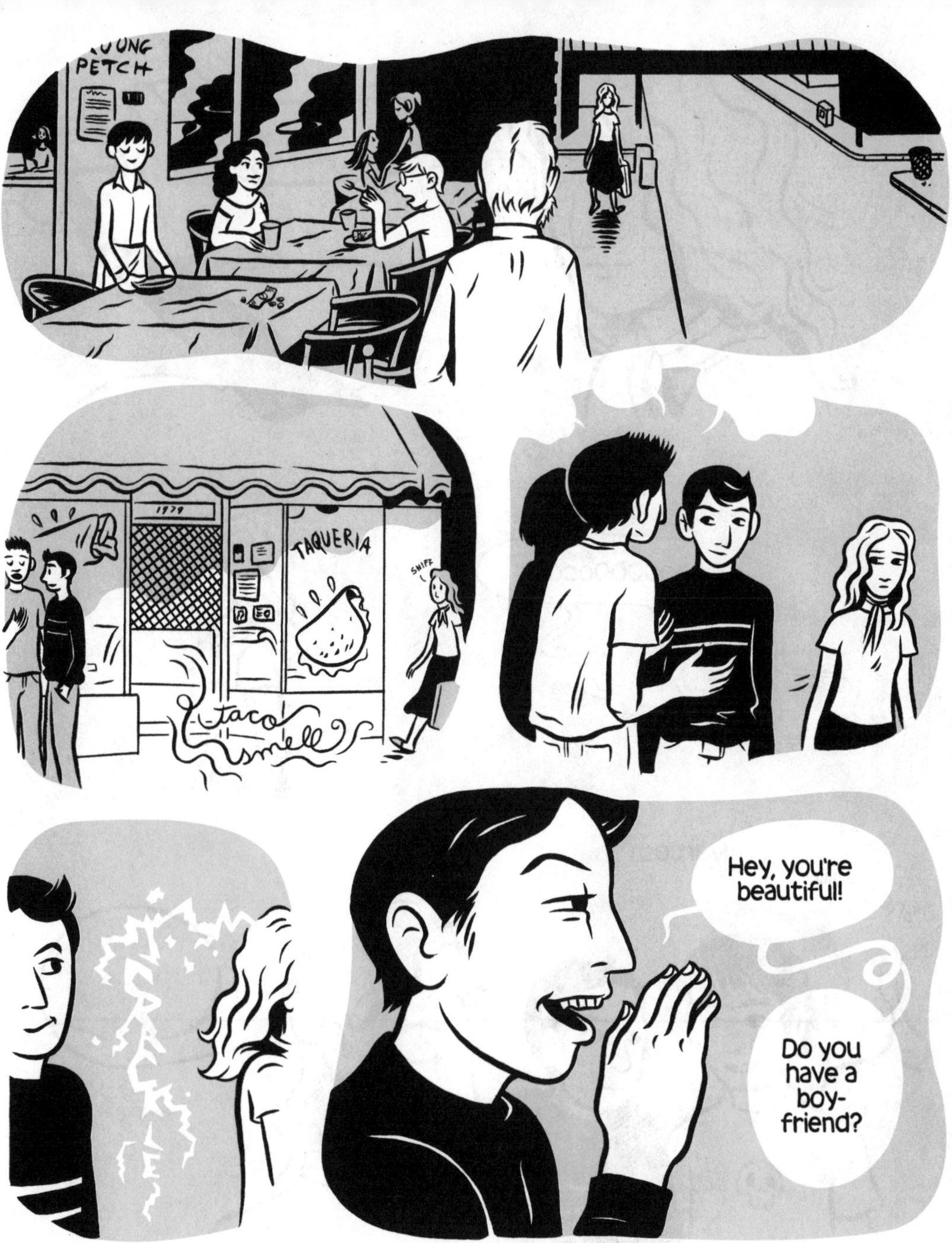
PETCH
1979
TAQUERIA
SNIFF
taco smell
CRACKLE
Hey, you're beautiful!
Do you have a boy-friend?

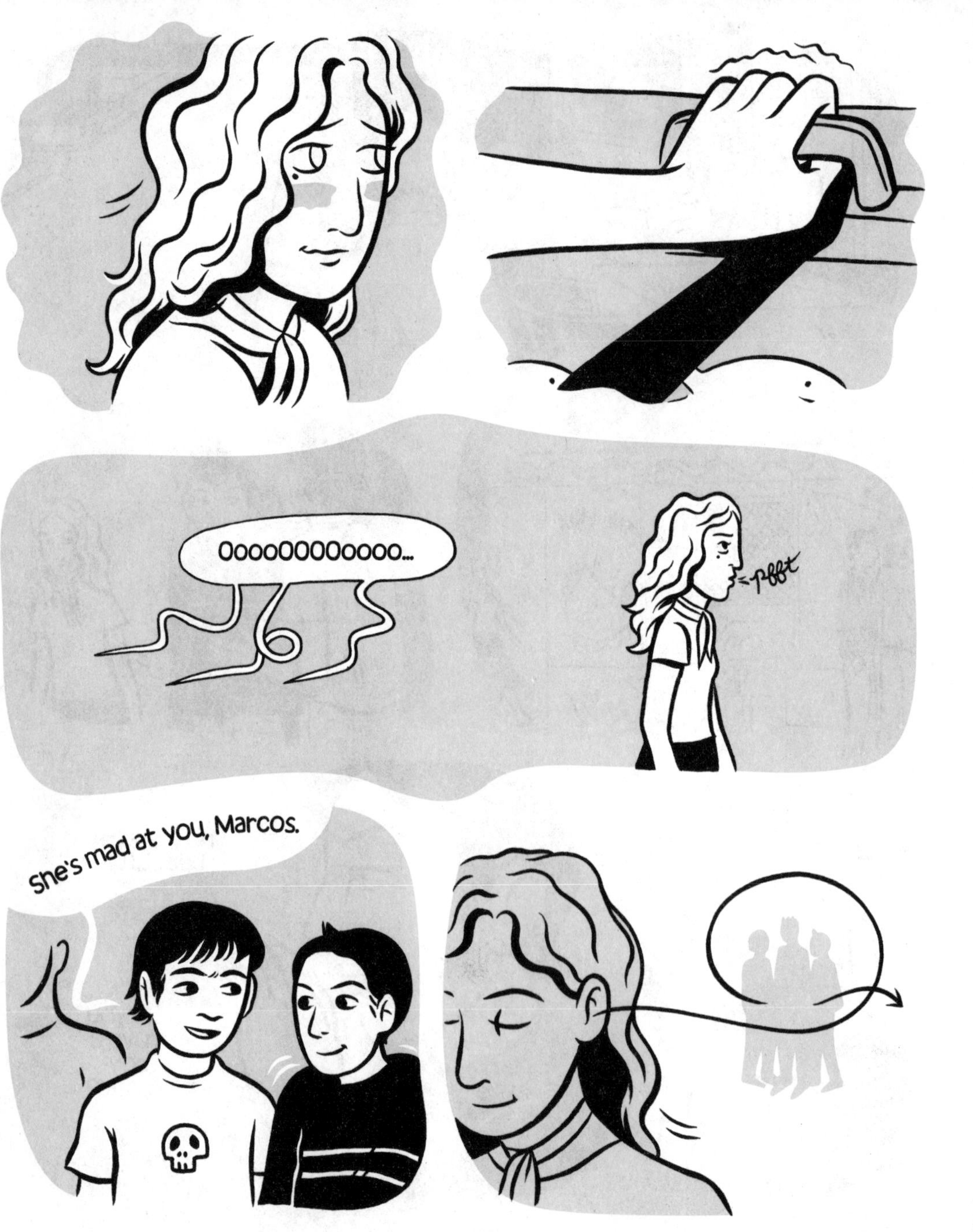
OooooOOOOoooo...
pfft
She's mad at you, Marcos.

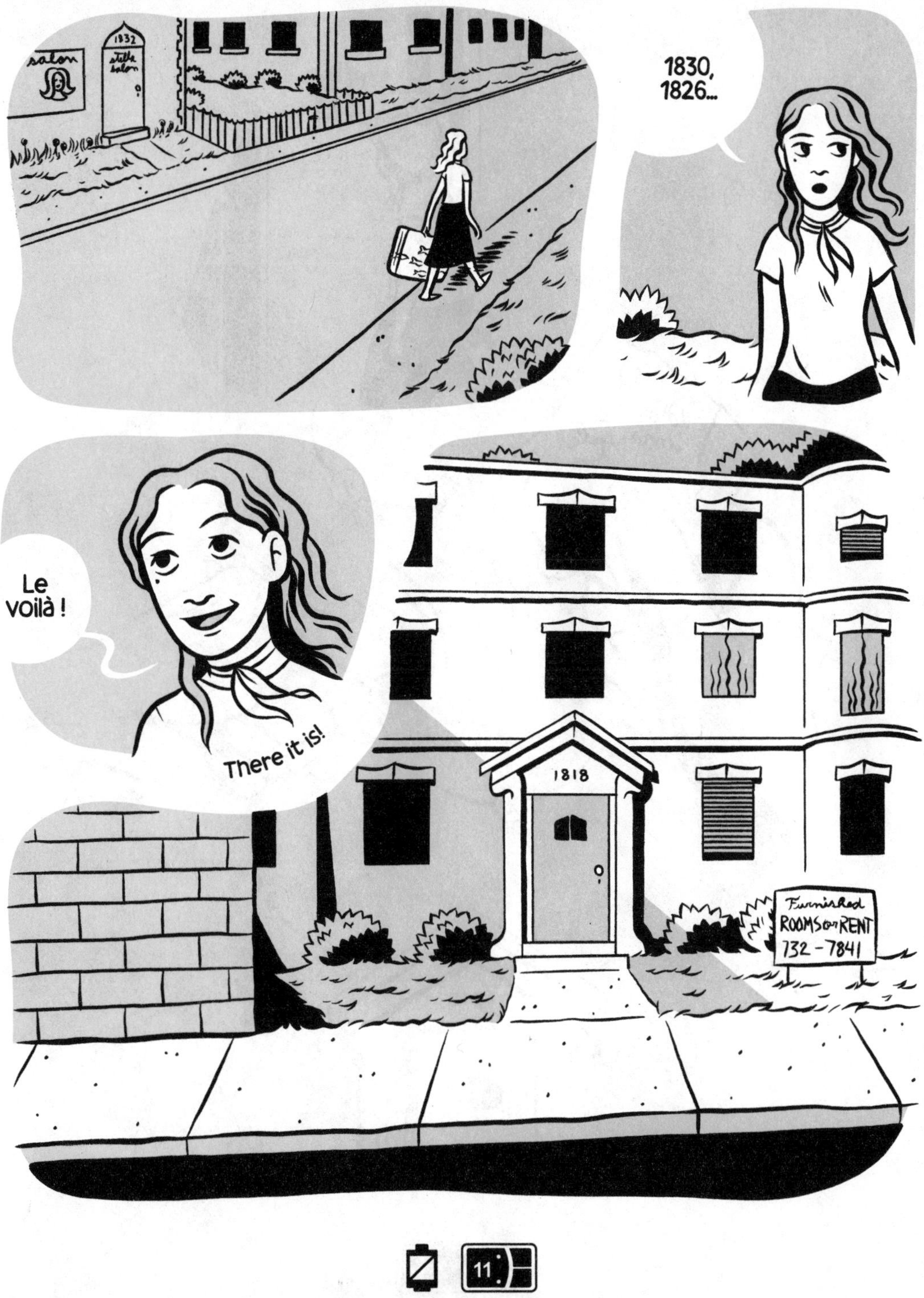
salon
1832
1830, 1826...
Le voilà !
There it is!
1818
Furnished ROOMS for RENT 732-7841

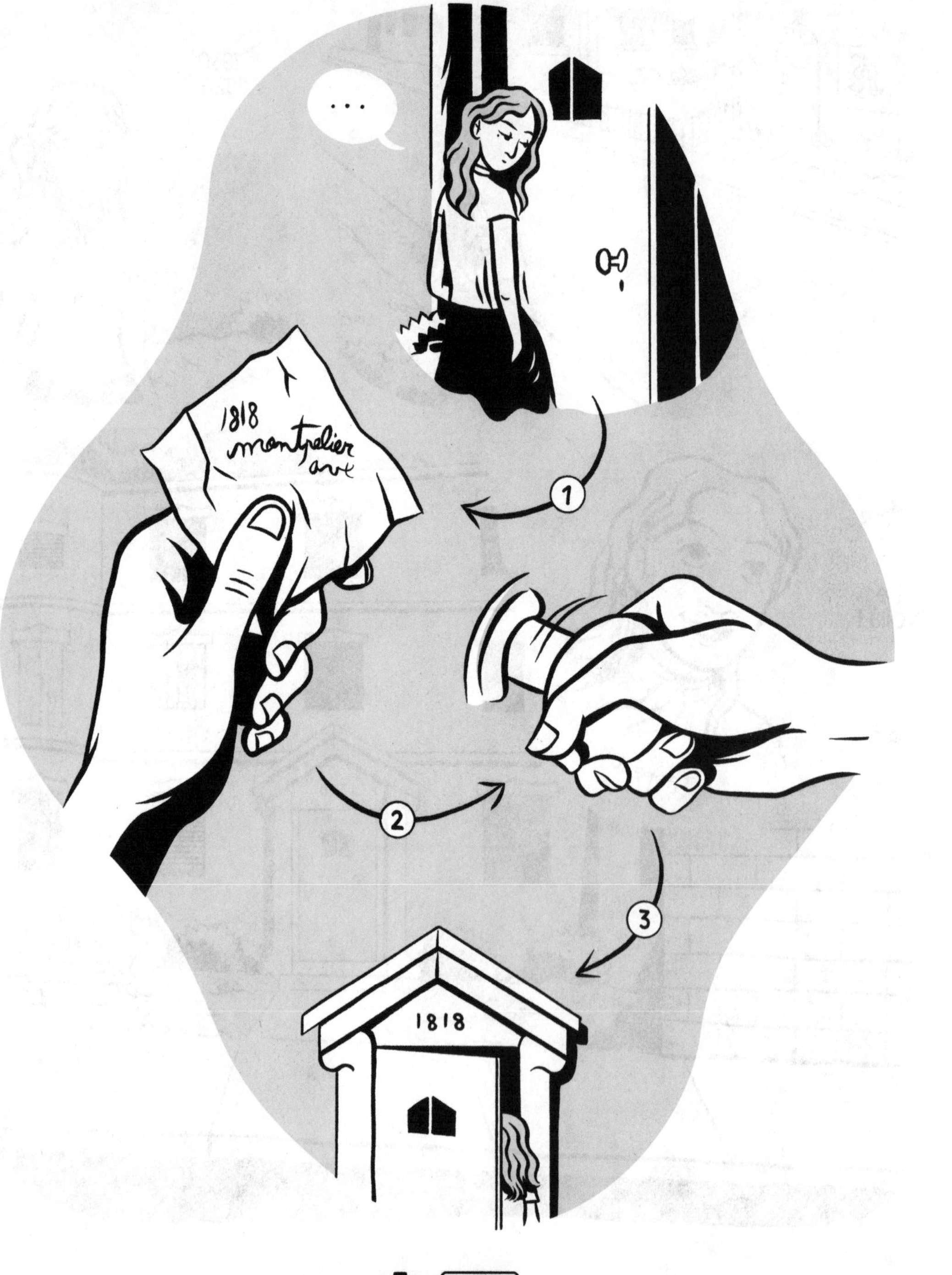

...
1818
montpelier
ave
1
2
3
1818

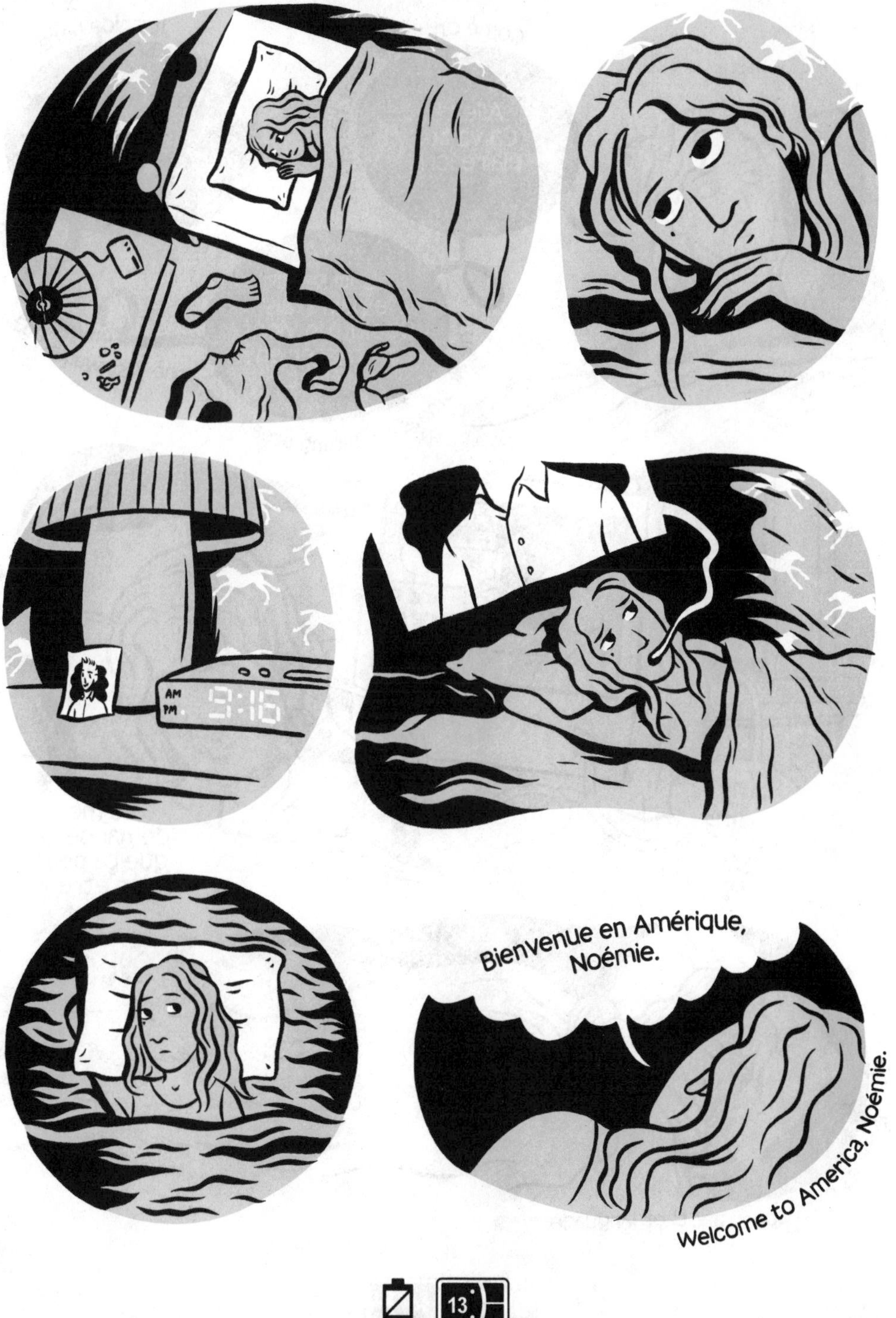
AM
PM
9:16
Bienvenue en Amérique, Noémie.
Welcome to America, Noémie.

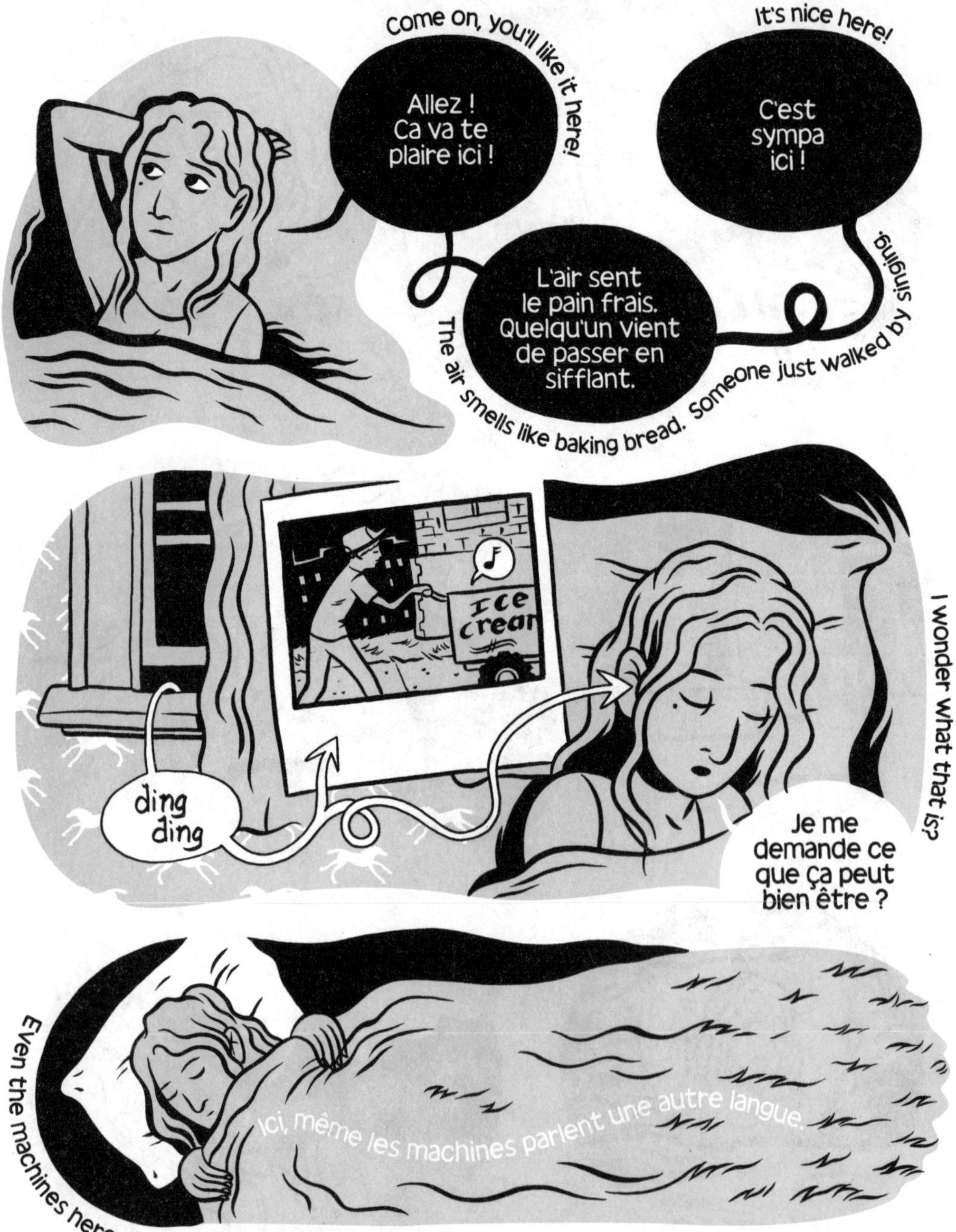
Allez ! Ca va te plaire ici !
Come on, you'll like it here!
C'est sympa ici !
It's nice here!
L'air sent le pain frais. Quelqu'un vient de passer en sifflant.
The air smells like baking bread. Someone just walked by singing.
Ice Crean
ding ding
Je me demande ce que ça peut bien être ?
I wonder what that is?
Ici, même les machines parlent une autre langue.
Even the machines here speak another language.

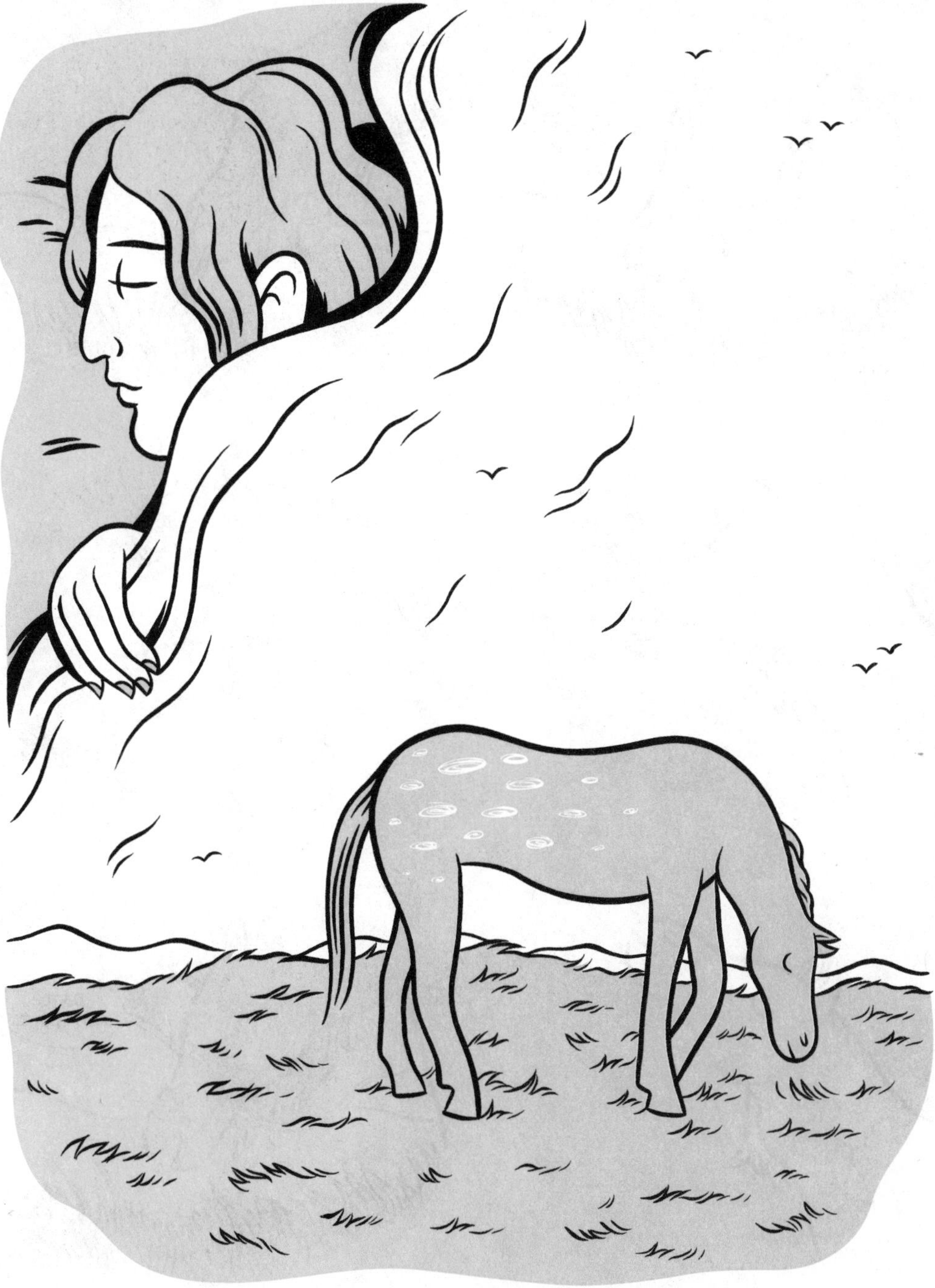

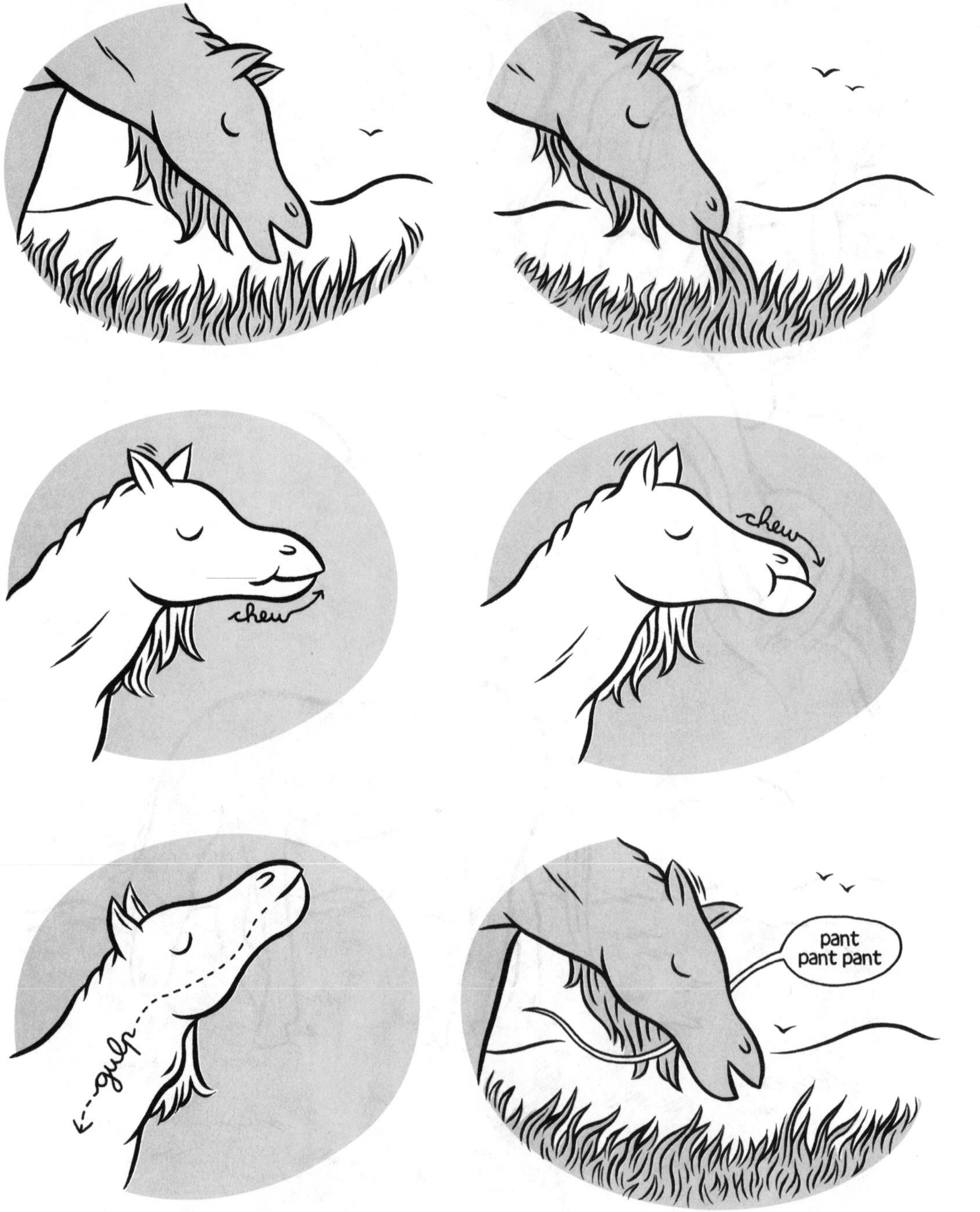
chew
chew
gulp
pant pant pant

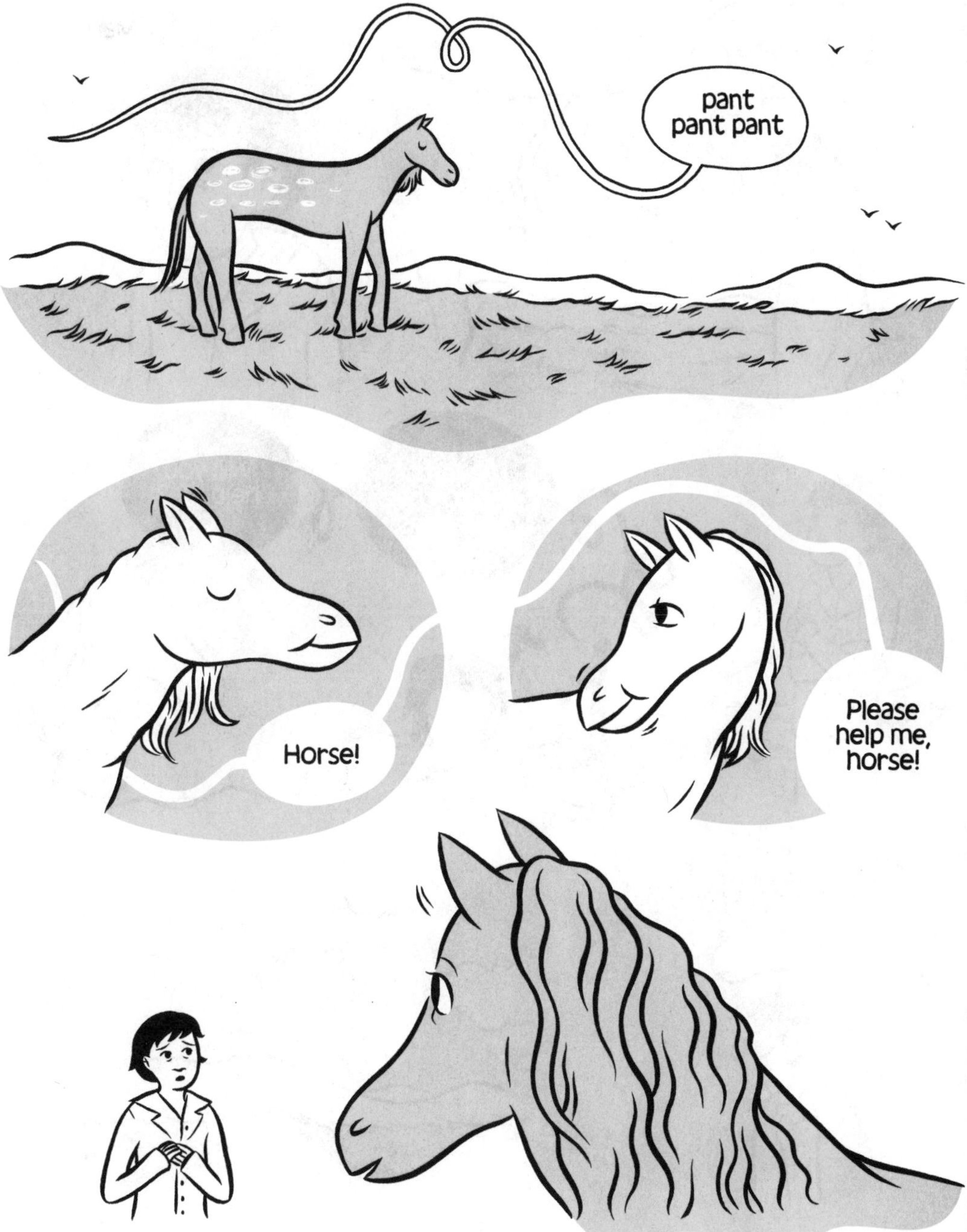
pant
pant pant
Horse!
Please help me, horse!

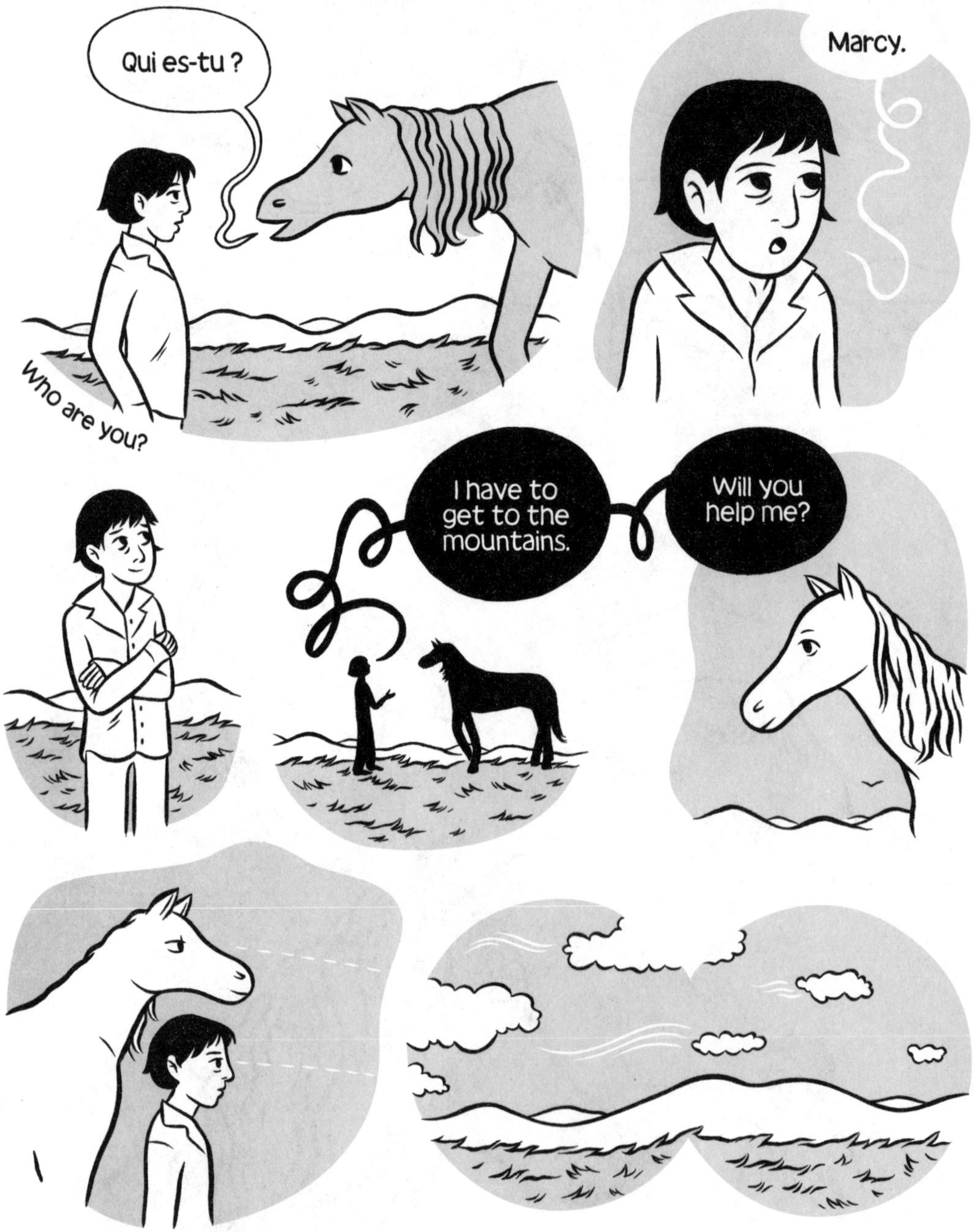
Qui es-tu ?
Who are you?
Marcy.
I have to get to the mountains.
Will you help me?

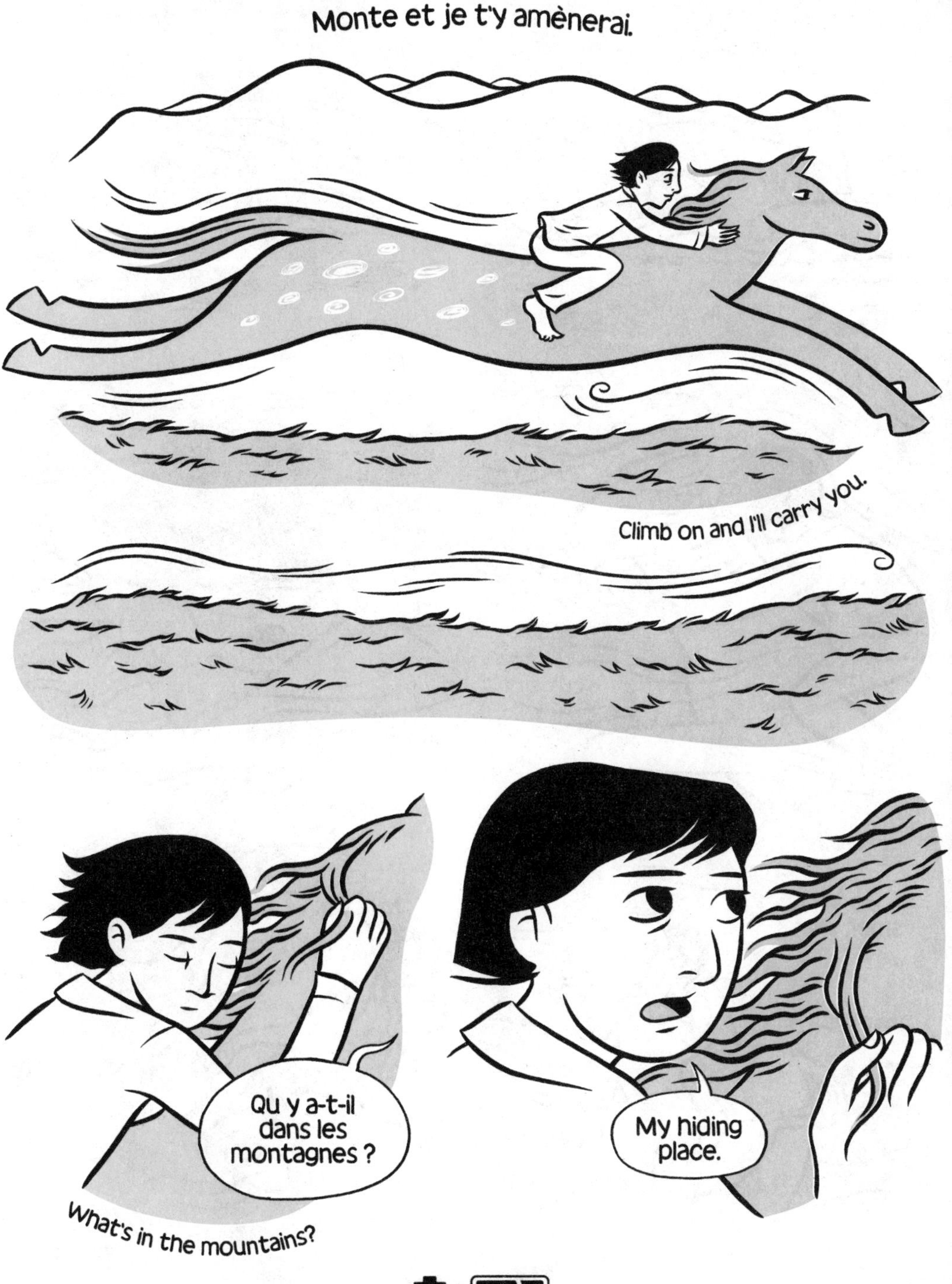

Monte et je t'y amènerai.
Climb on and I'll carry you.
Qu y a-t-il dans les montagnes ?
What's in the mountains?
My hiding place.

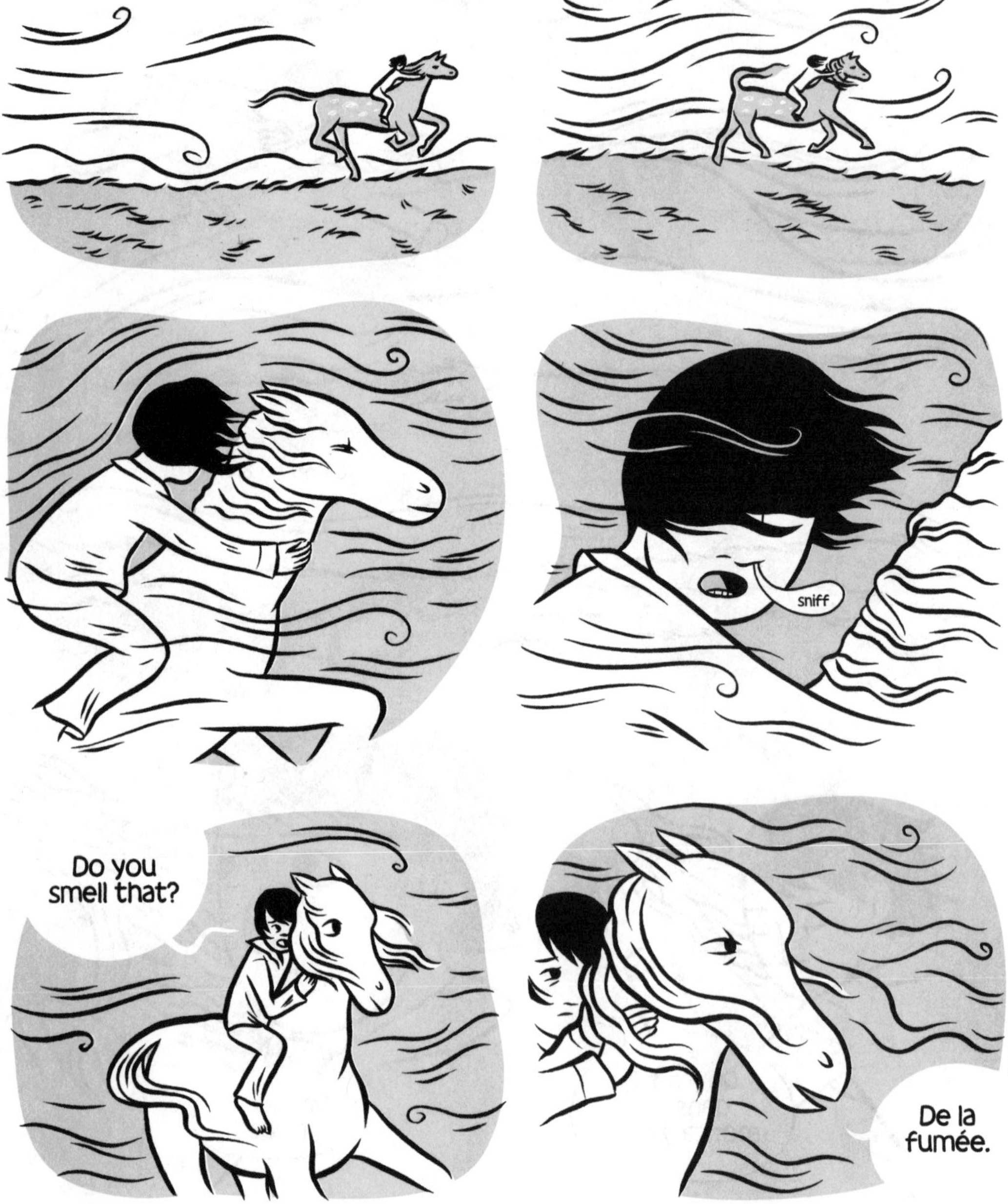
sniff
Do you smell that?
De la fumée.
Smoke.

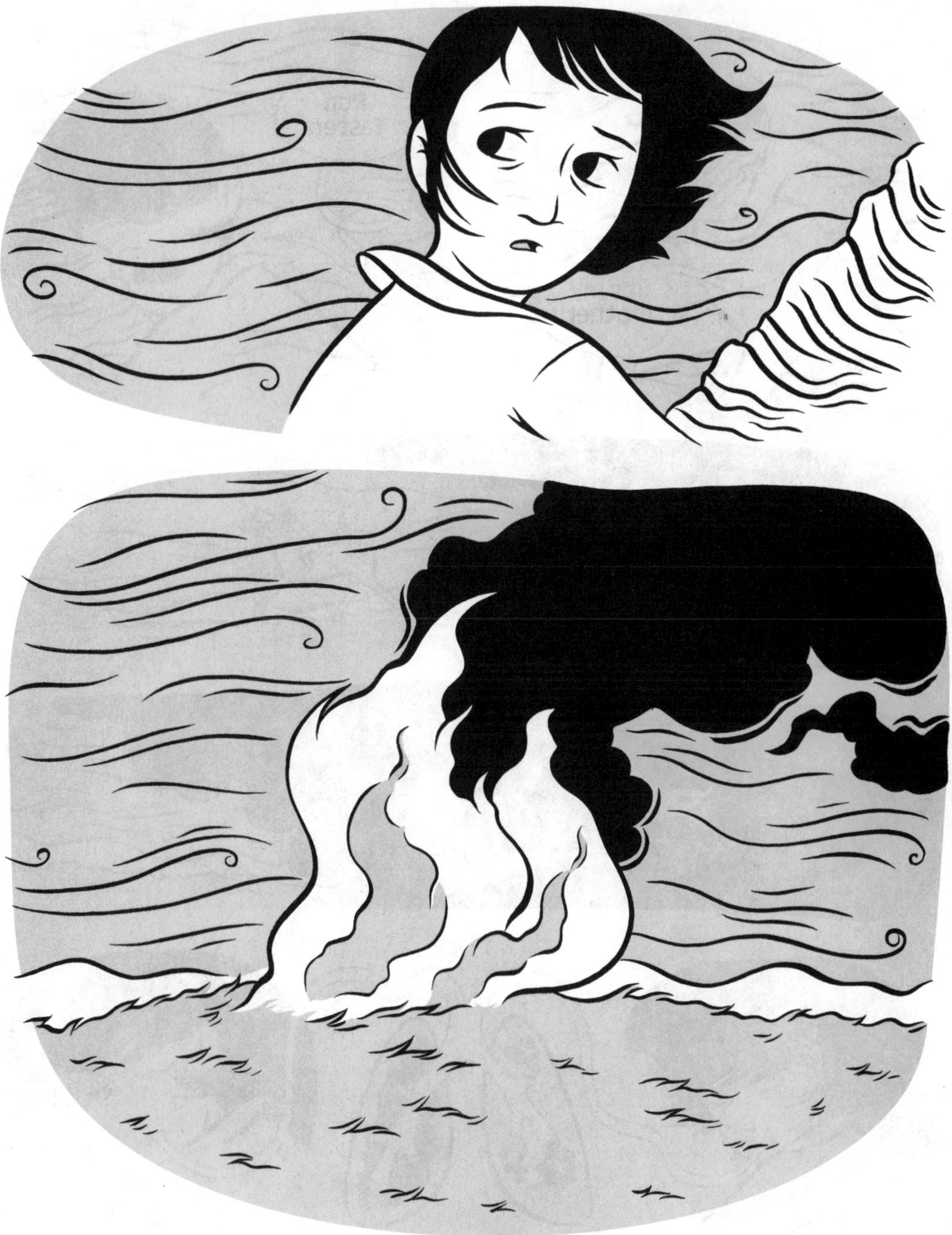

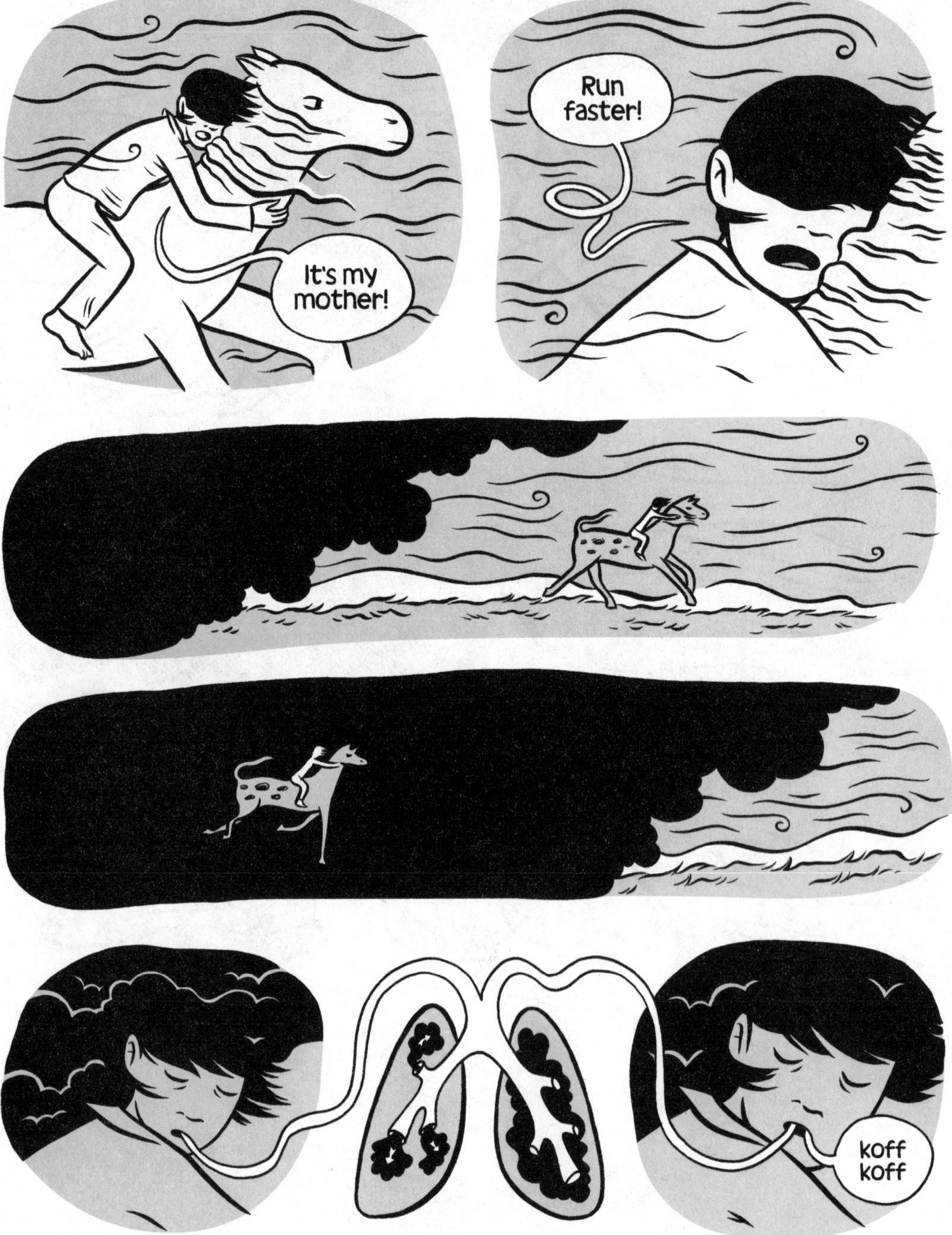
It's my mother!
Run faster!
koff koff

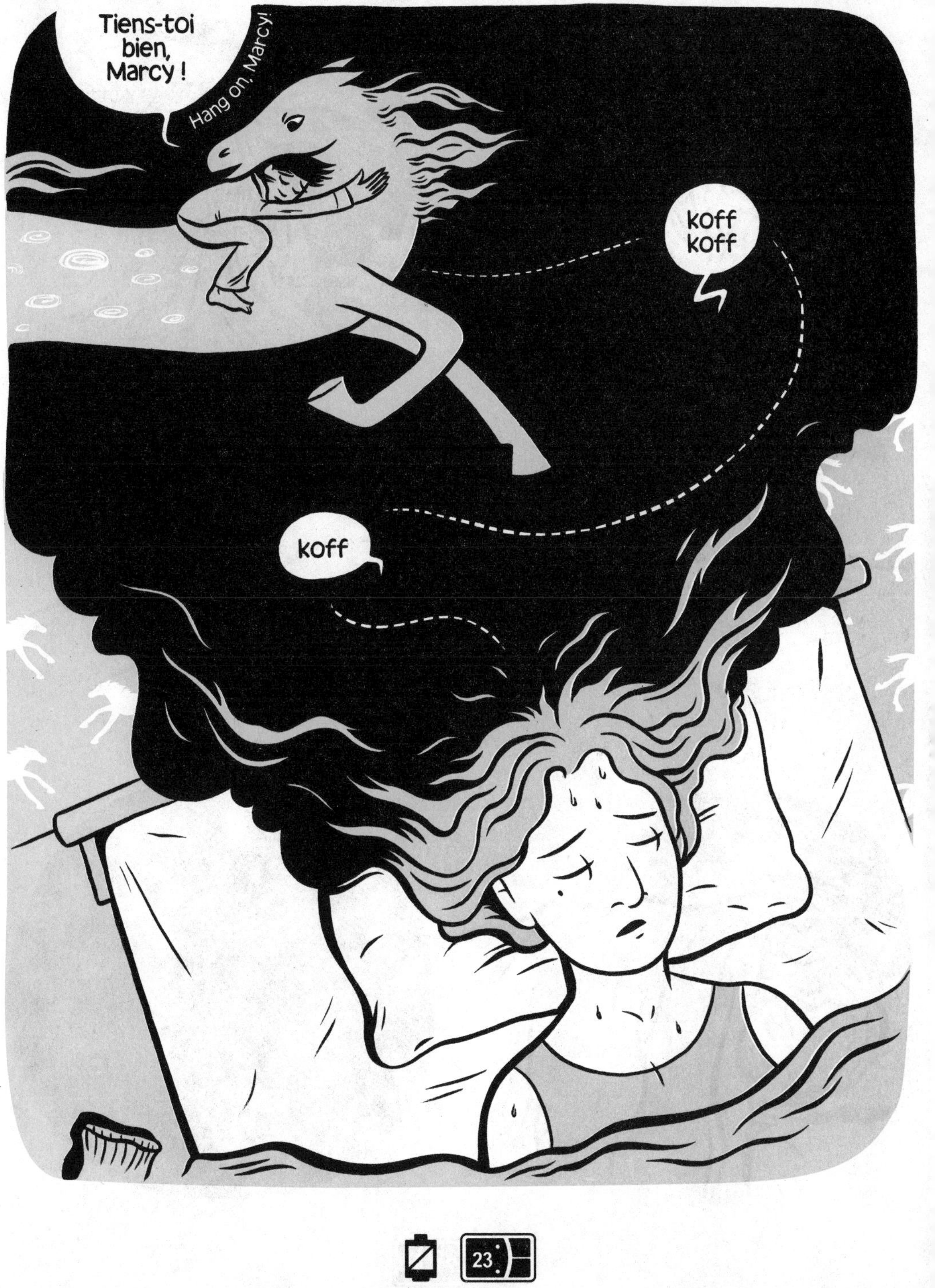
Tiens-toi bien, Marcy !
Hang on, Marcy!
koff koff
koff

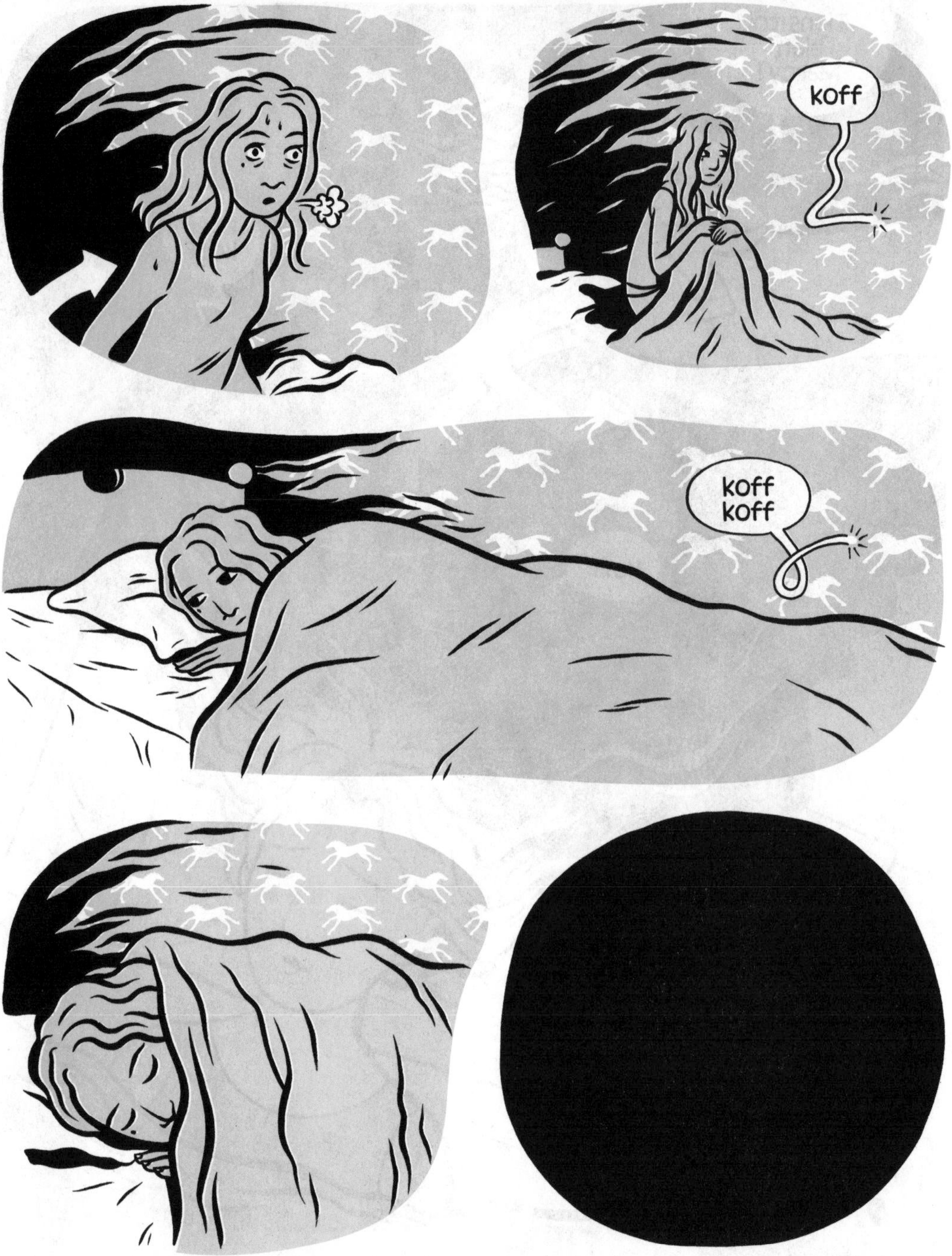
koff
koff koff

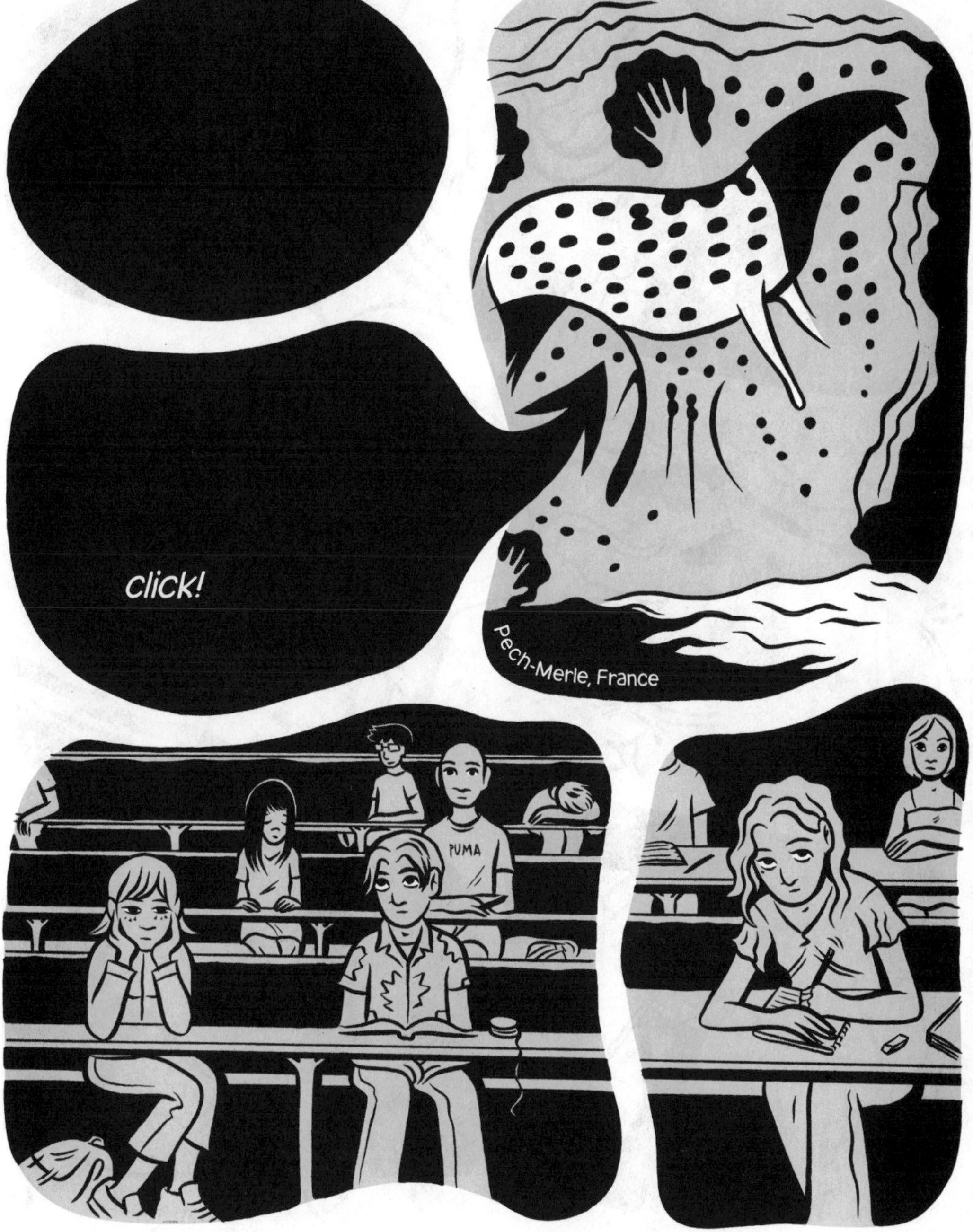
click!
Pech-Merle, France
PUMA

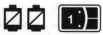

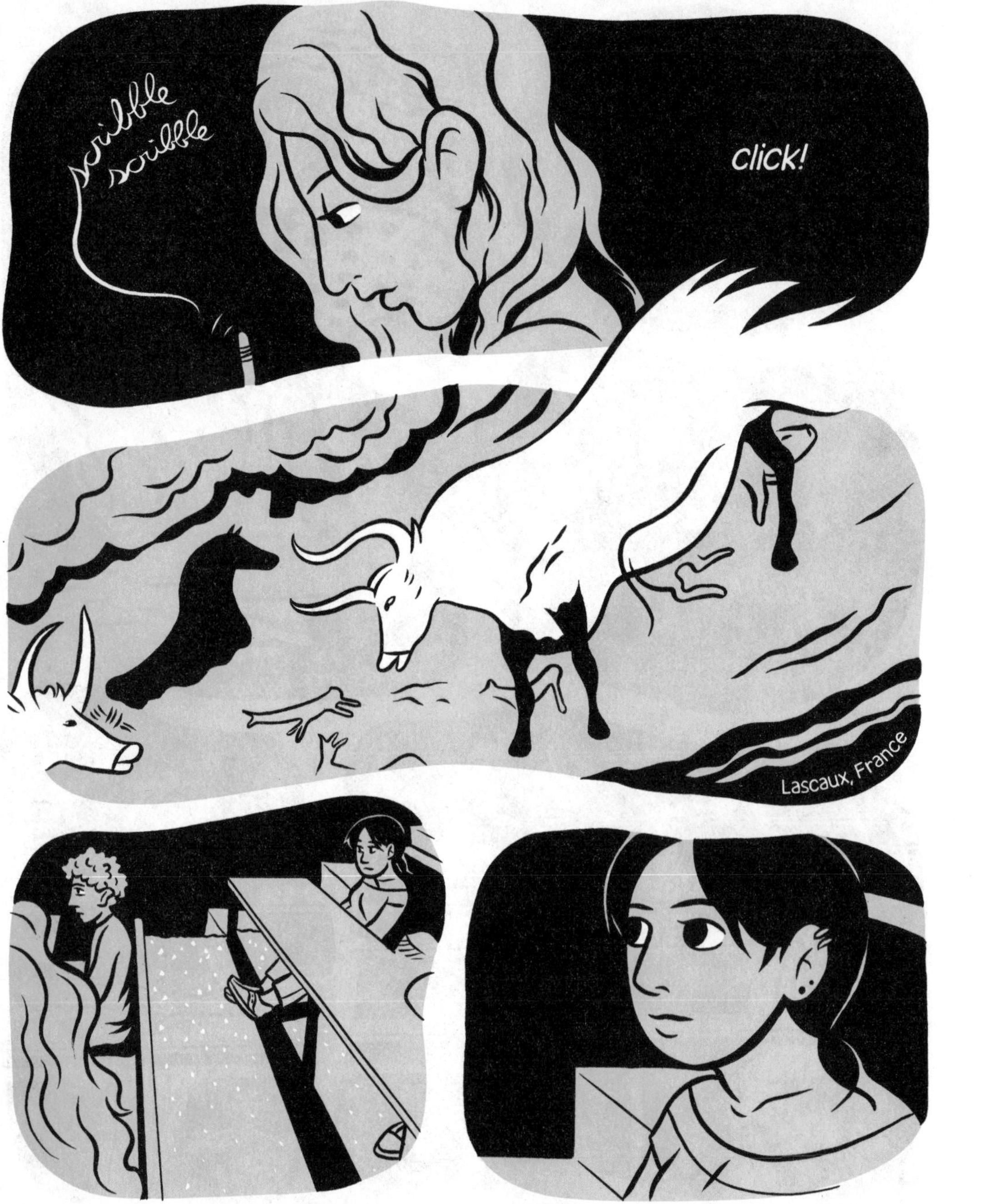
scribble
scribble
click!
Lascaux, France

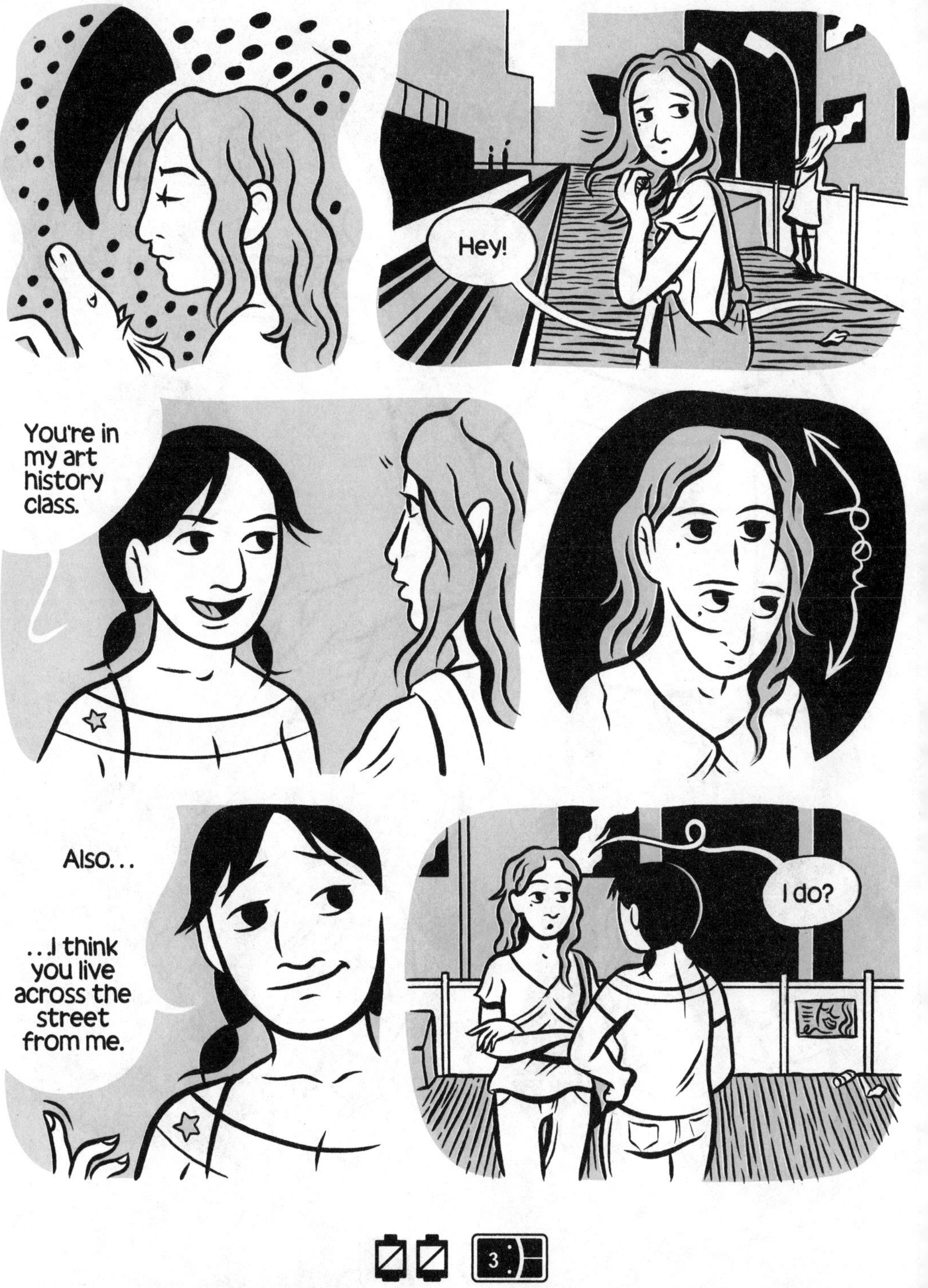
Hey!
You're in my art history class.
Also...
...I think you live across the street from me.
I do?

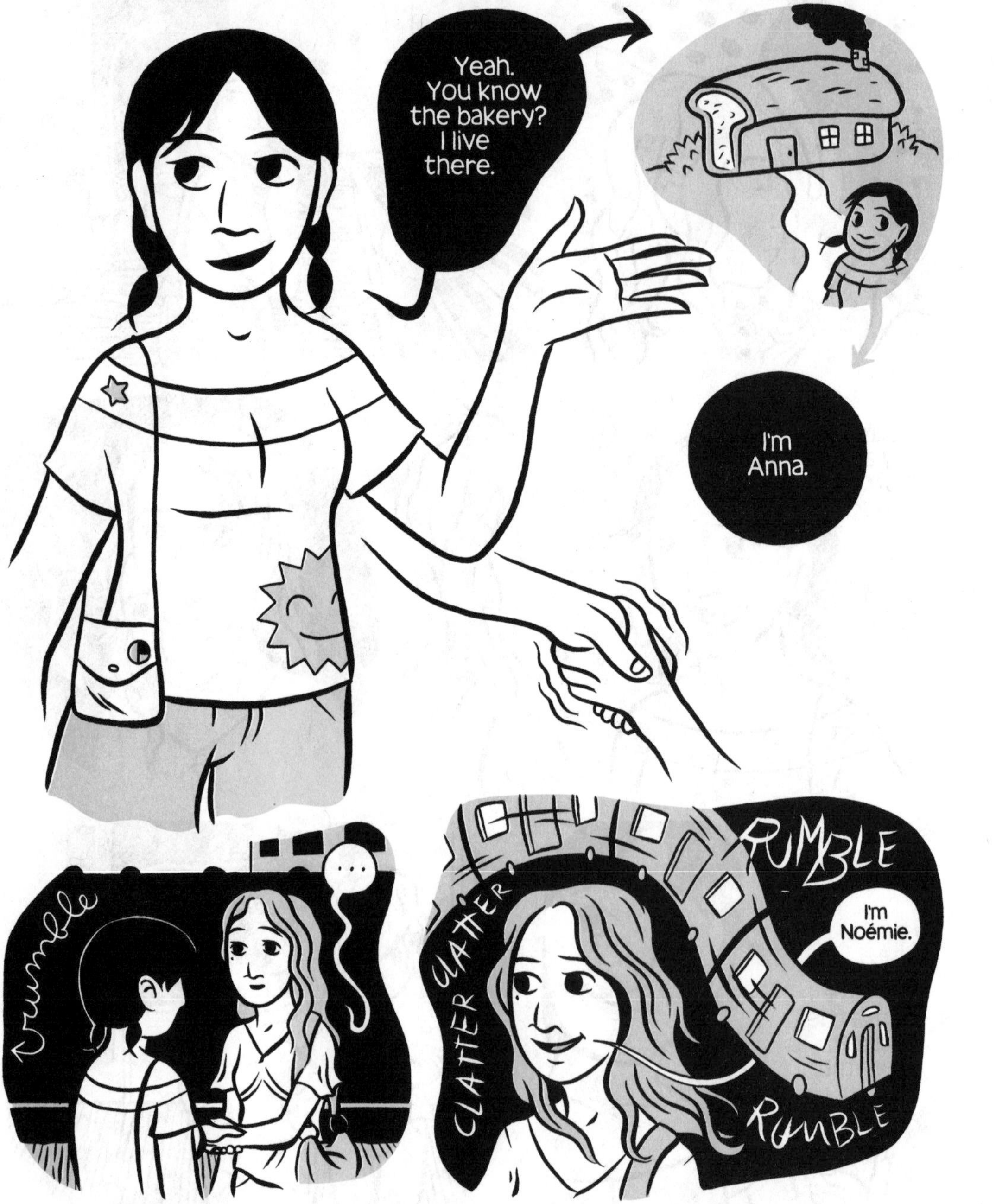
Yeah.
You know
the bakery?
I live
there.
I'm
Anna.
rumble
...
CLATTER CLATTER
RUMBLE
I'm
Noémie.
RUMBLE

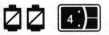

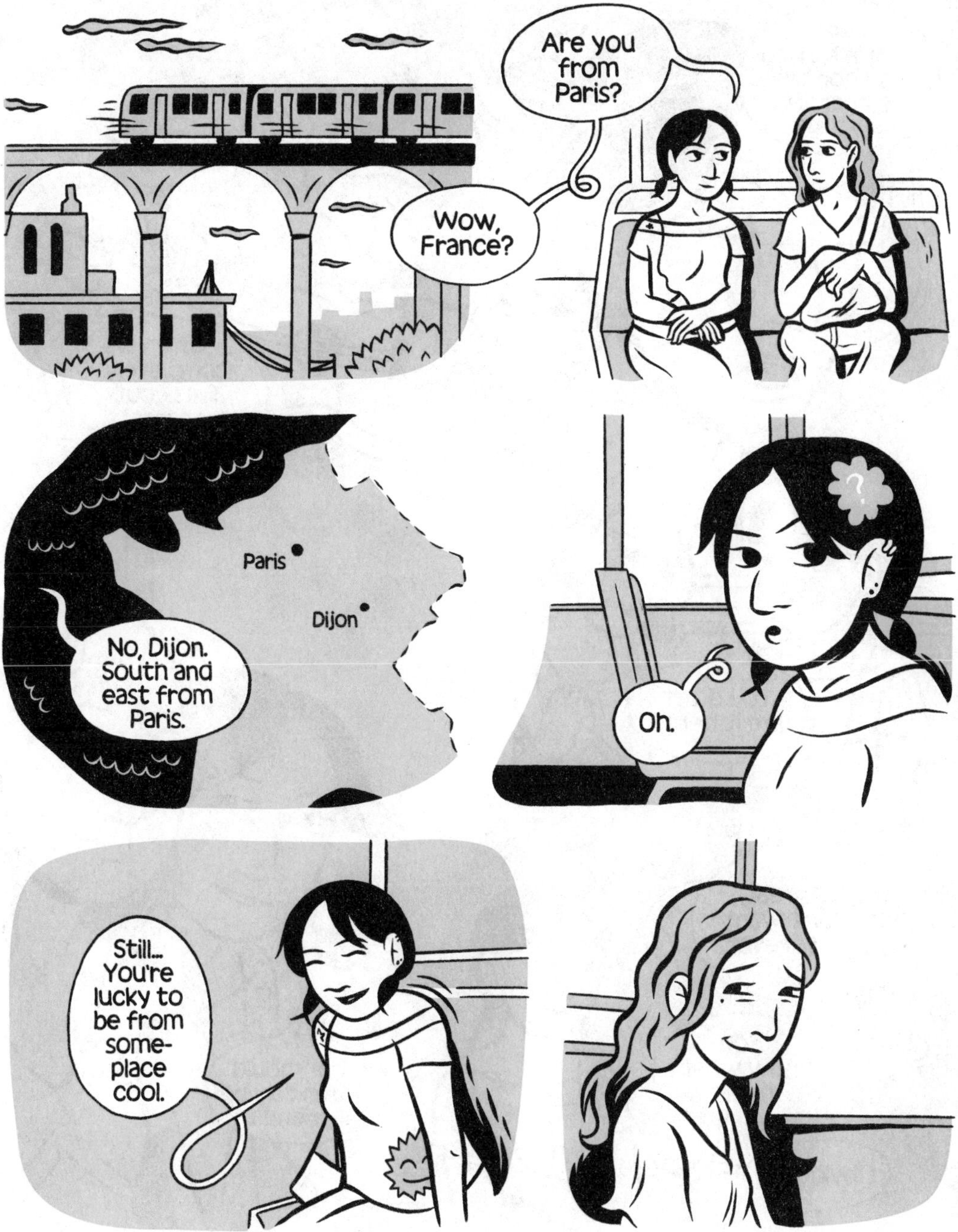
Wow, France?
Are you from Paris?
Paris
Dijon
No, Dijon. South and east from Paris.
Oh.
Still... You're lucky to be from some-place cool.

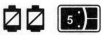

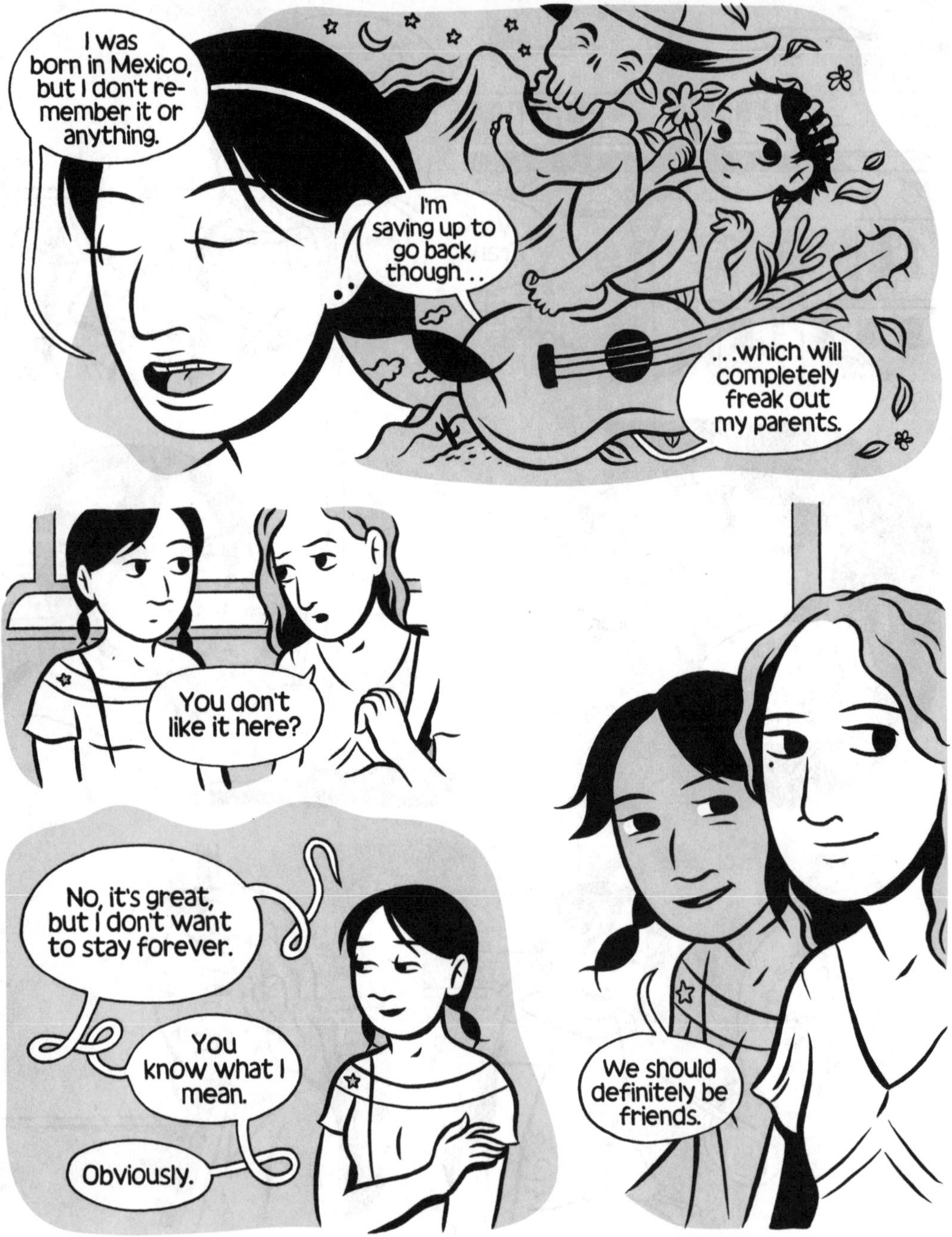
I was born in Mexico, but I don't re-member it or anything.
I'm saving up to go back, though. . .
. . .which will completely freak out my parents.
You don't like it here?
No, it's great, but I don't want to stay forever.
You know what I mean.
Obviously.
We should definitely be friends.

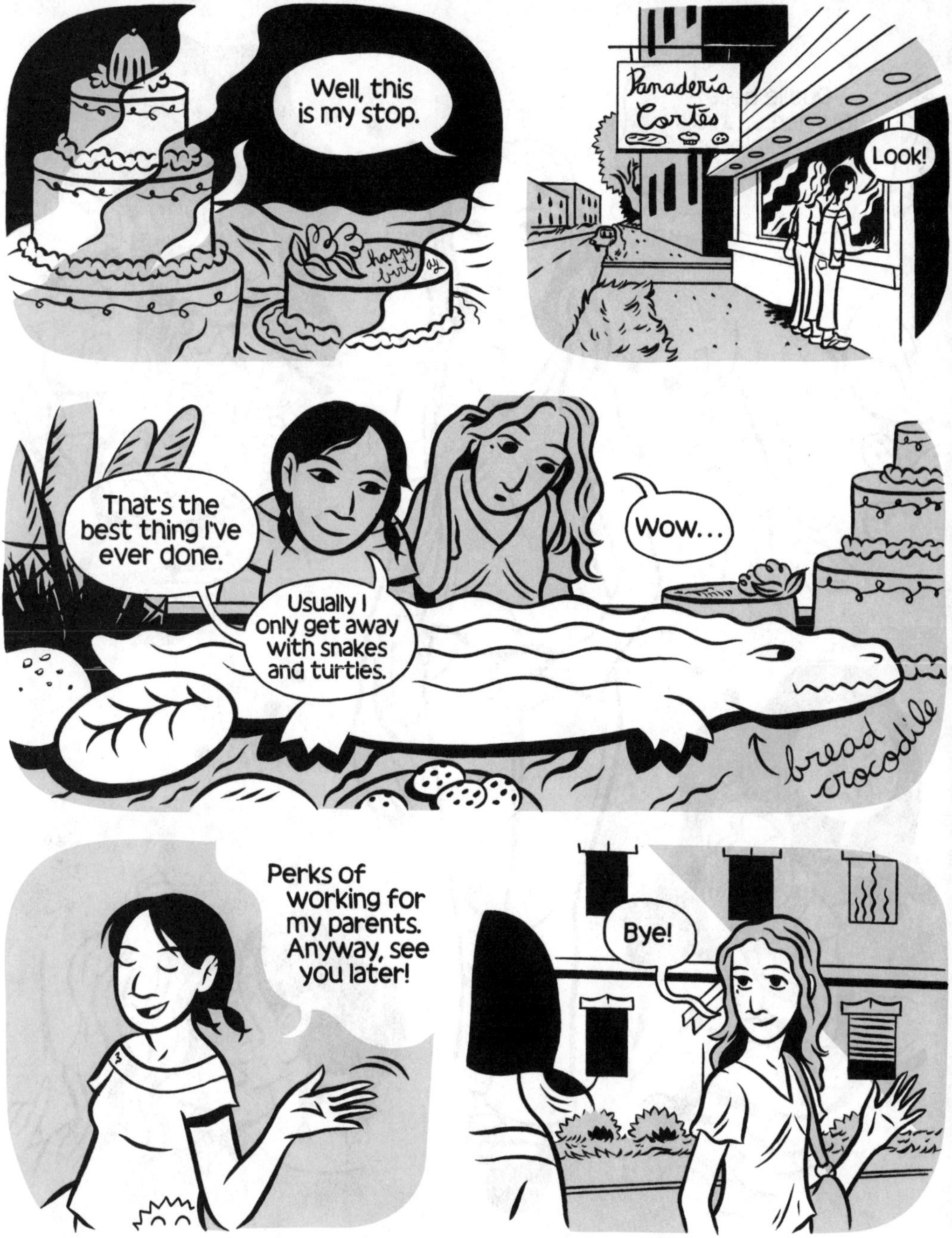
Well, this is my stop.
Panadería Cortés
Look!
That's the best thing I've ever done.
Usually I only get away with snakes and turtles.
Wow...
bread crocodile
Perks of working for my parents. Anyway, see you later!
Bye!

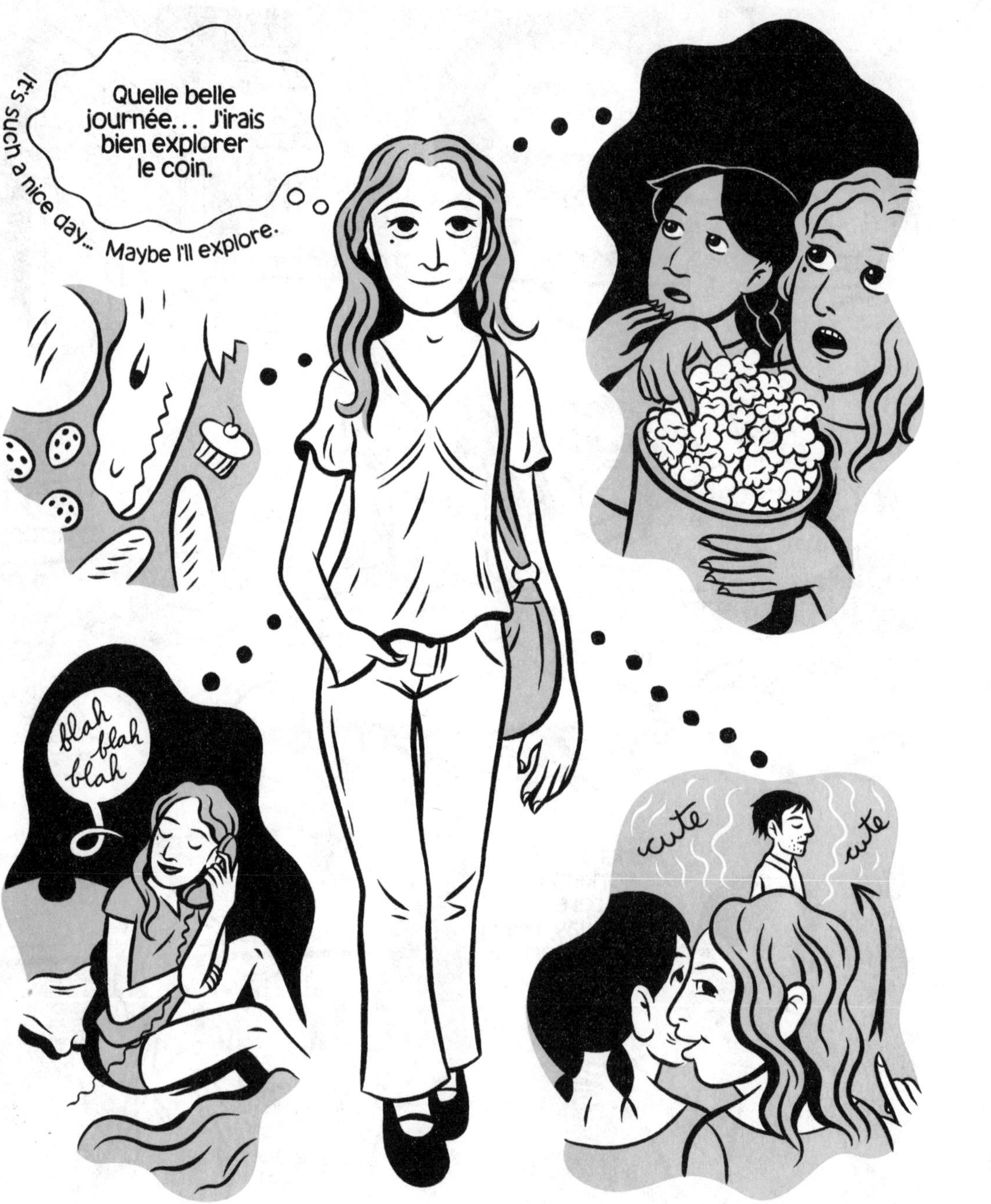
Quelle belle journée... J'irais bien explorer le coin.
It's such a nice day... Maybe I'll explore.
blah blah blah
cute
cute

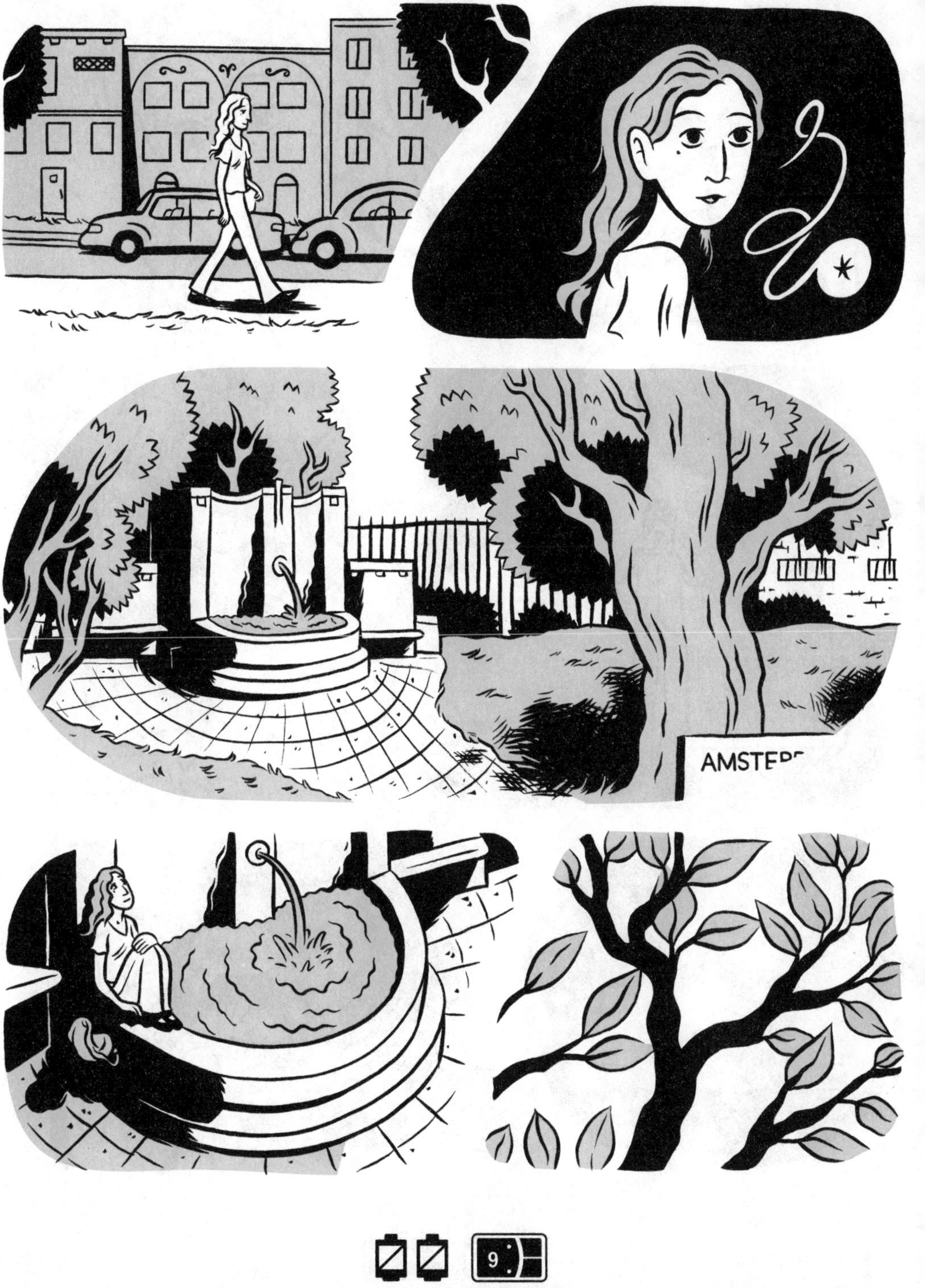
AMSTE

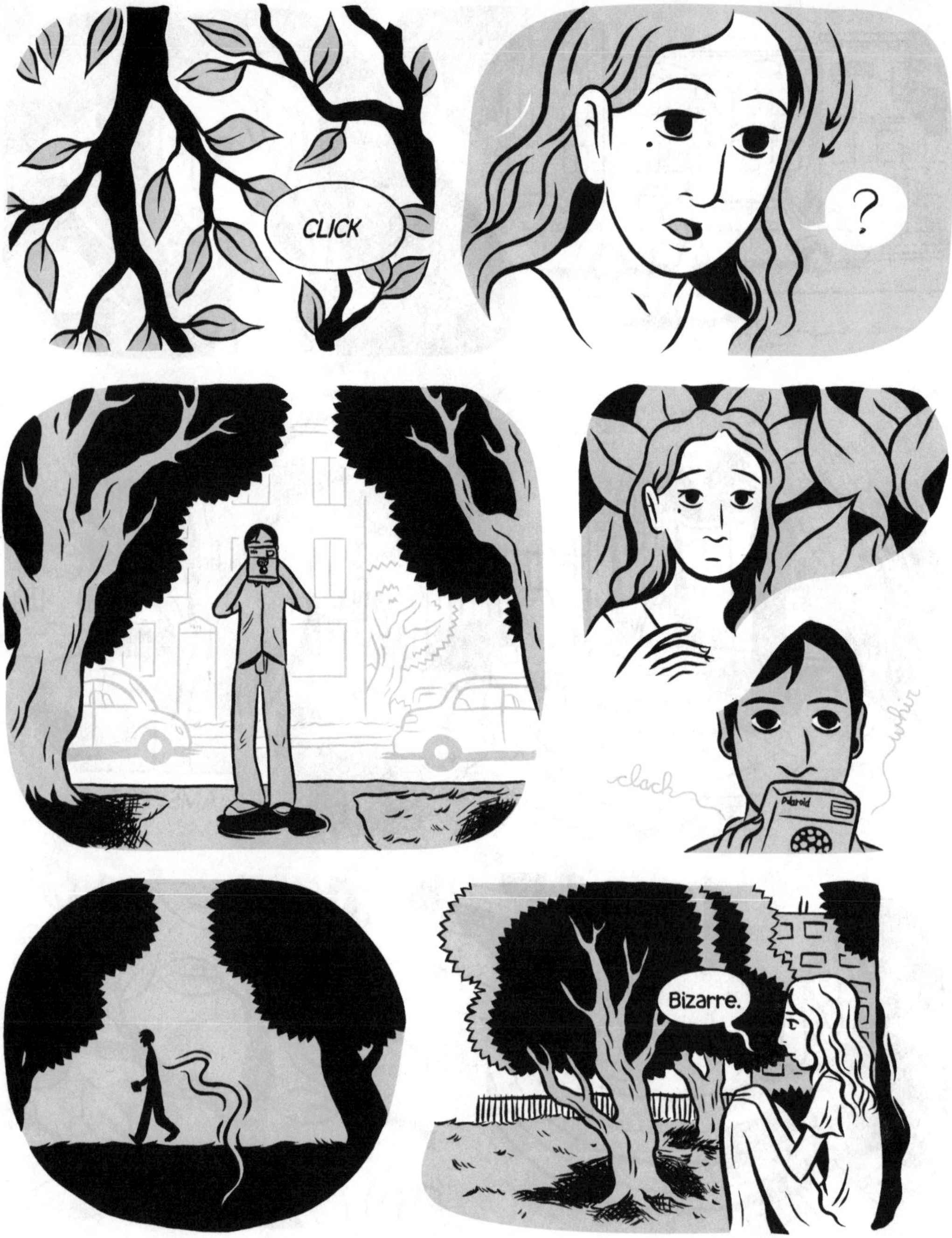
CLICK
?
clack
whir
Bizarre.

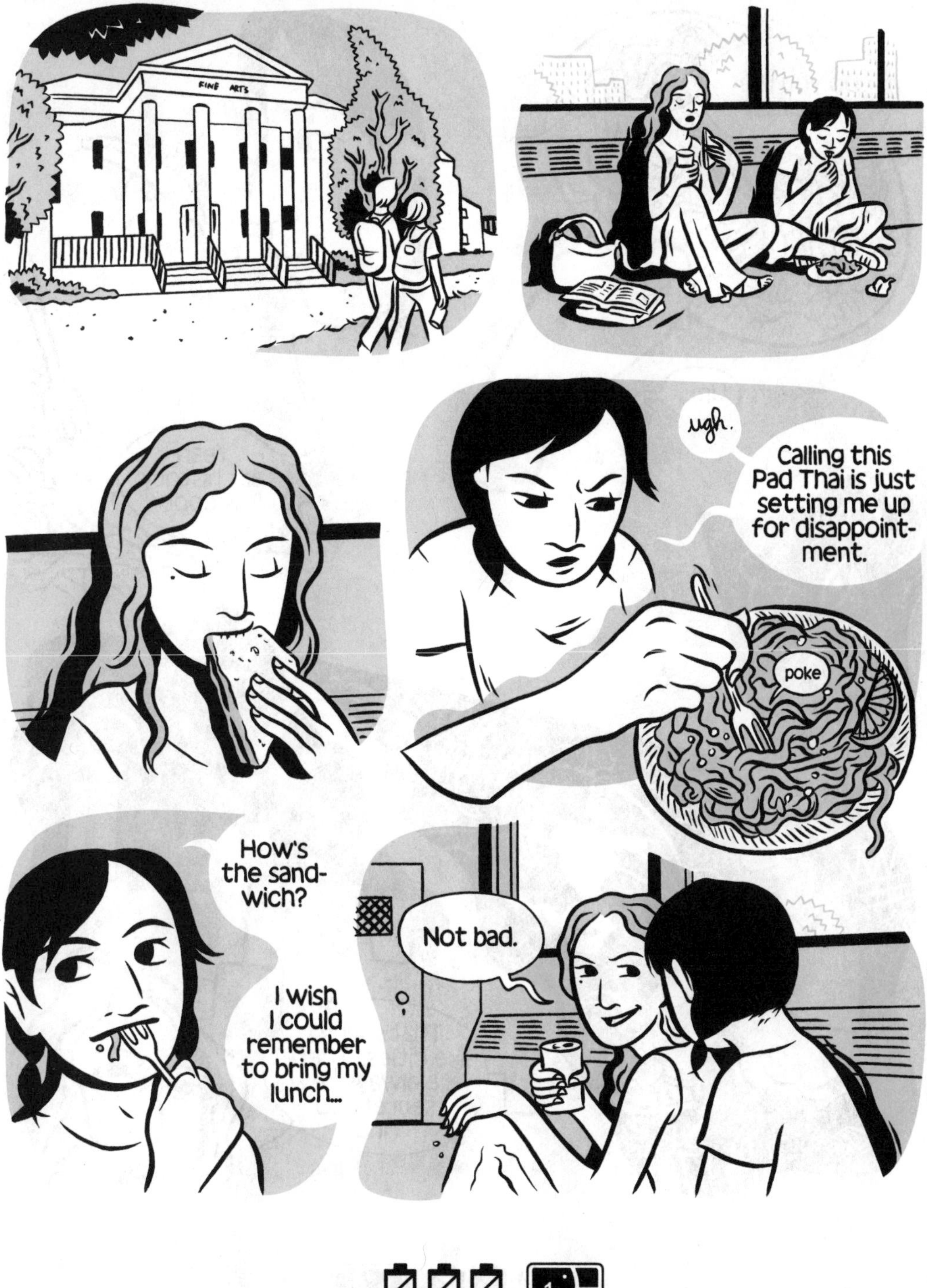
FINE ARTS
ugh.
Calling this Pad Thai is just setting me up for disappoint-ment.
poke
How's the sand-wich?
I wish I could remember to bring my lunch...
Not bad.

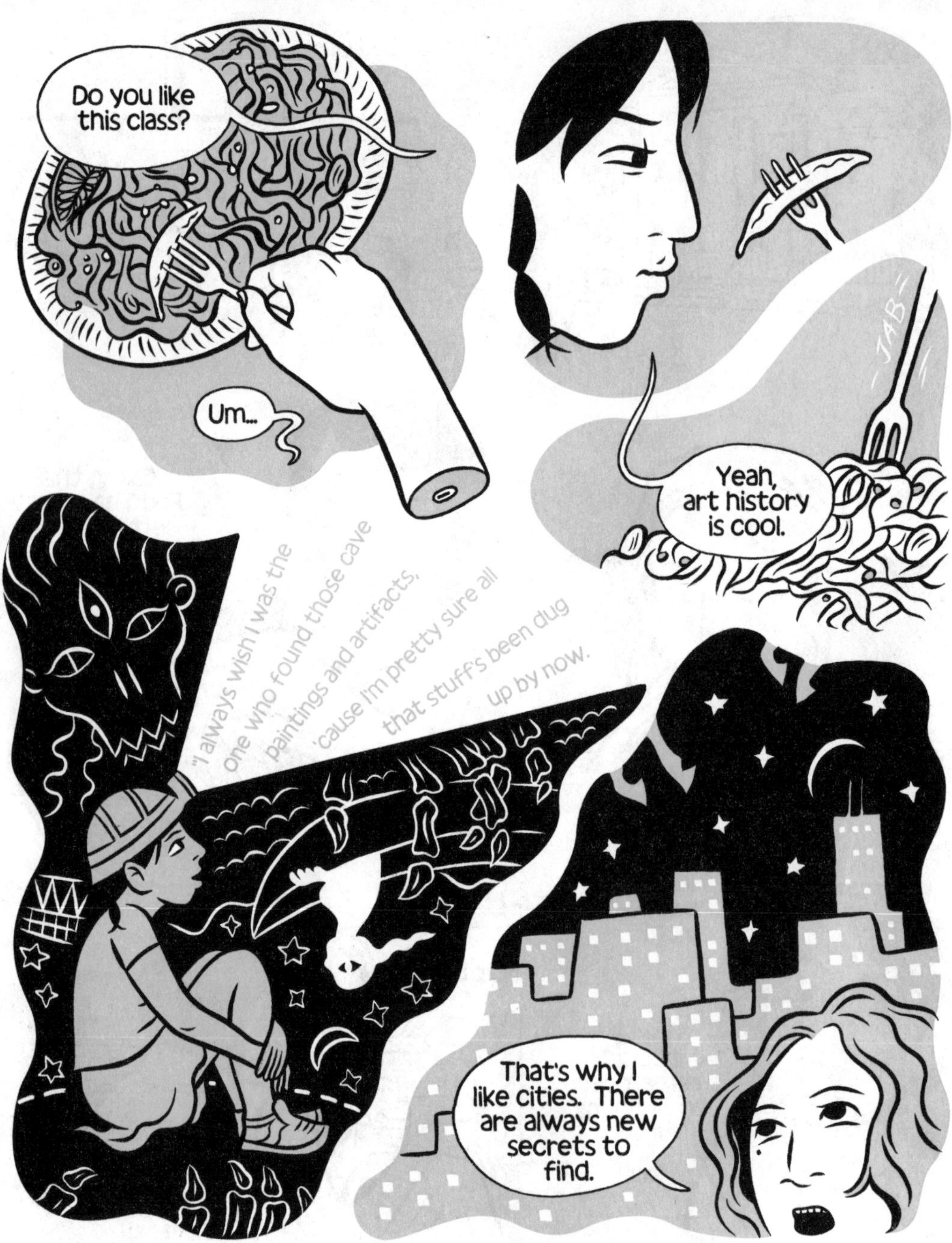
Do you like this class?
Um...
Yeah, art history is cool.
JAB
"I always wish I was the one who found those cave paintings and artifacts, 'cause I'm pretty sure all that stuff's been dug up by now.
That's why I like cities. There are always new secrets to find.

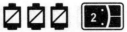

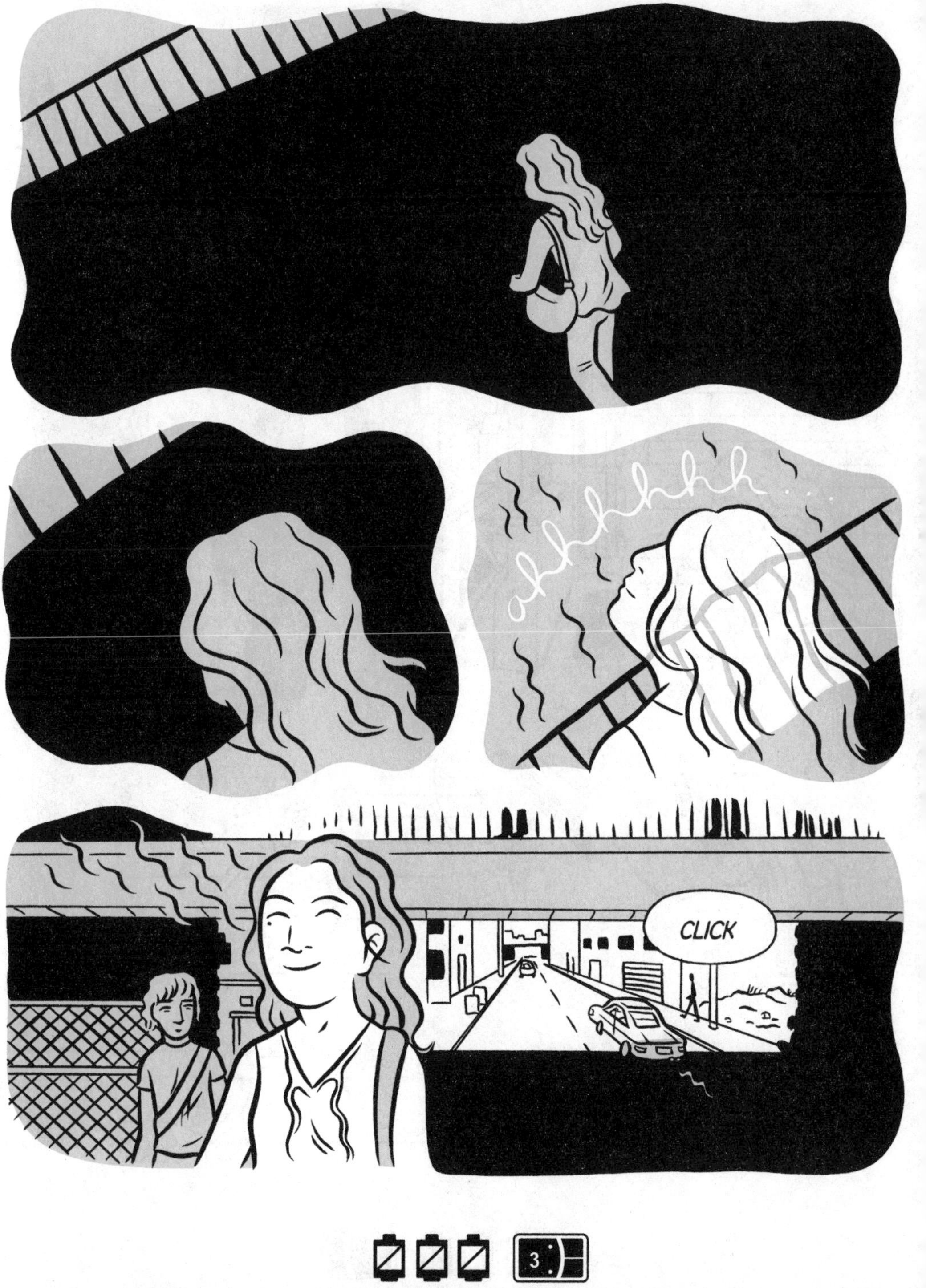
ahhhhhh...
CLICK

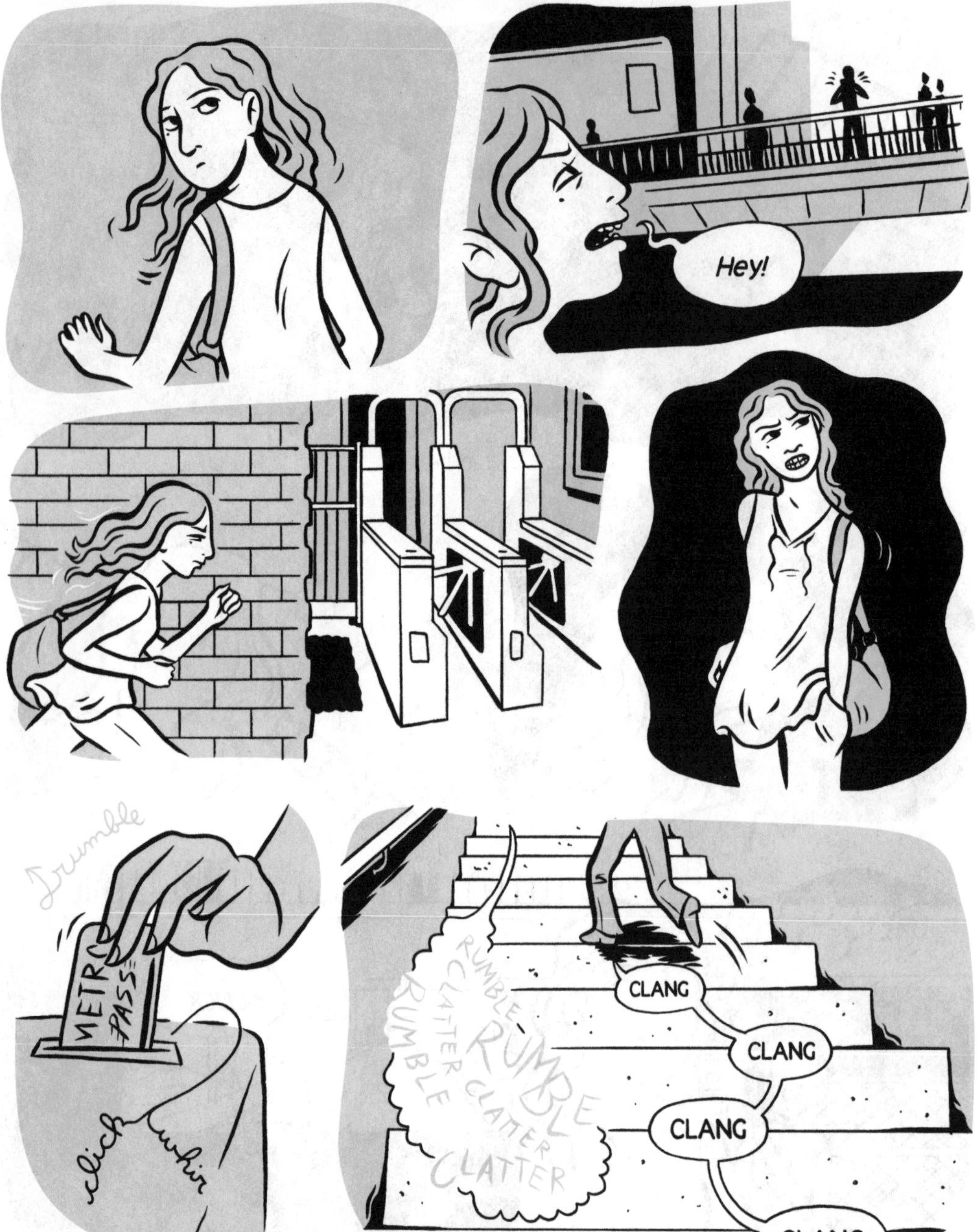
Hey!
rumble
METRO PASS
click
whir
RUMBLE RUMBLE RUMBLE
CLATTER CLATTER CLATTER CLATTER
CLANG
CLANG
CLANG
CLANG

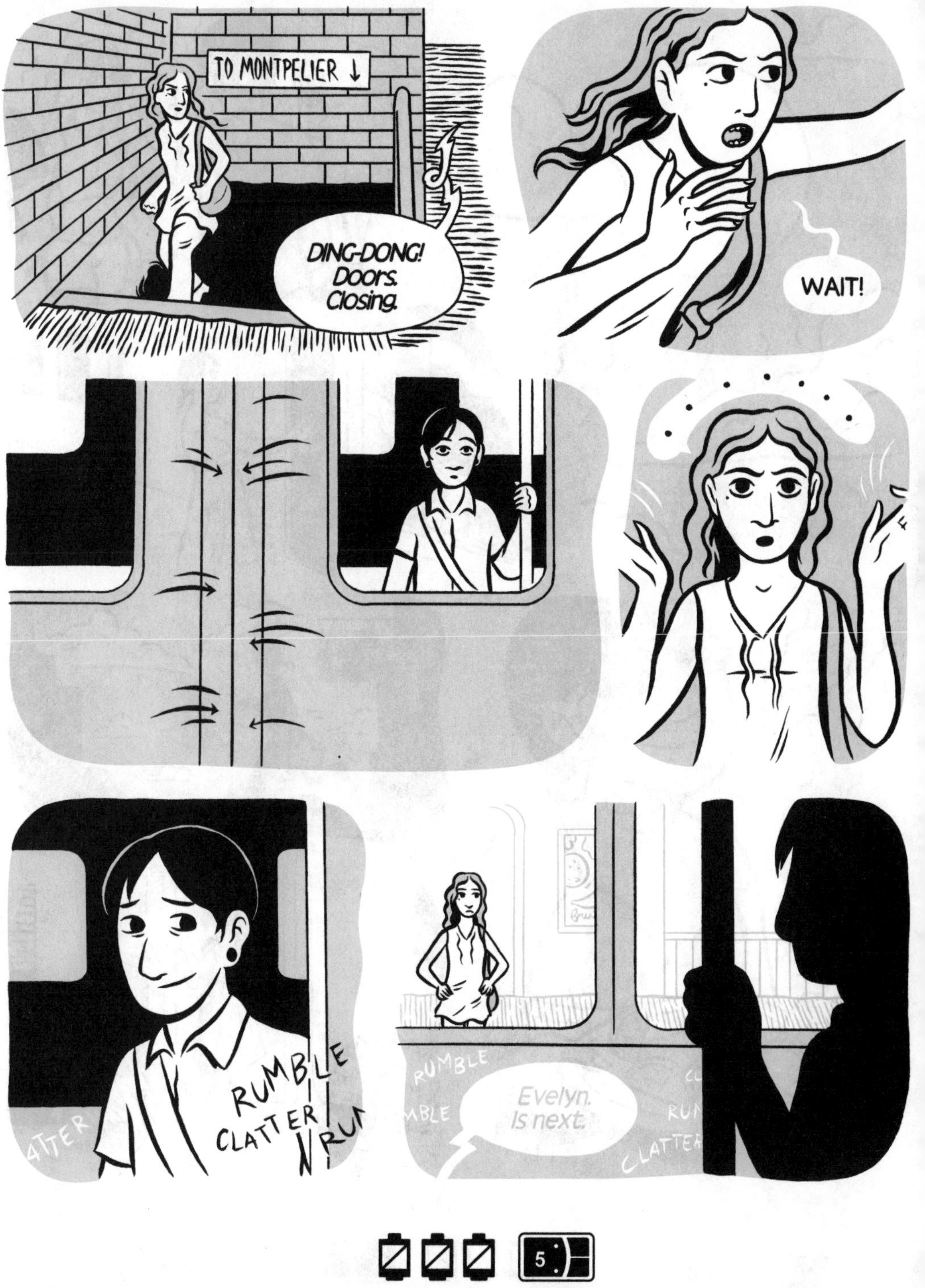
TO MONTPELIER ↓
DING-DONG! Doors. Closing.
WAIT!
RUMBLE
CLATTER
RUMBLE
Evelyn. Is next.
CLATTER

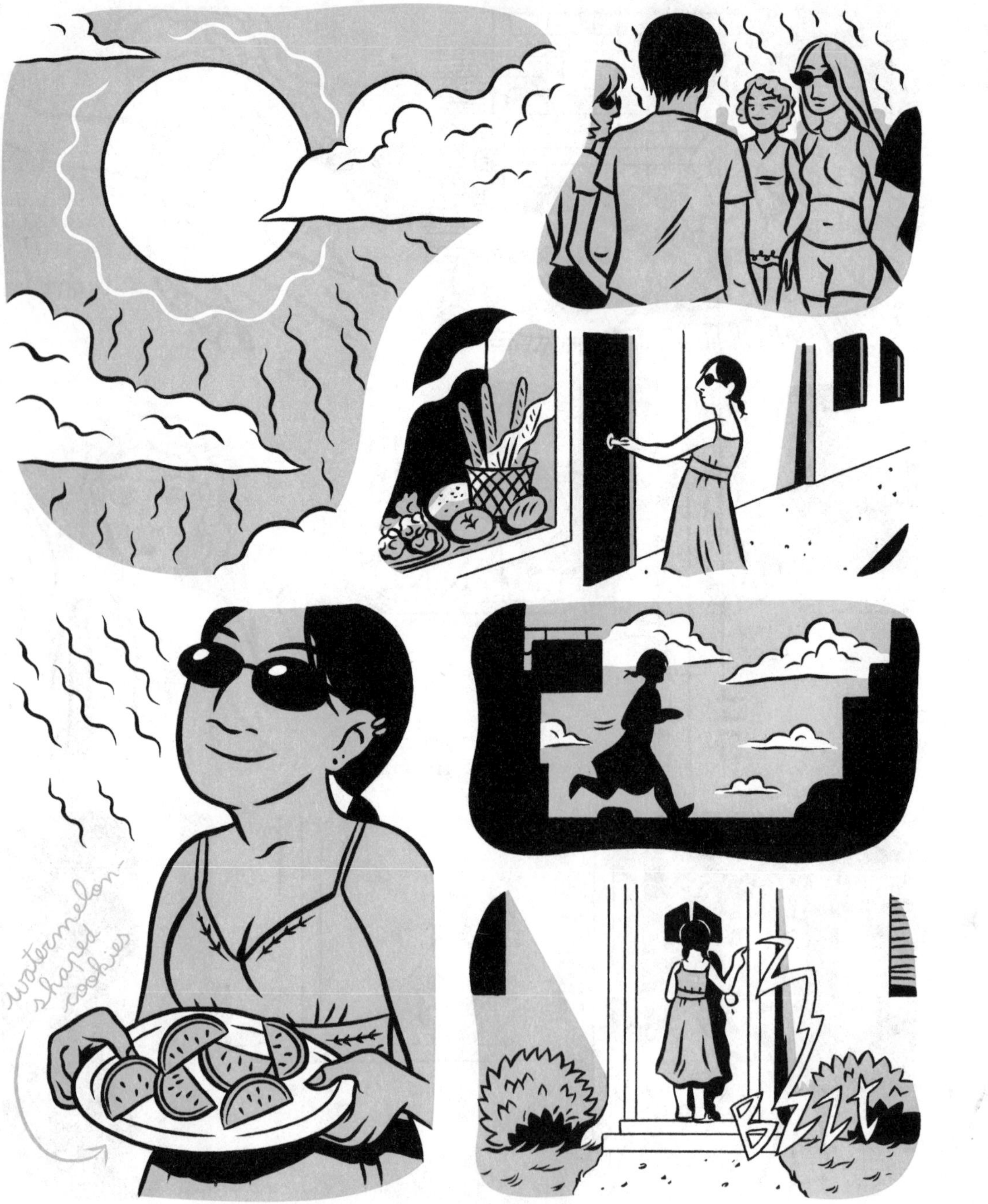
watermelon-shaped cookies
BZZZt

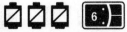

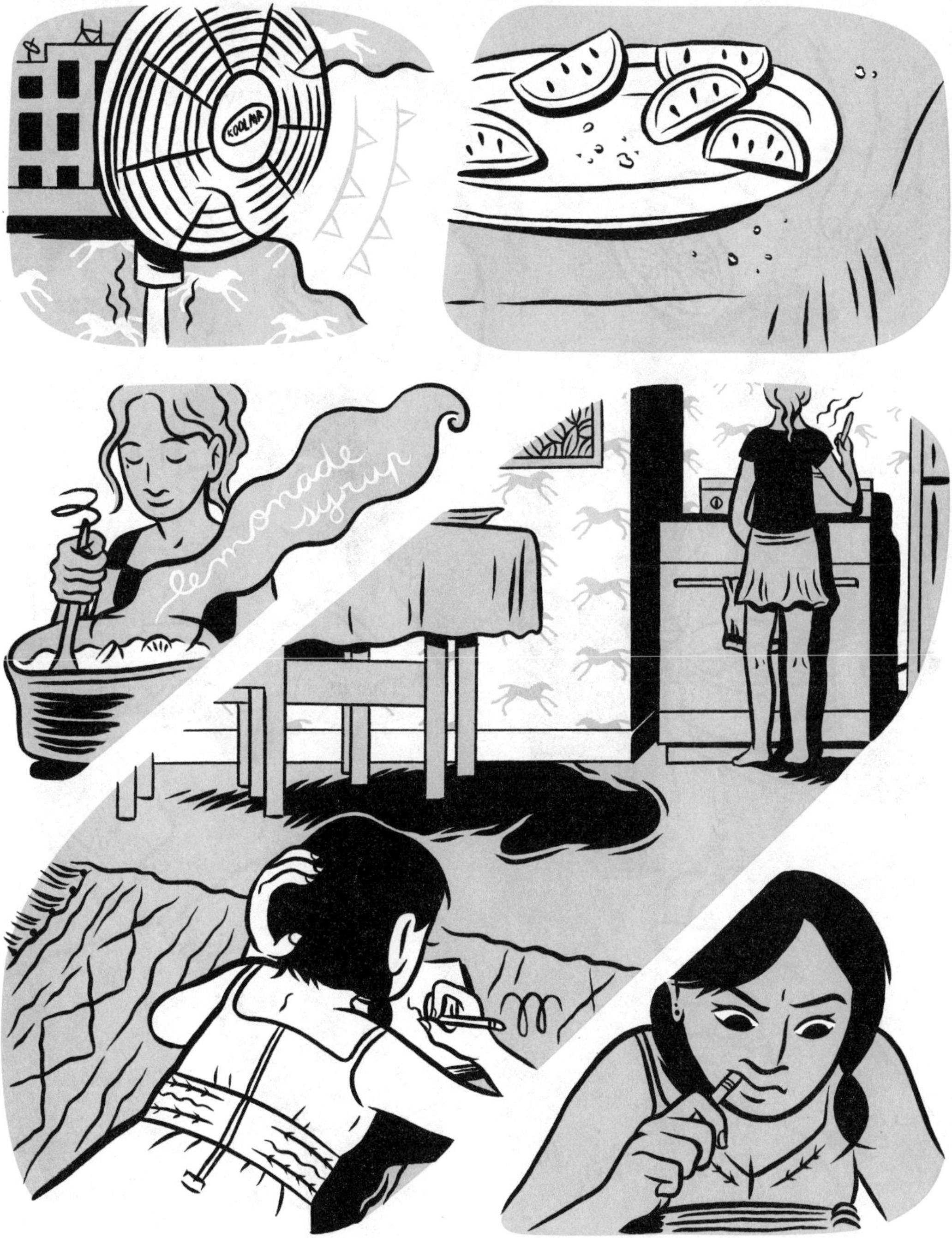
KOOL AIR
lemonade syrup

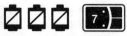

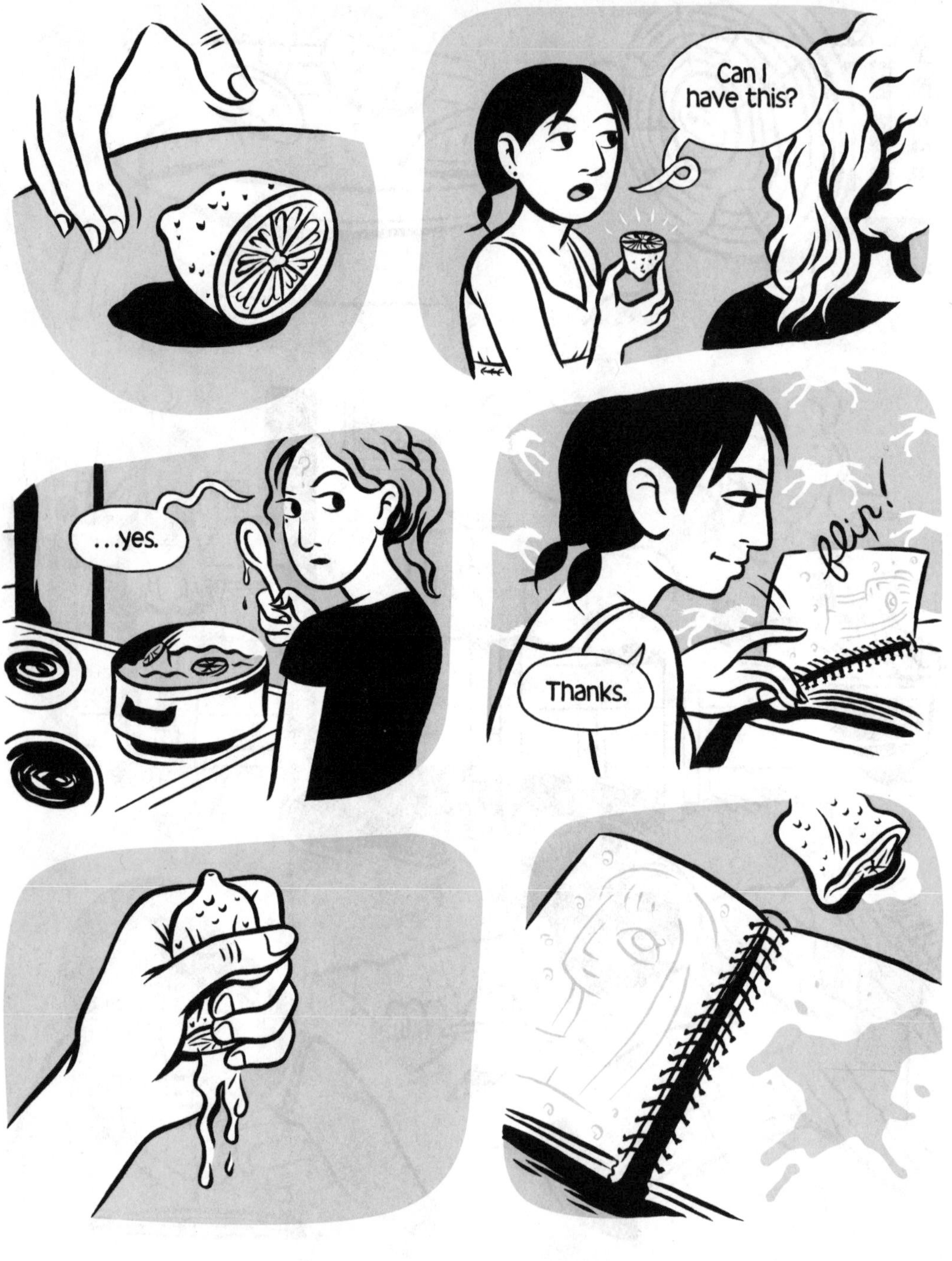
Can I have this?
...yes.
flip!
Thanks.

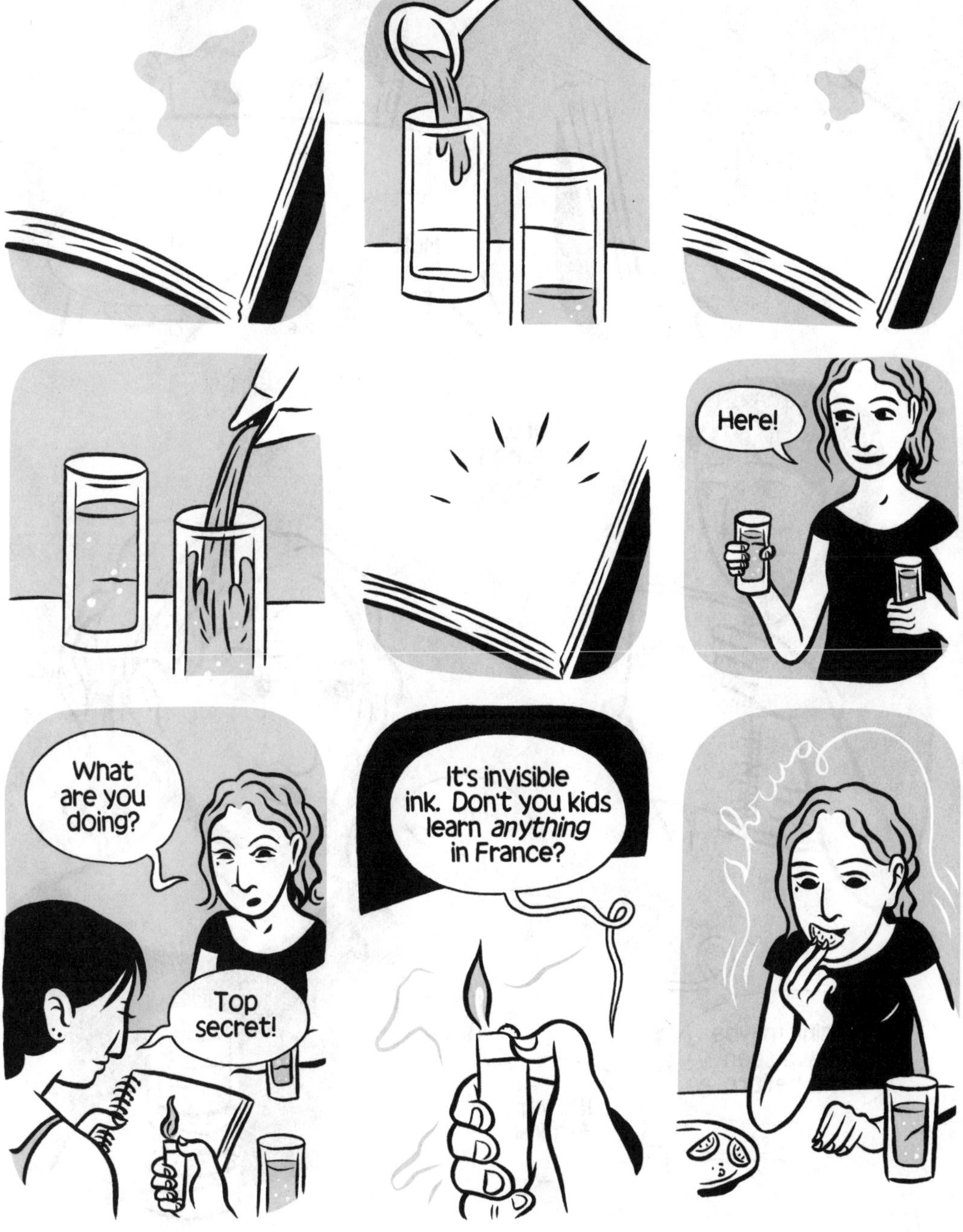
Here!
What are you doing?
Top secret!
It's invisible ink. Don't you kids learn *anything* in France?
shrug

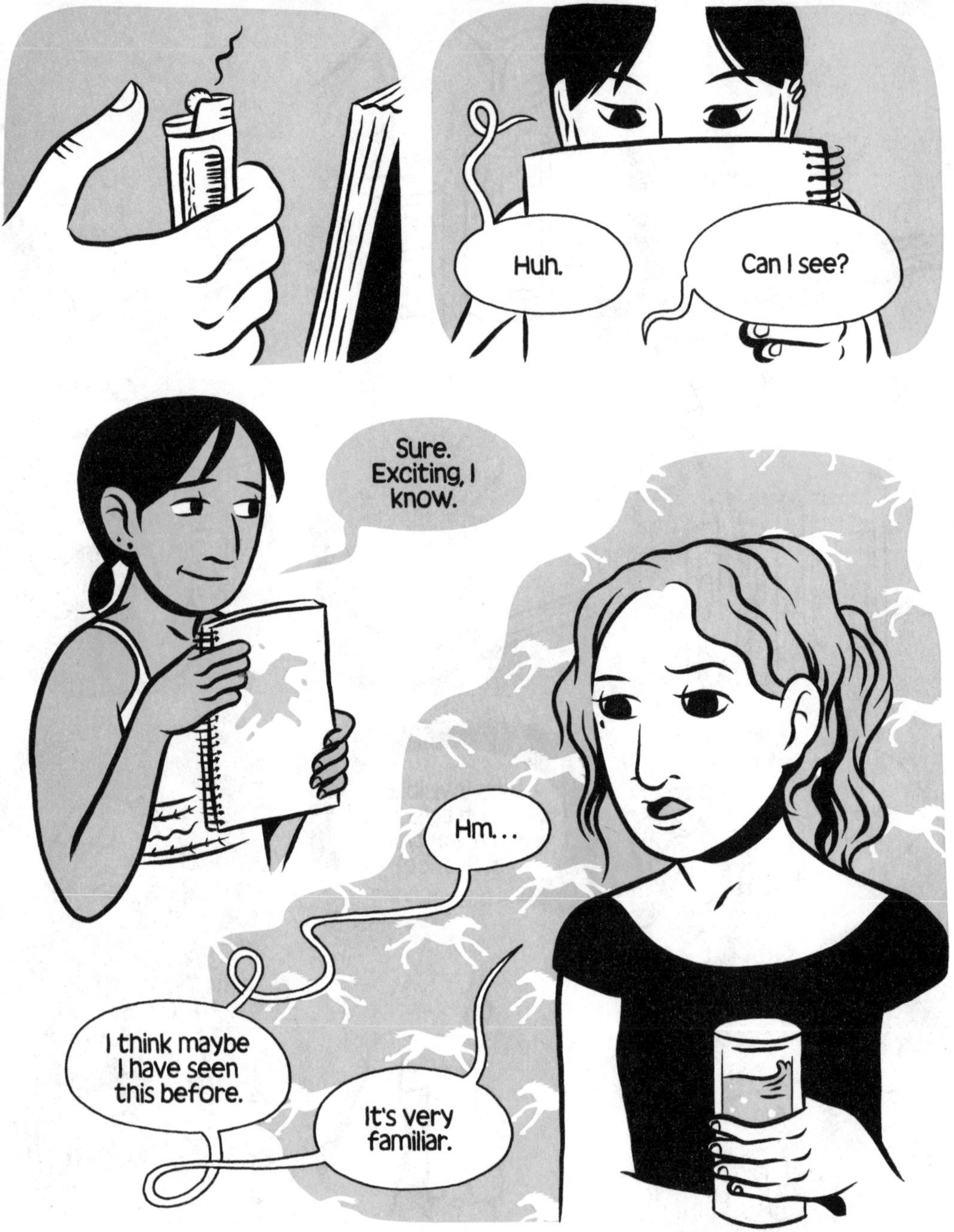
Huh.
Can I see?
Sure. Exciting, I know.
Hm...
I think maybe I have seen this before.
It's very familiar.

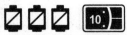

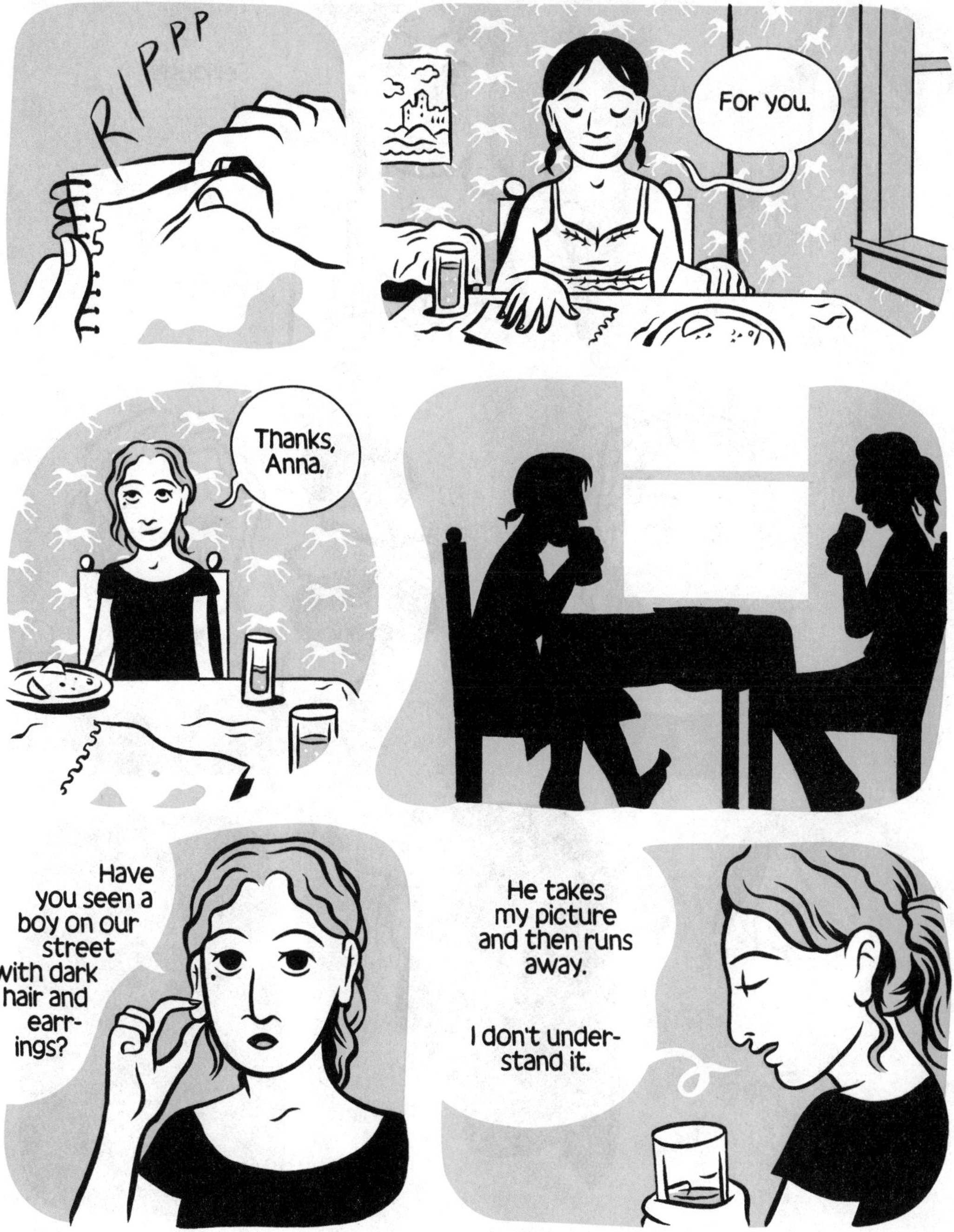
RIPPP
For you.
Thanks, Anna.
Have you seen a boy on our street with dark hair and earr-ings?
He takes my picture and then runs away.
I don't under-stand it.

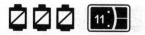

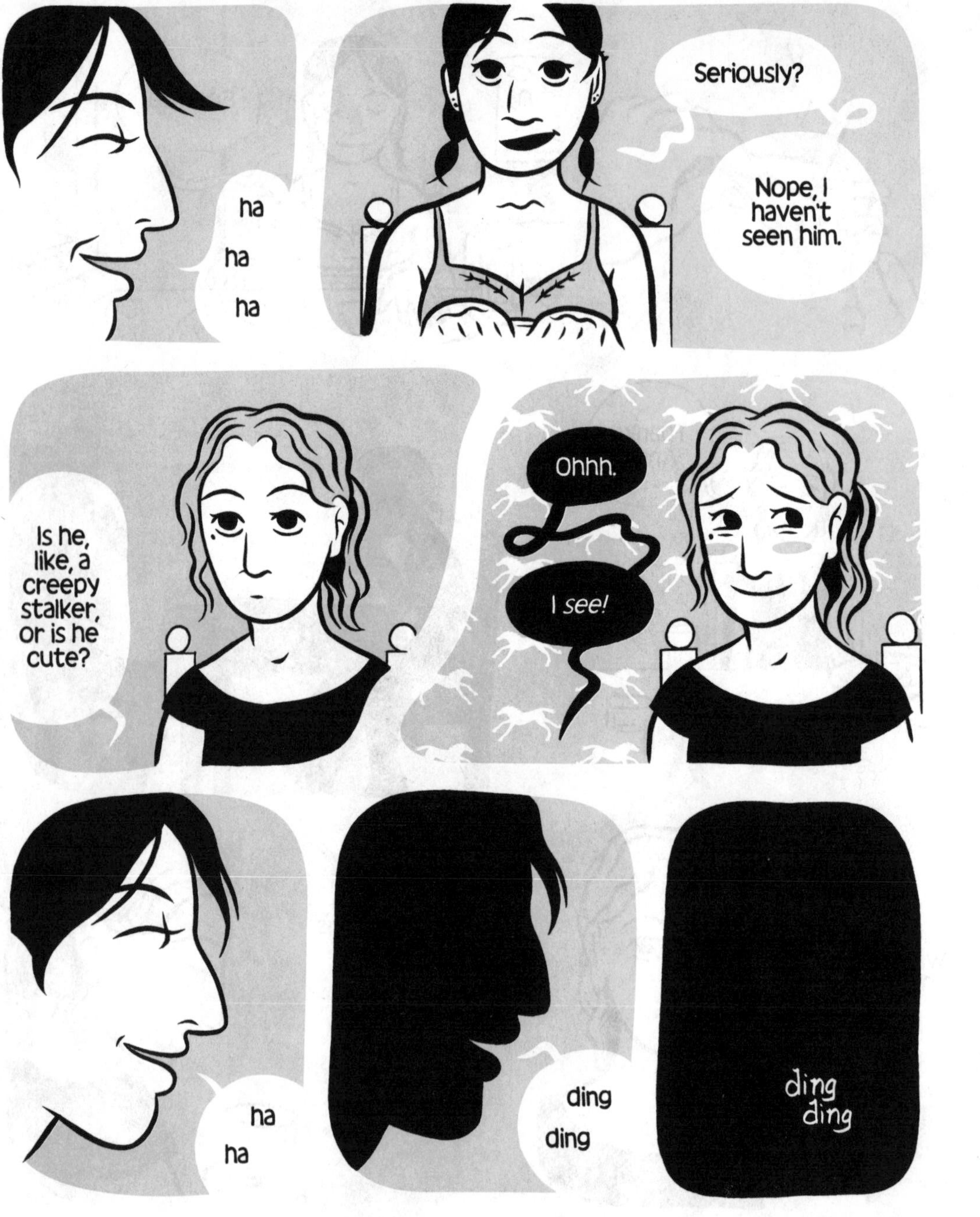

ha
ha
ha
Seriously?
Nope, I haven't seen him.
Is he, like, a creepy stalker, or is he cute?
Ohhh.
I *see!*
ha
ha
ding
ding
ding
ding

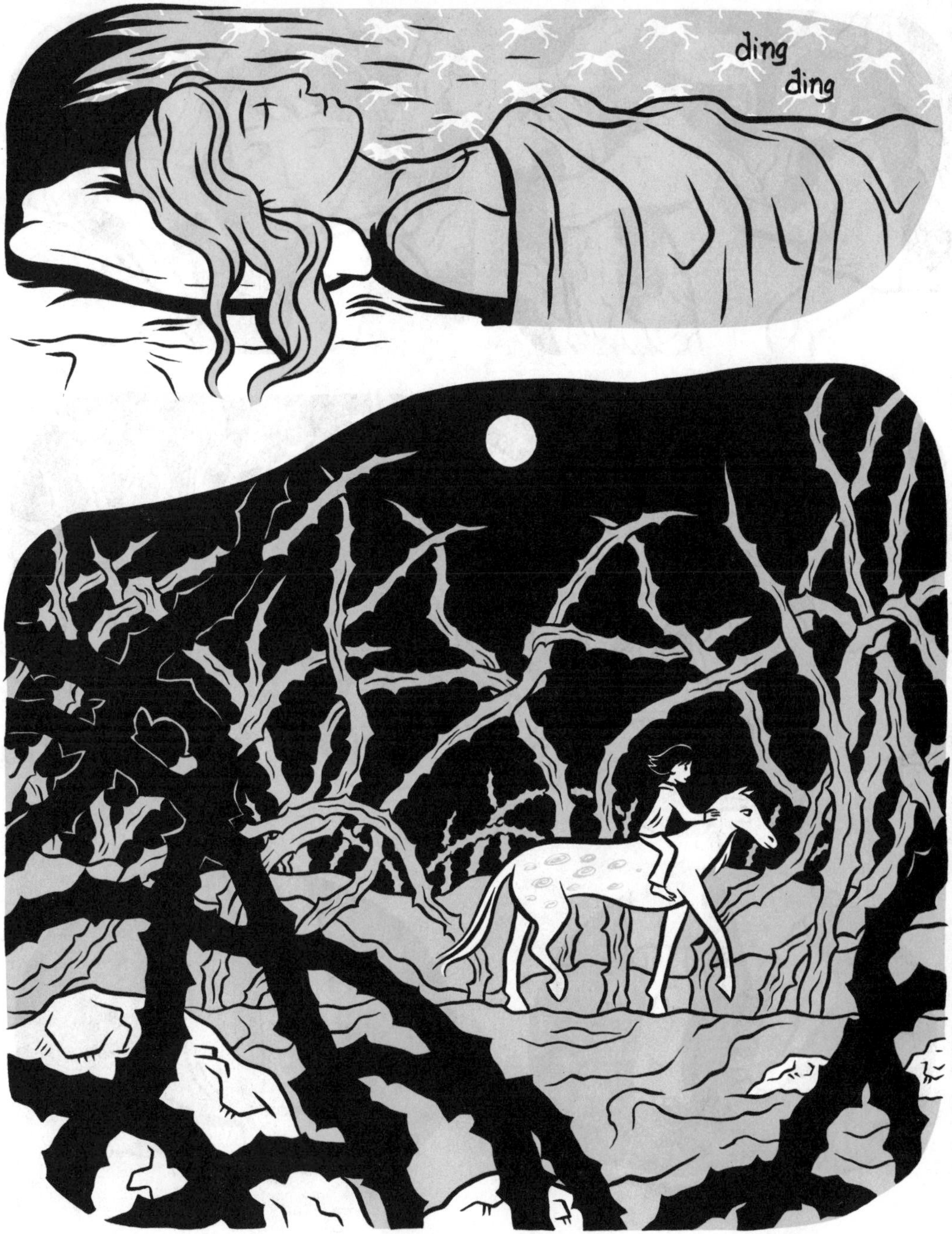
ding
ding

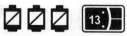

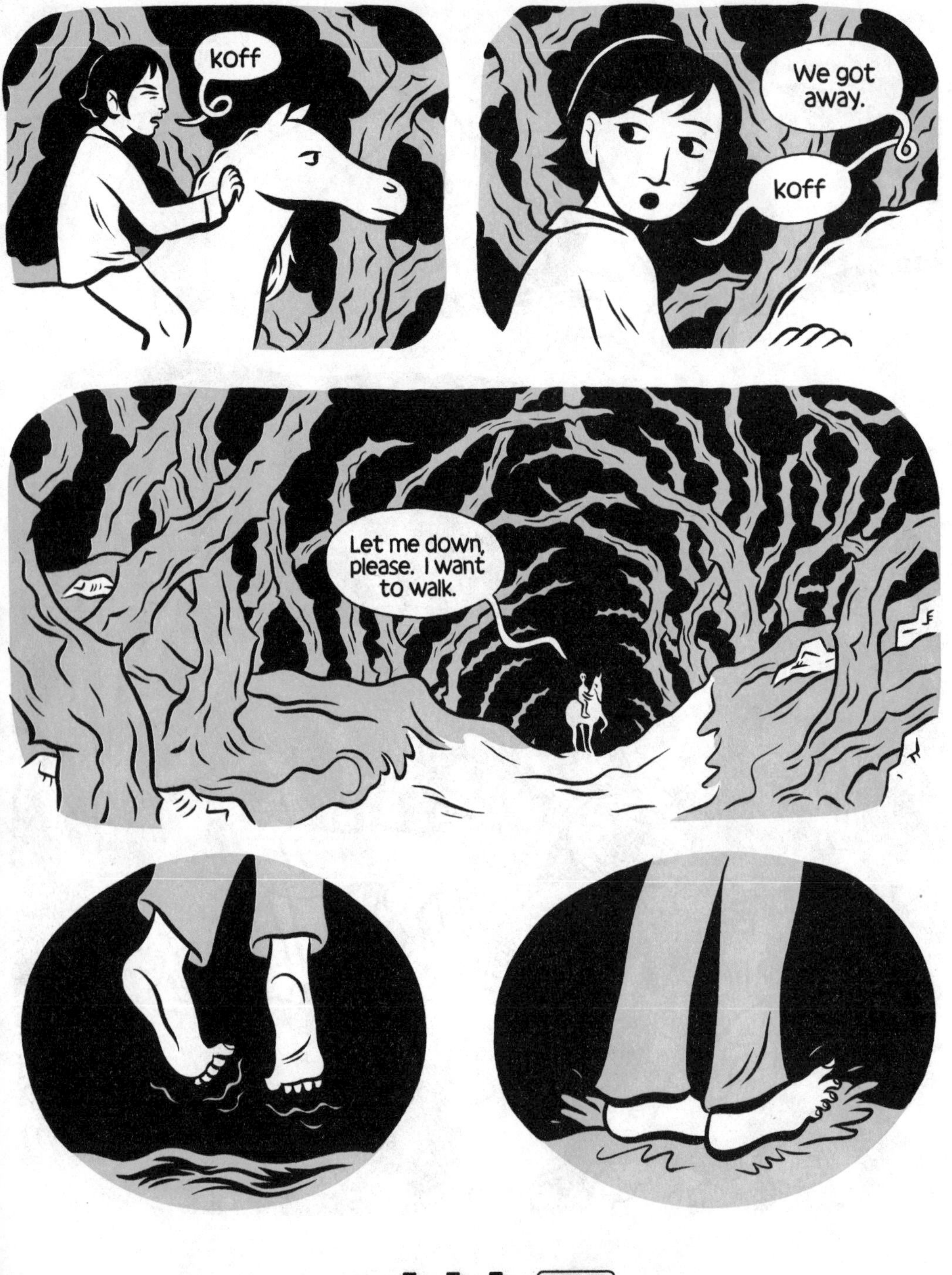
koff
We got away.
koff
Let me down, please. I want to walk.

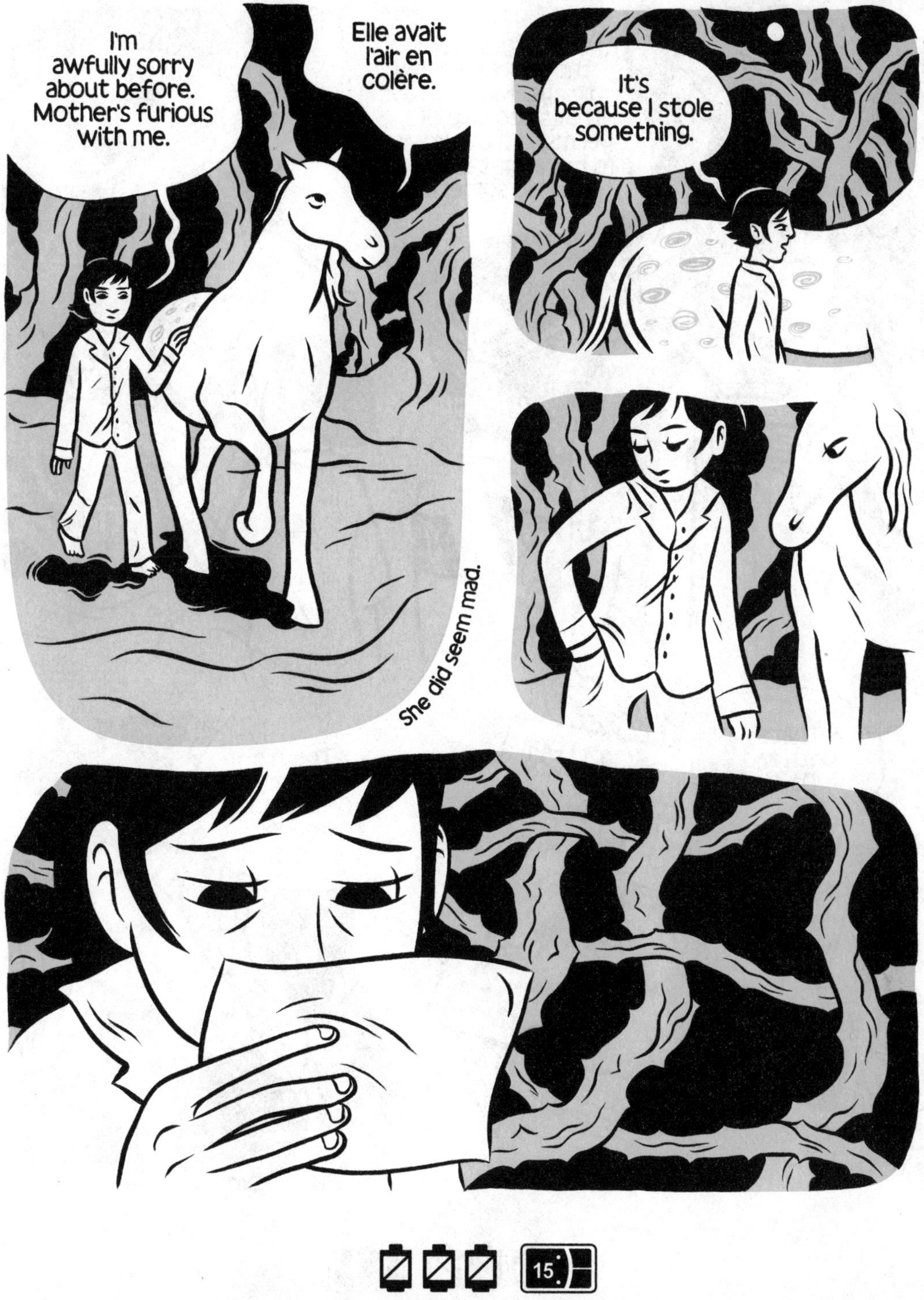

I'm awfully sorry about before. Mother's furious with me.
Elle avait l'air en colère.
She did seem mad.
It's because I stole something.

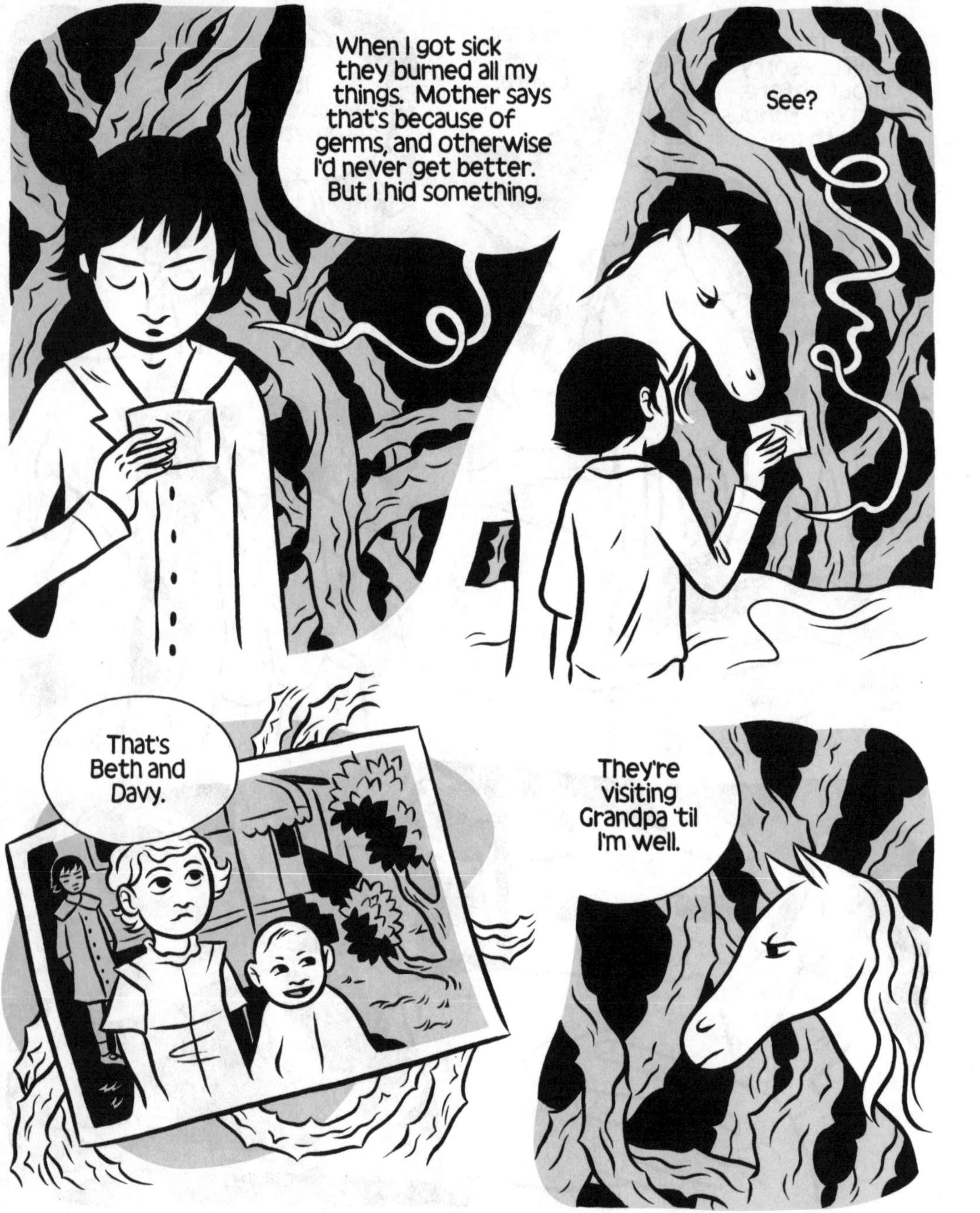
When I got sick they burned all my things. Mother says that's because of germs, and otherwise I'd never get better. But I hid something.
See?
That's Beth and Davy.
They're visiting Grandpa 'til I'm well.

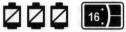

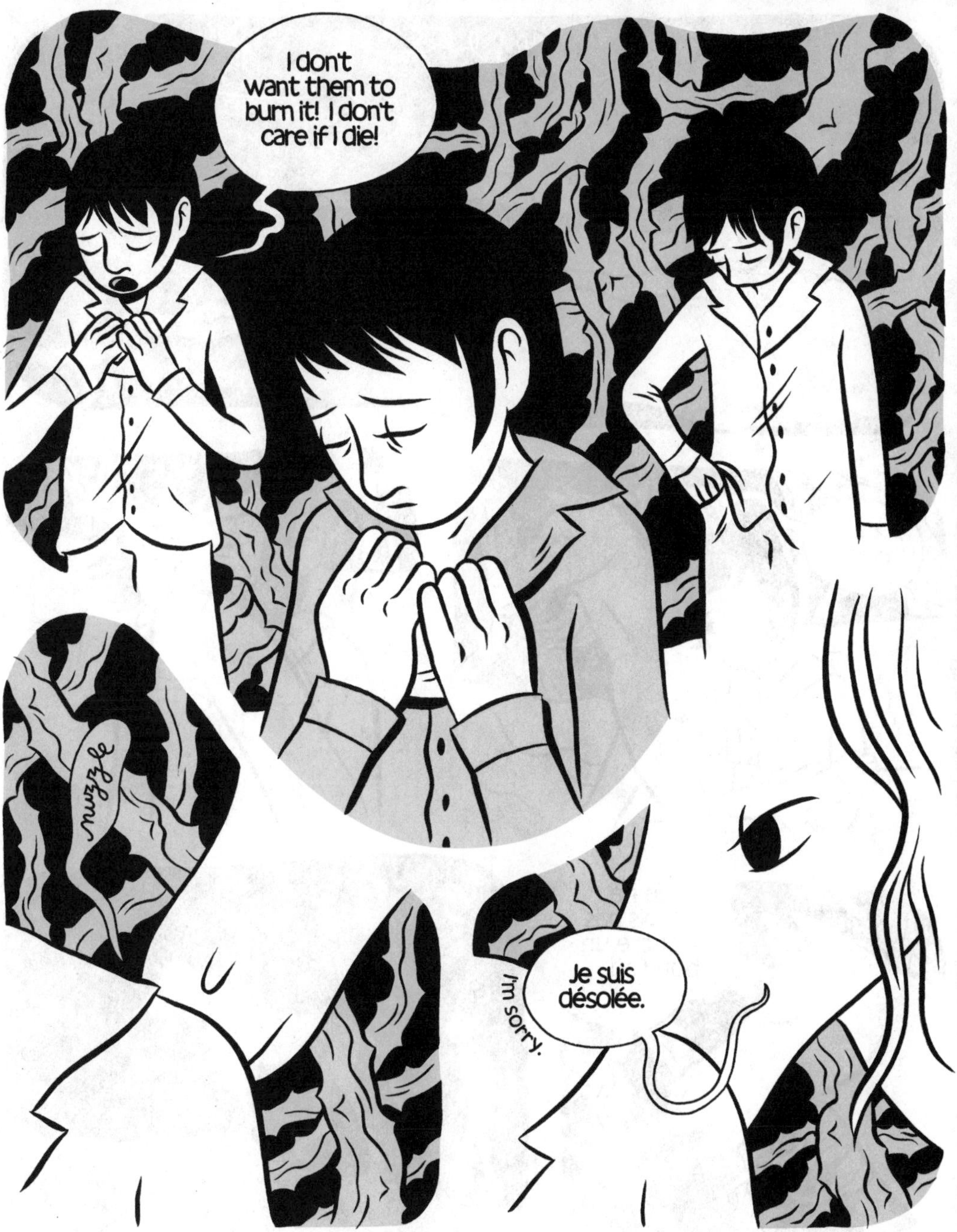

I don't want them to burn it! I don't care if I die!
muzzle
Je suis désolée.
I'm sorry.

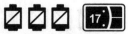

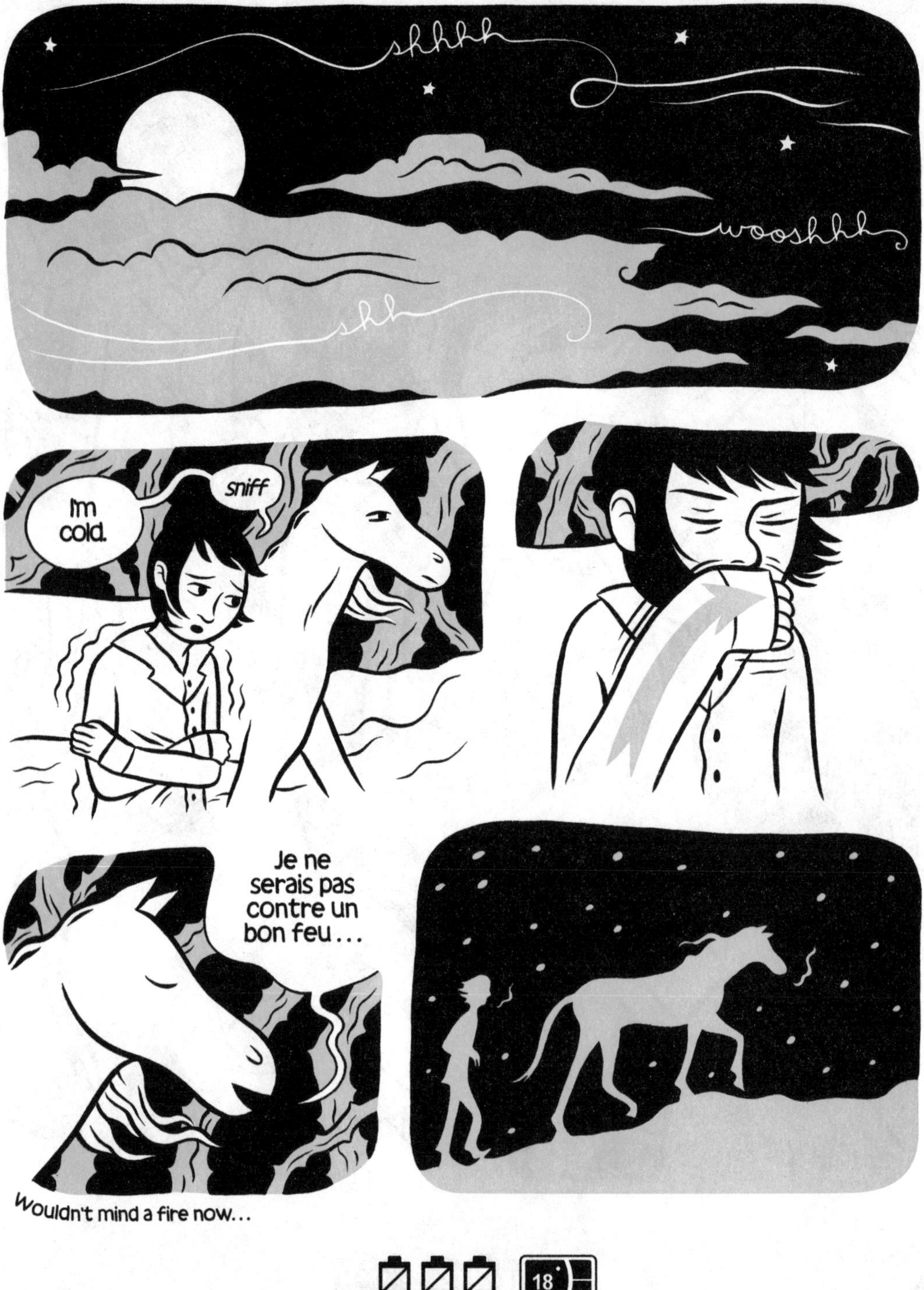
shhhh
wooshhh
shh
I'm cold.
sniff
Je ne serais pas contre un bon feu...
Wouldn't mind a fire now...

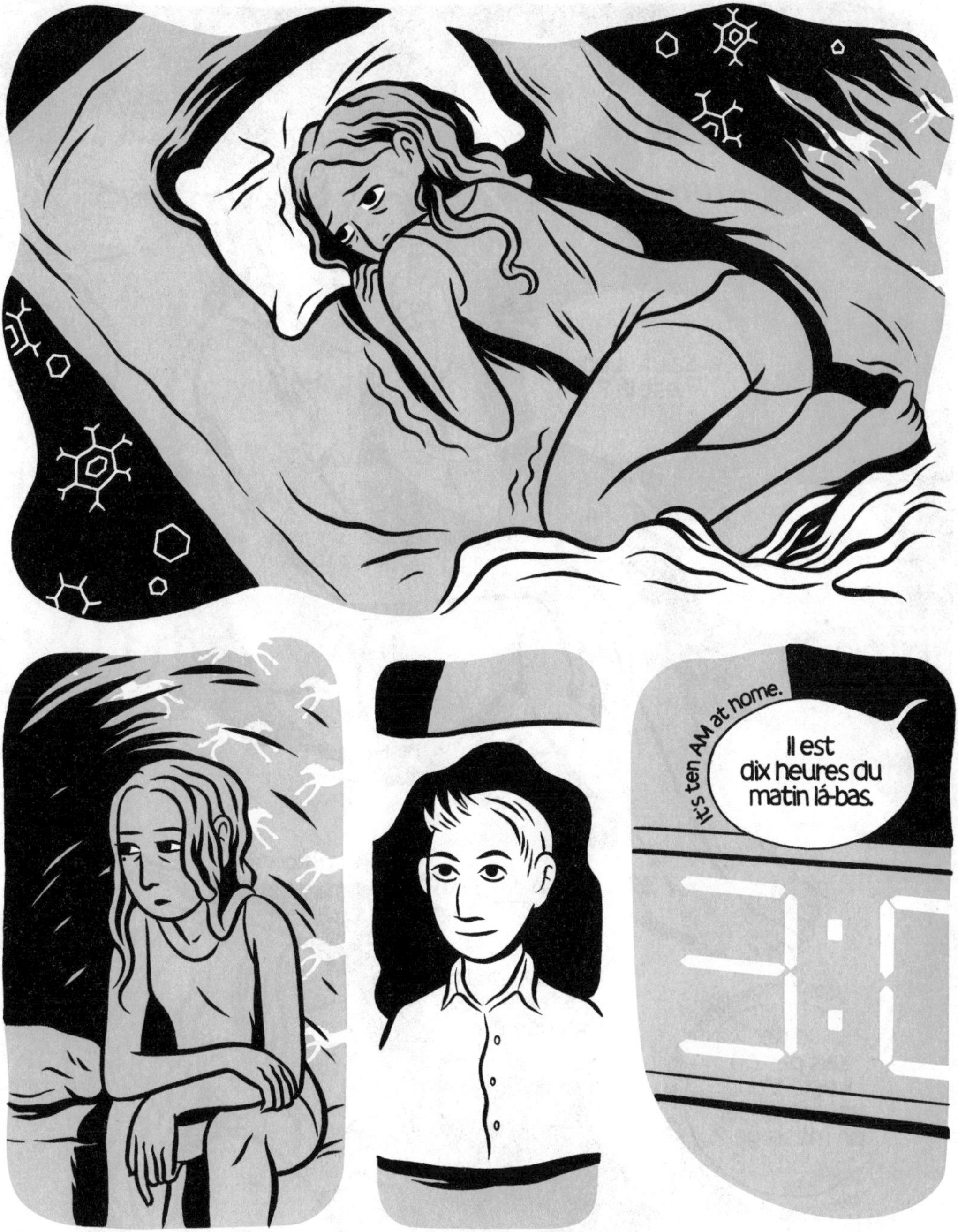
Il est dix heures du matin lá-bas.
It's ten AM at home.

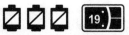

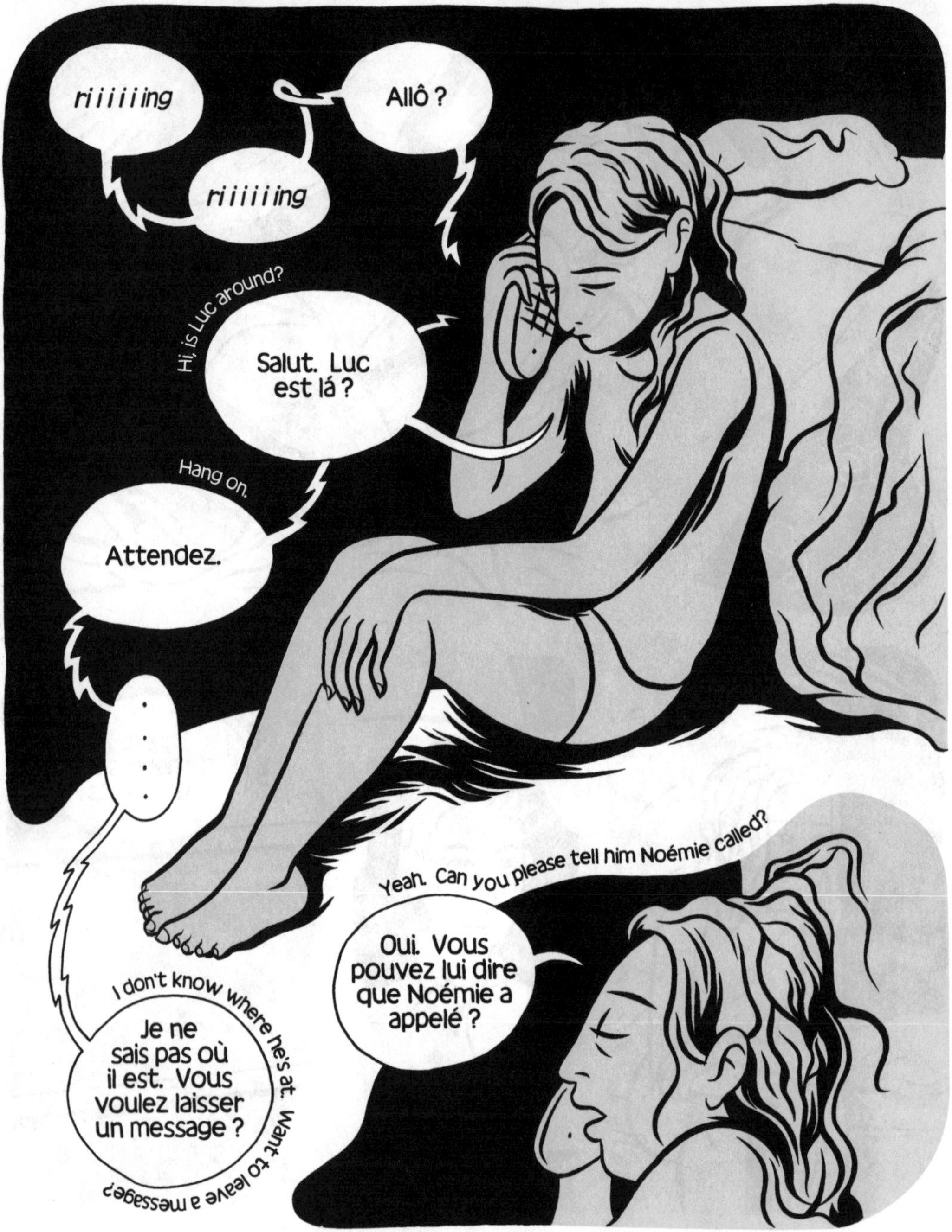
riiiiiing
riiiiiing
Allô ?
Hi, is Luc around?
Salut. Luc est lá ?
Hang on.
Attendez.
. . . .
Yeah. Can you please tell him Noémie called?
Oui. Vous pouvez lui dire que Noémie a appelé ?
I don't know where he's at. Want to leave a message?
Je ne sais pas où il est. Vous voulez laisser un message ?

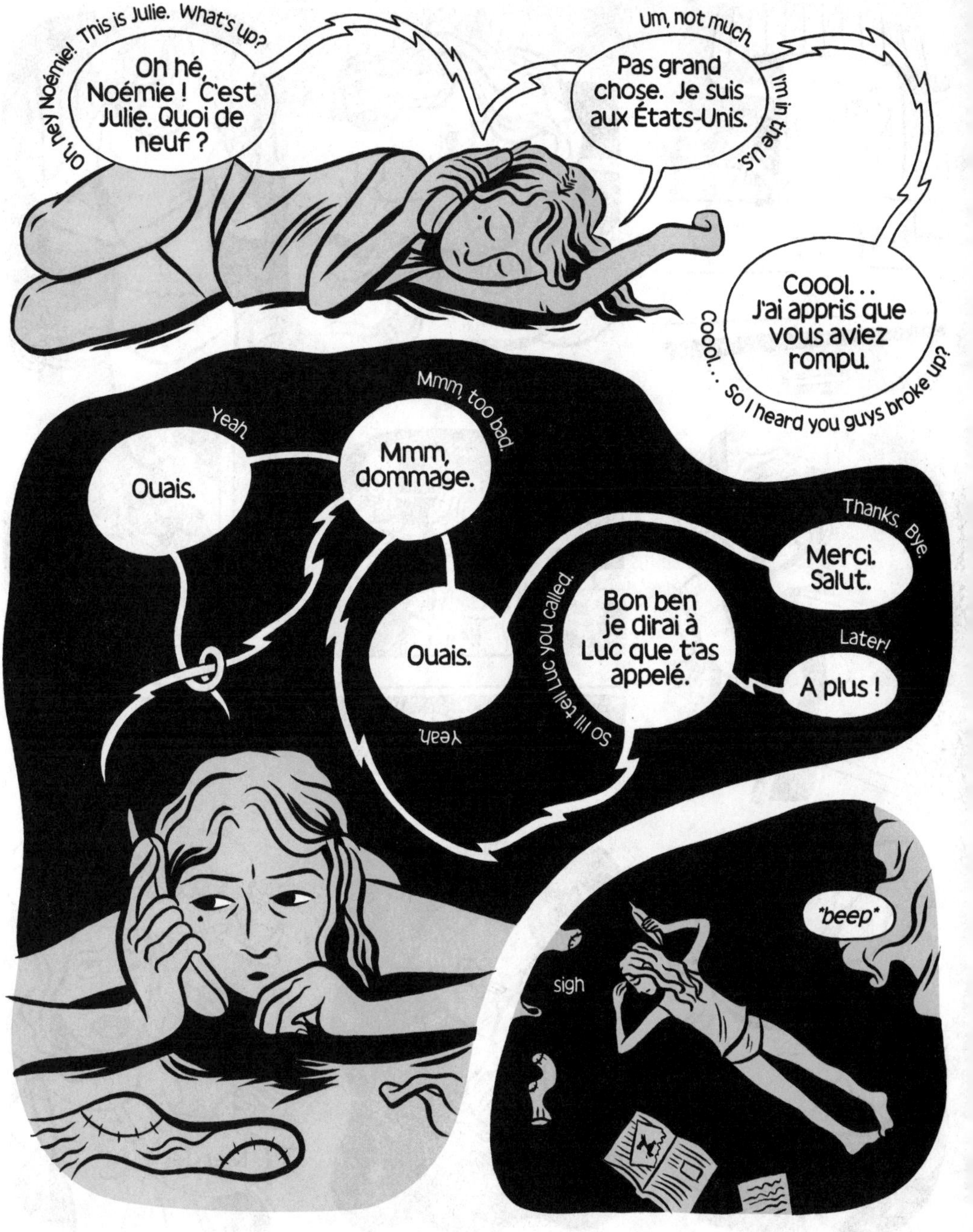
Oh hé, Noémie ! C'est Julie. Quoi de neuf ?
Oh, hey Noémie! This is Julie. What's up?
Pas grand chose. Je suis aux États-Unis.
Um, not much. I'm in the U.S.
Coool... J'ai appris que vous aviez rompu.
Coool... So I heard you guys broke up?
Ouais.
Yeah.
Mmm, dommage.
Mmm, too bad.
Ouais.
Yeah.
Bon ben je dirai à Luc que t'as appelé.
So I'll tell Luc you called.
Merci. Salut.
Thanks. Bye.
A plus !
Later!
beep
sigh

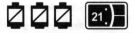

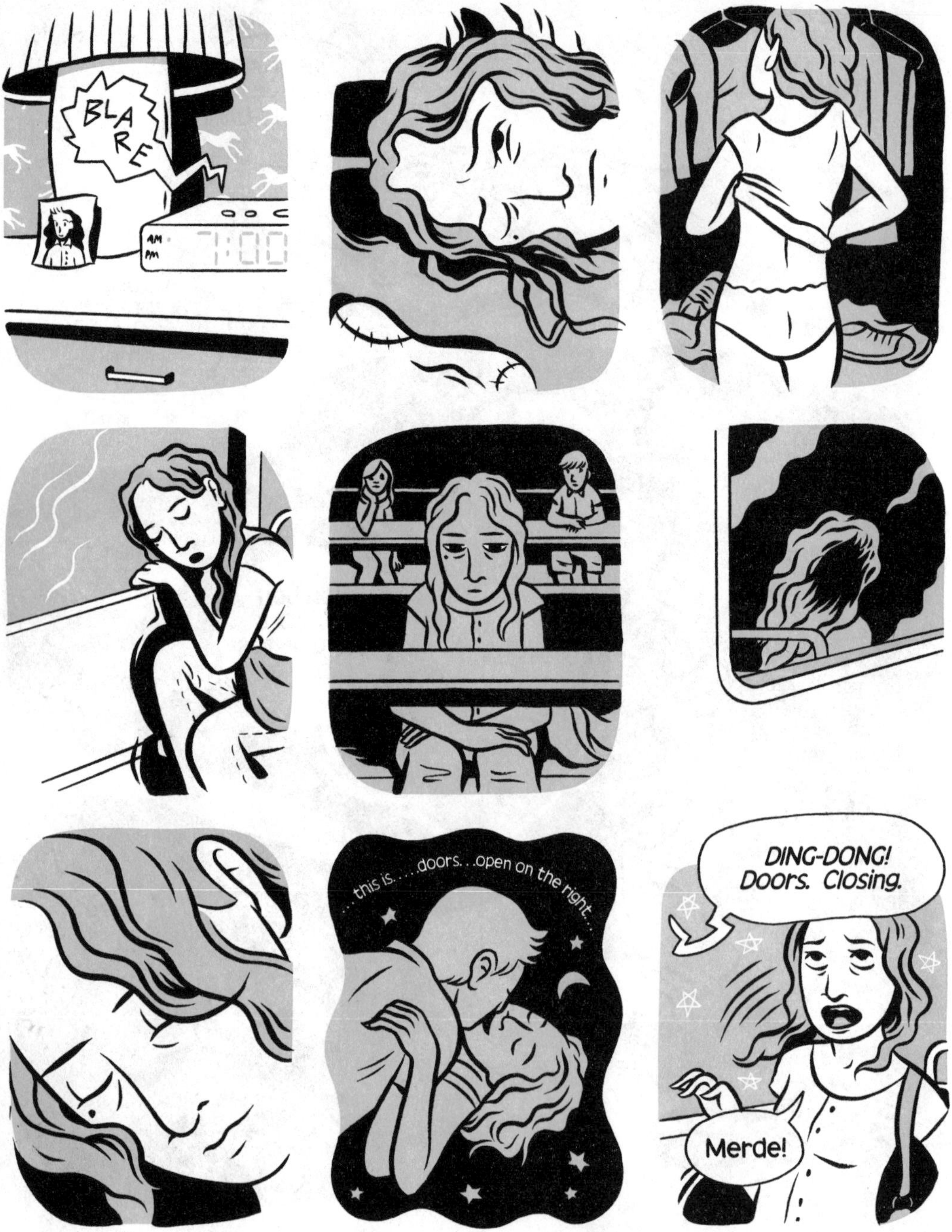
BLARE
AM
PM
7:00
. . this is. . . . .doors. . .open on the right. . . .
DING-DONG! Doors. Closing.
Merde!

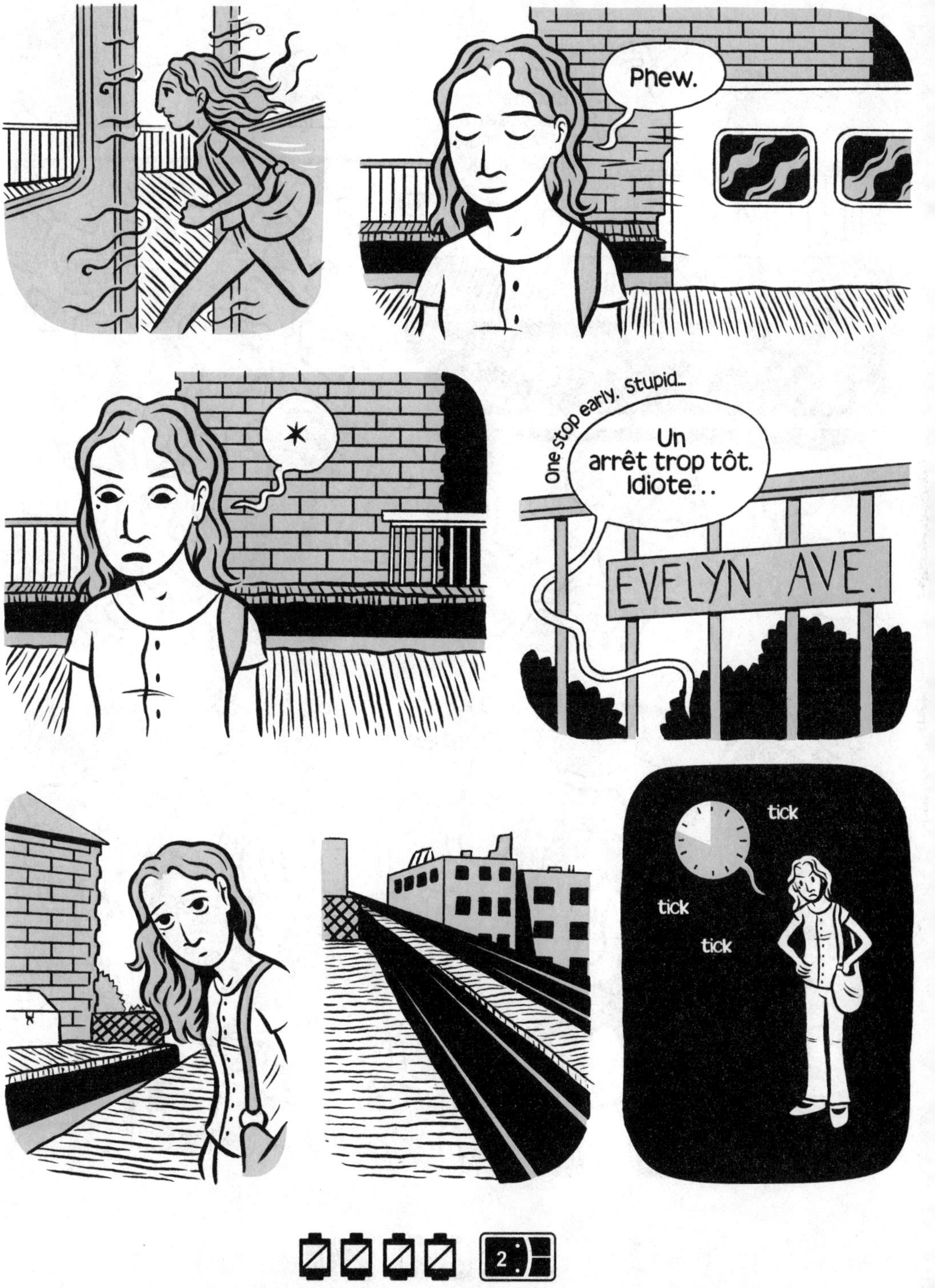
Phew.
*
One stop early. Stupid...
Un arrêt trop tôt. Idiote...
EVELYN AVE.
tick
tick
tick

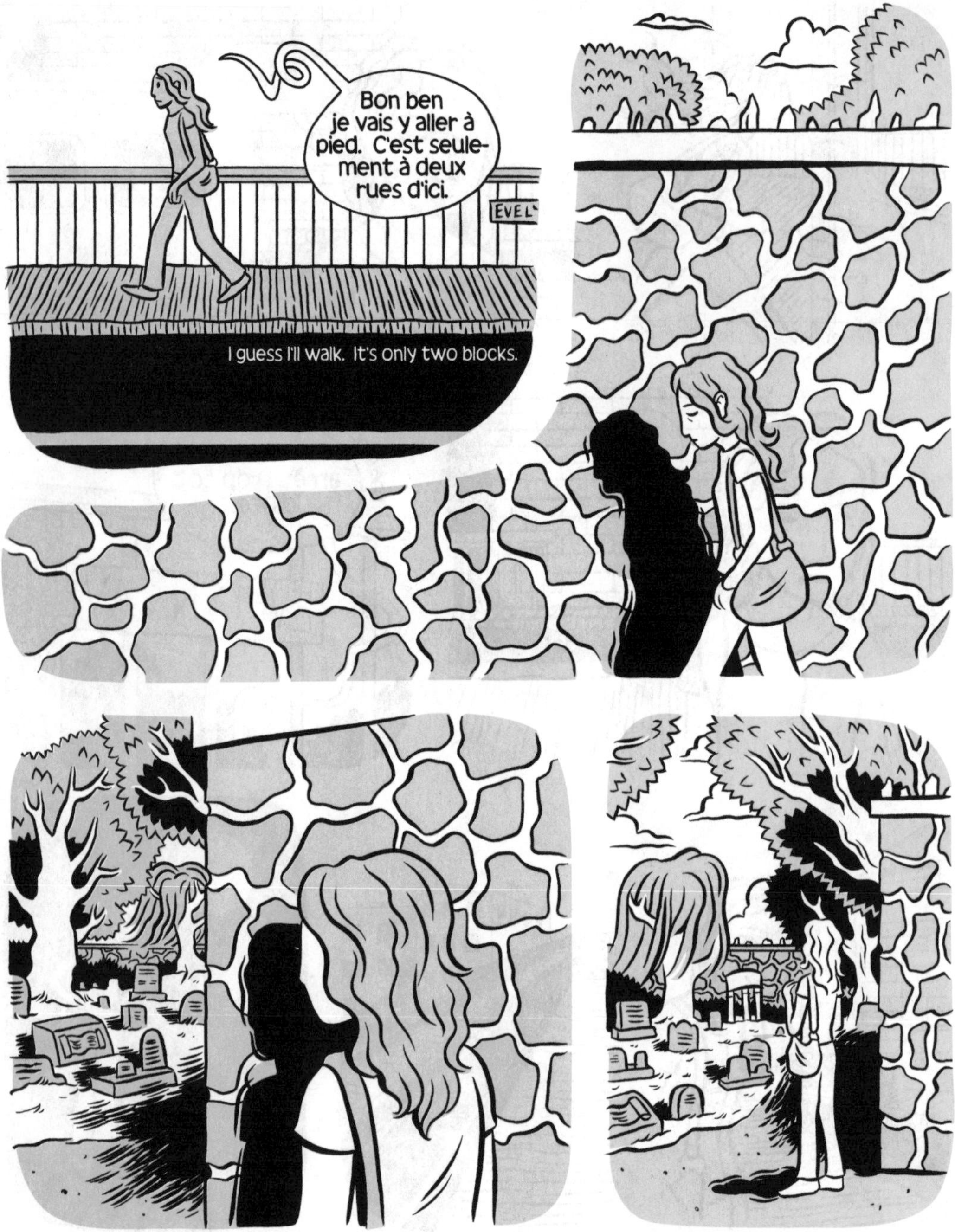
Bon ben je vais y aller à pied. C'est seulement à deux rues d'ici.
EVEL
I guess I'll walk. It's only two blocks.

C'est calme ici, pas comme au centre ville.
It's quiet here, not like the middle of a city.
shh
shhhh

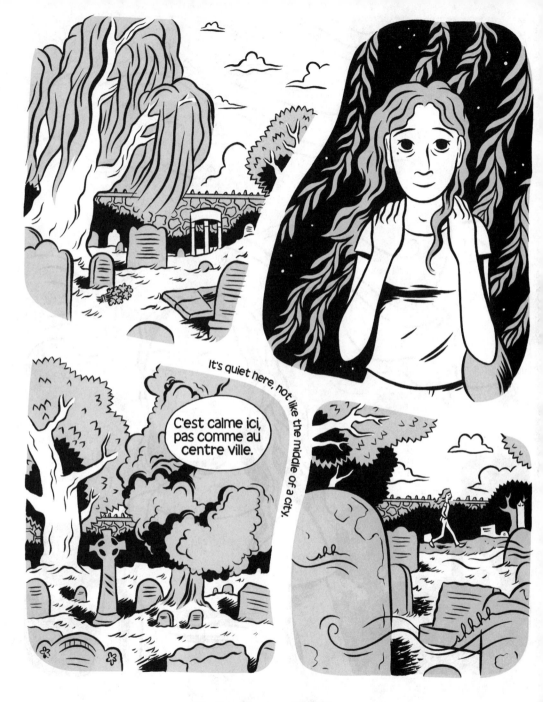

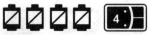

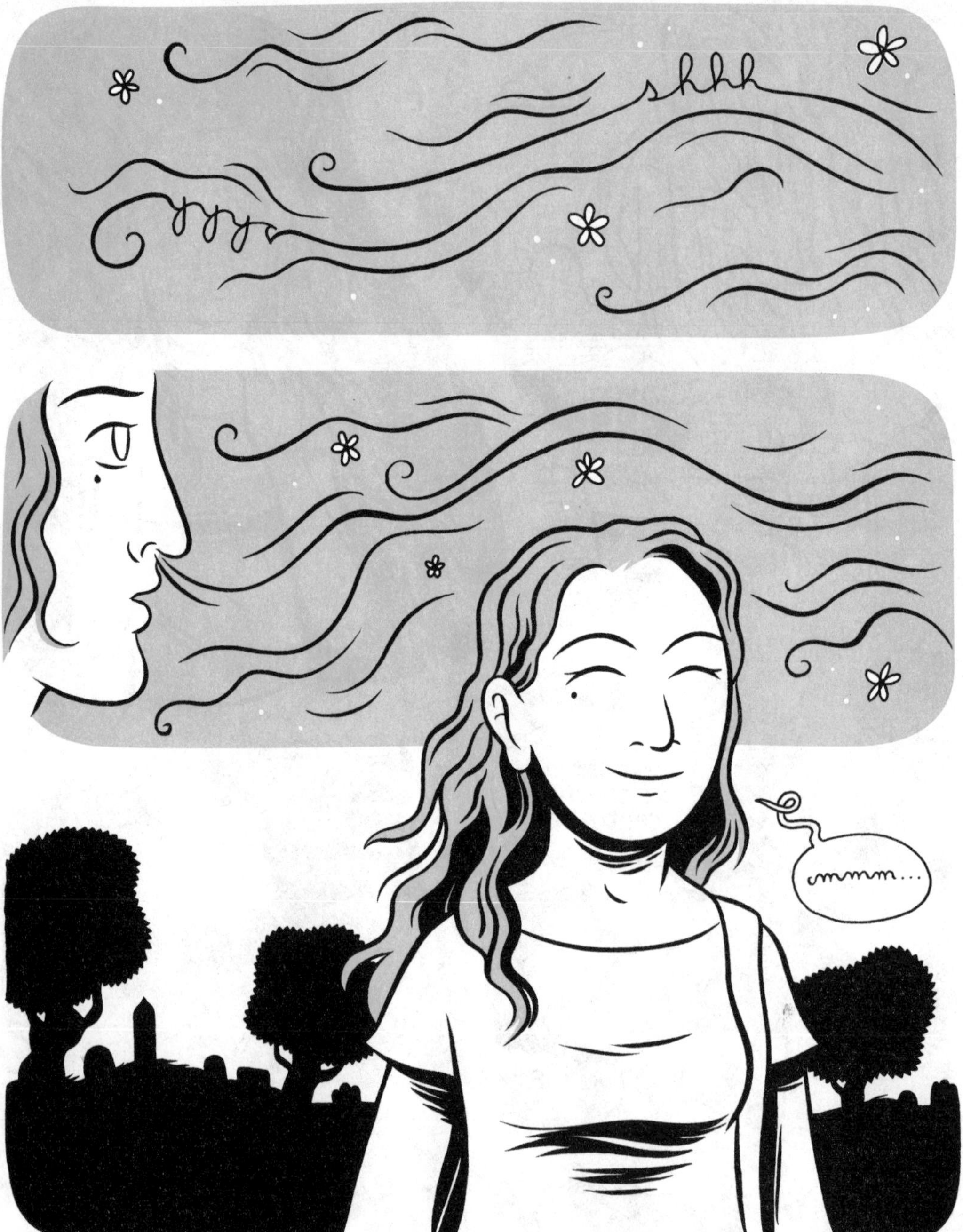
shhh
yyyy
mmmm...

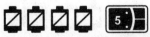

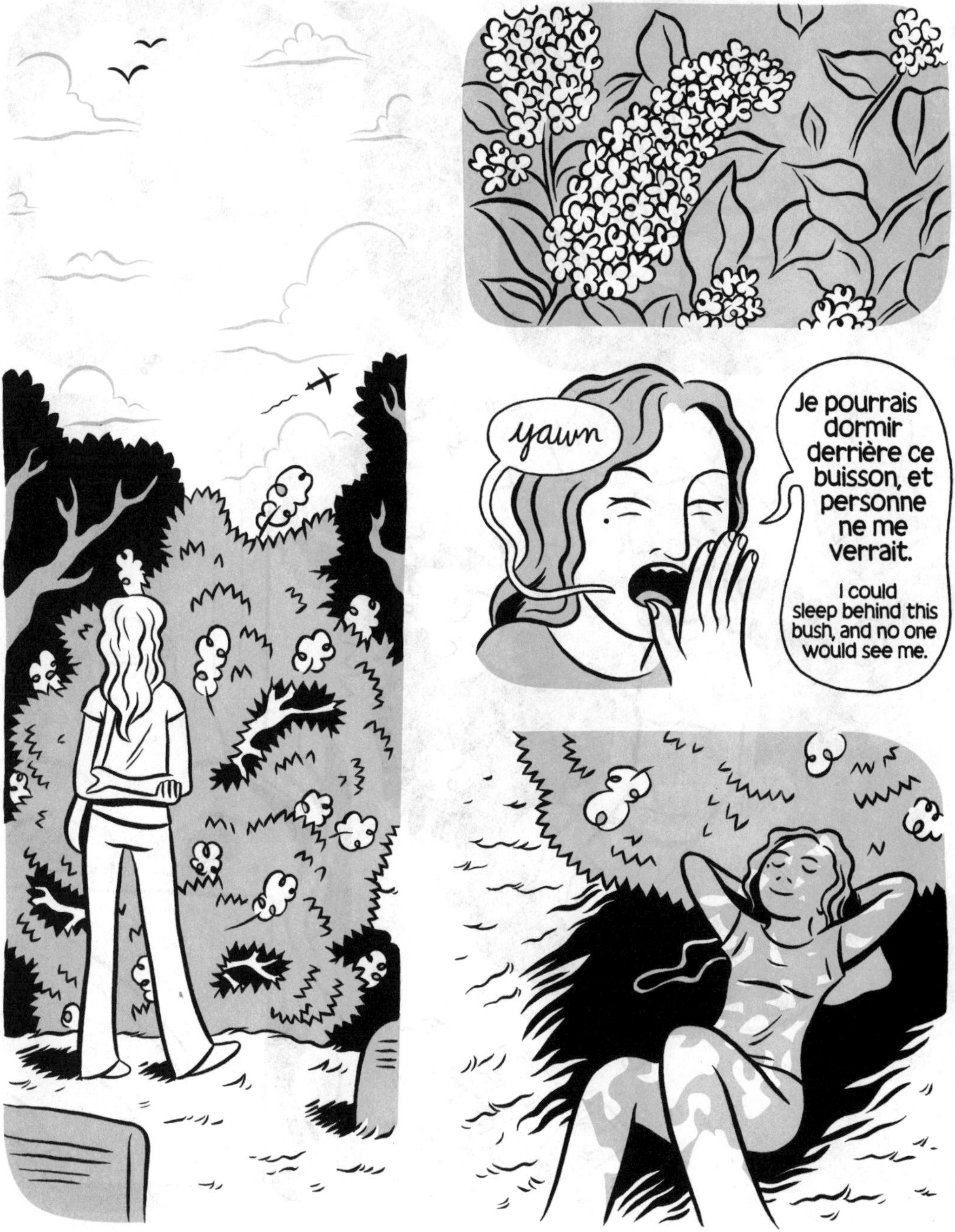
yawn
Je pourrais dormir derrière ce buisson, et personne ne me verrait.
I could sleep behind this bush, and no one would see me.

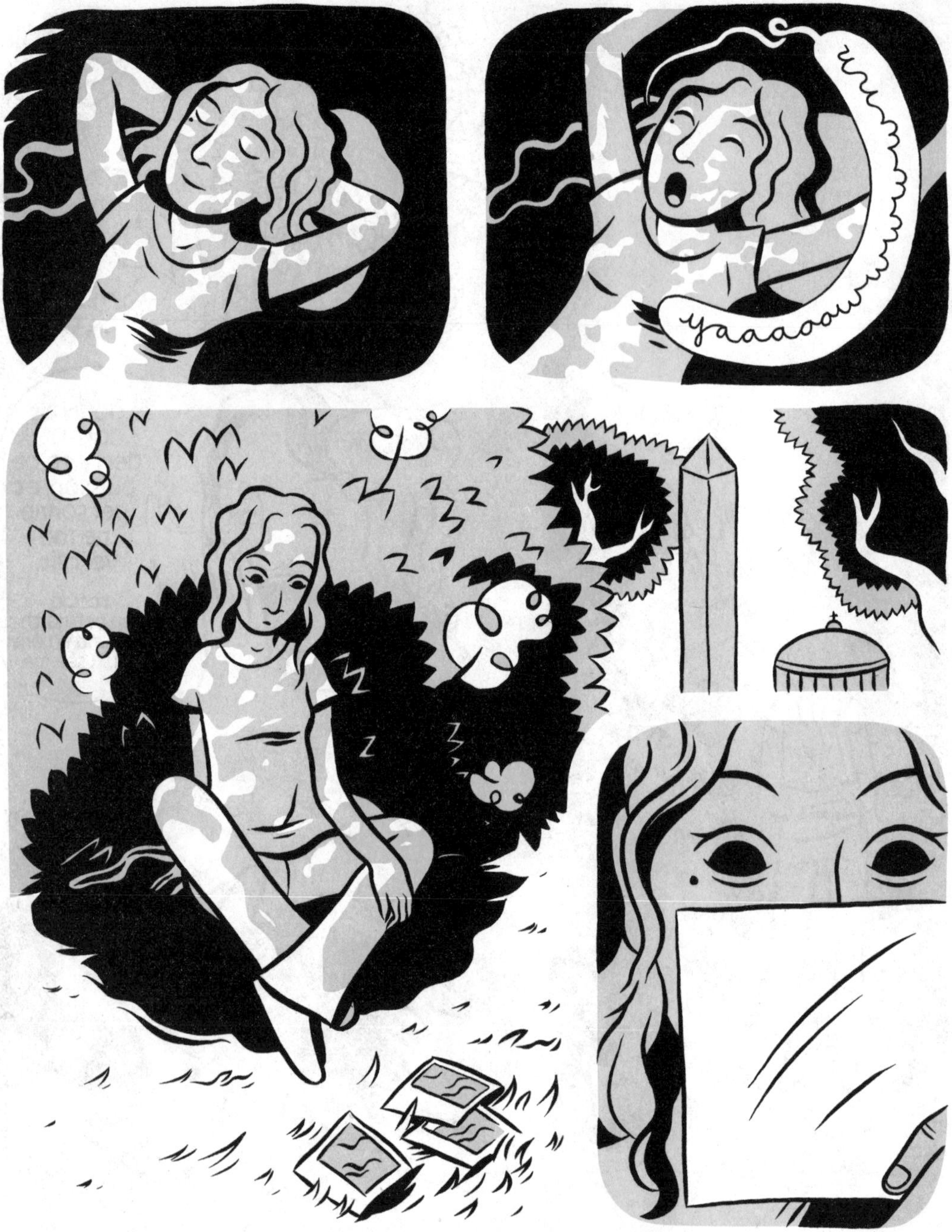
yaaaaowwwwwwn

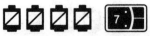

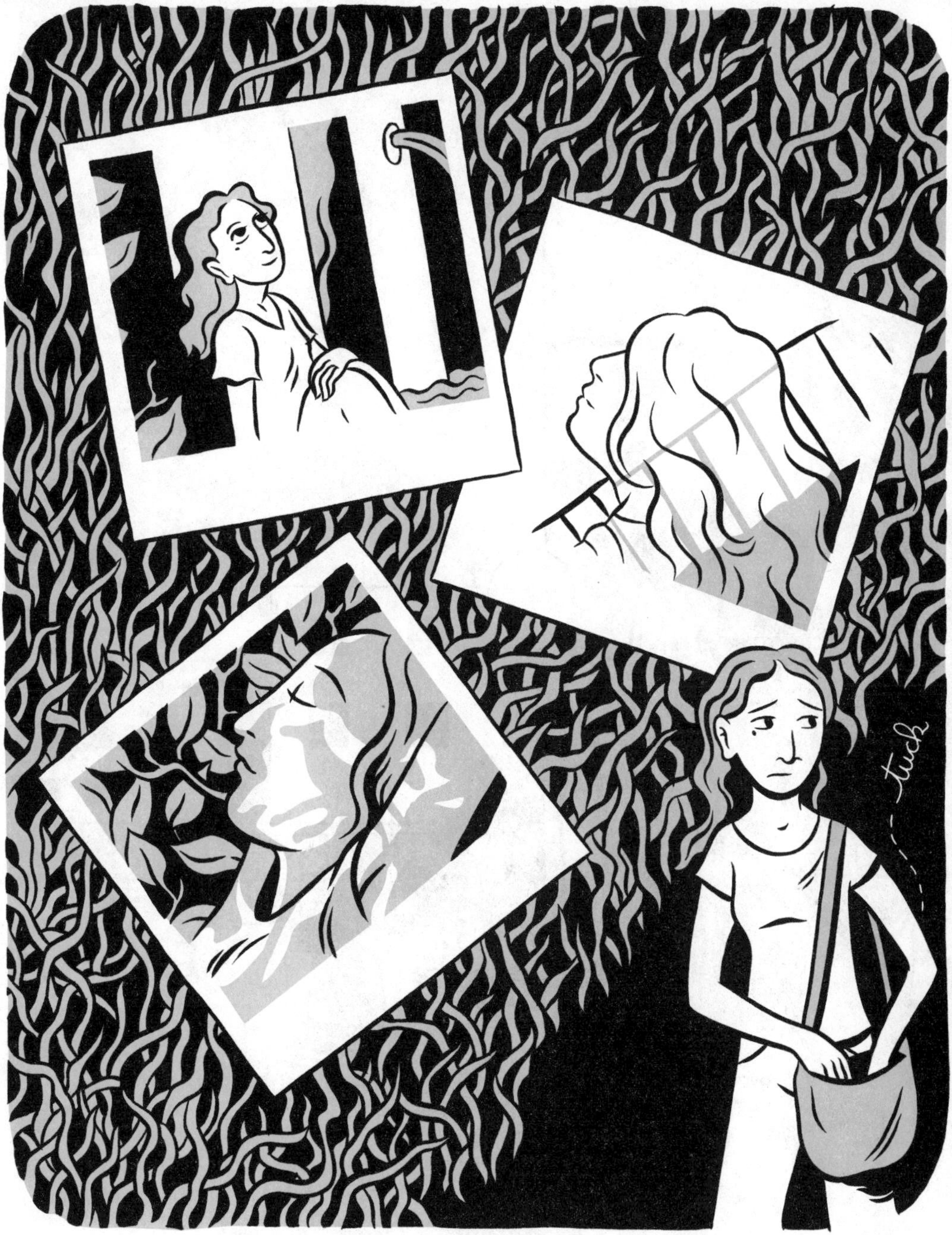
tuck

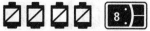

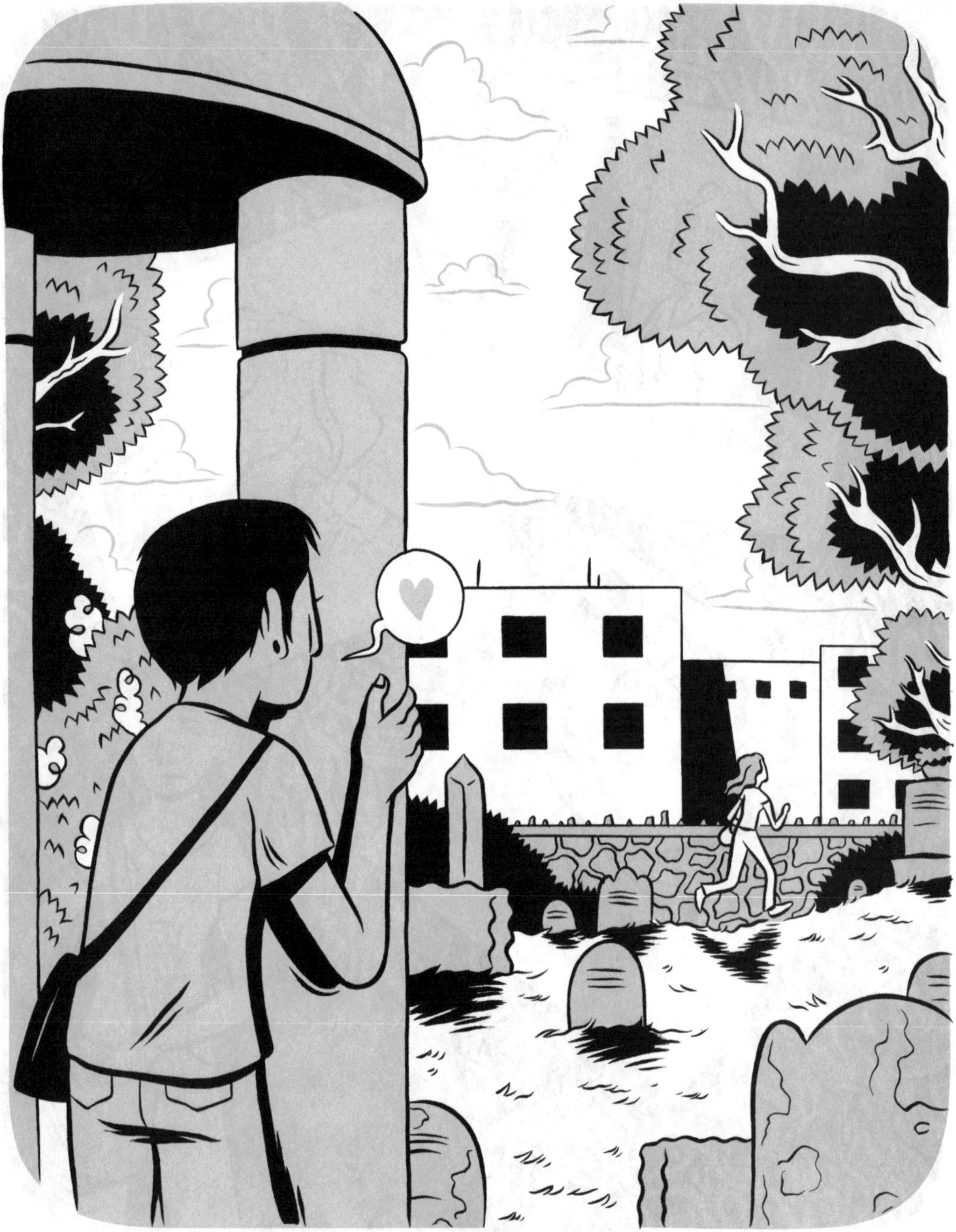

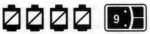

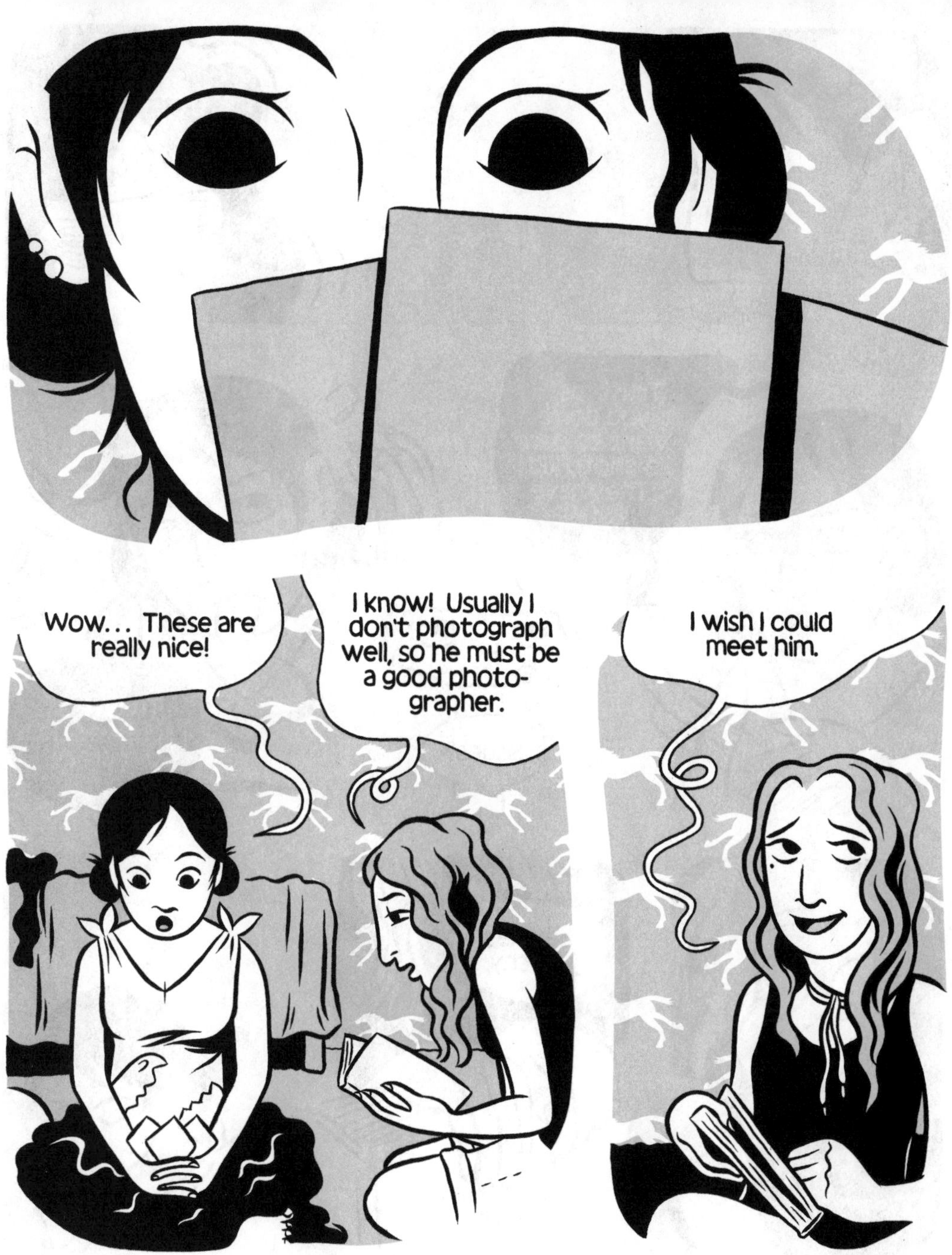
Wow... These are really nice!
I know! Usually I don't photograph well, so he must be a good photographer.
I wish I could meet him.

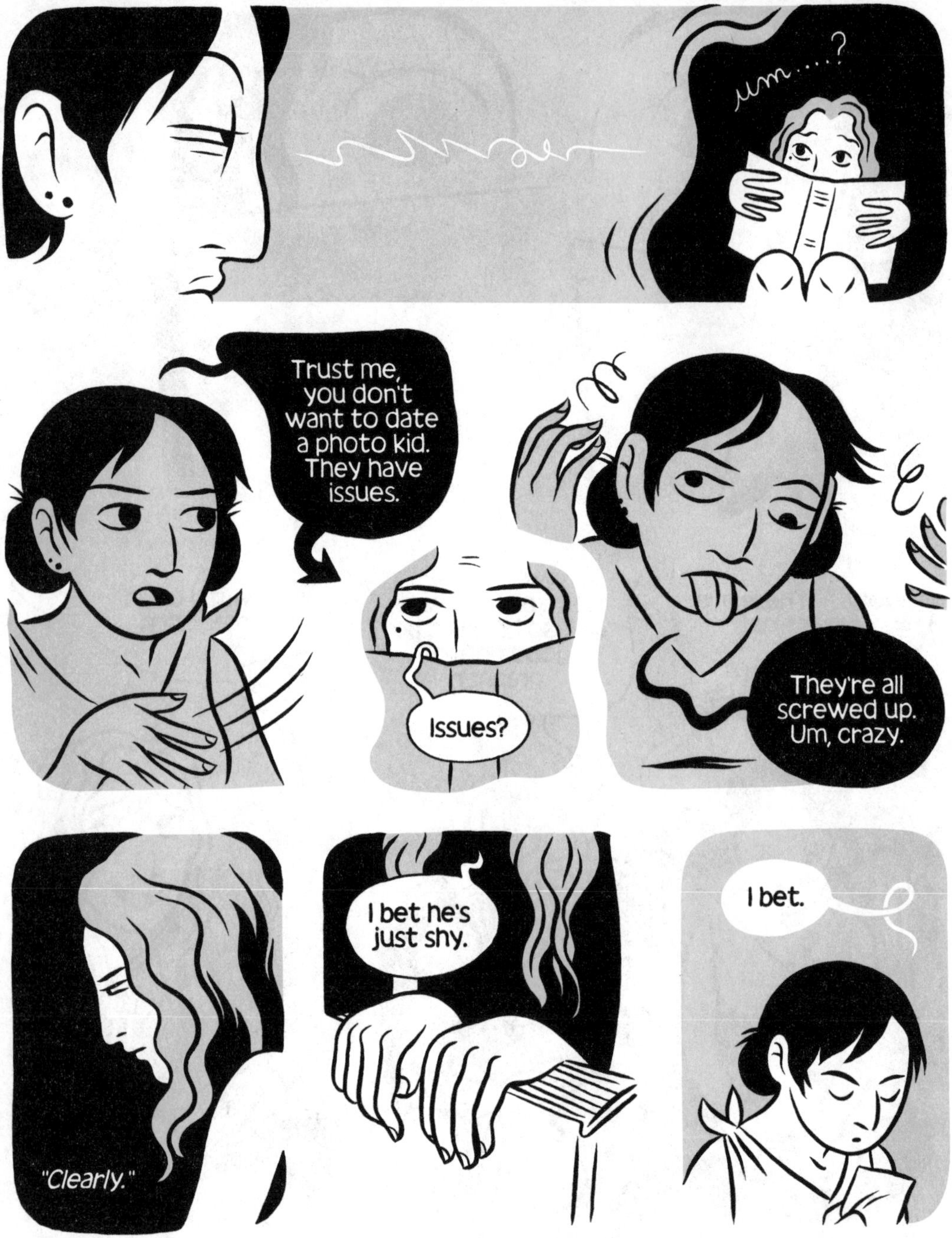

um....?
Trust me, you don't want to date a photo kid. They have issues.
Issues?
They're all screwed up. Um, crazy.
"Clearly."
I bet he's just shy.
I bet.

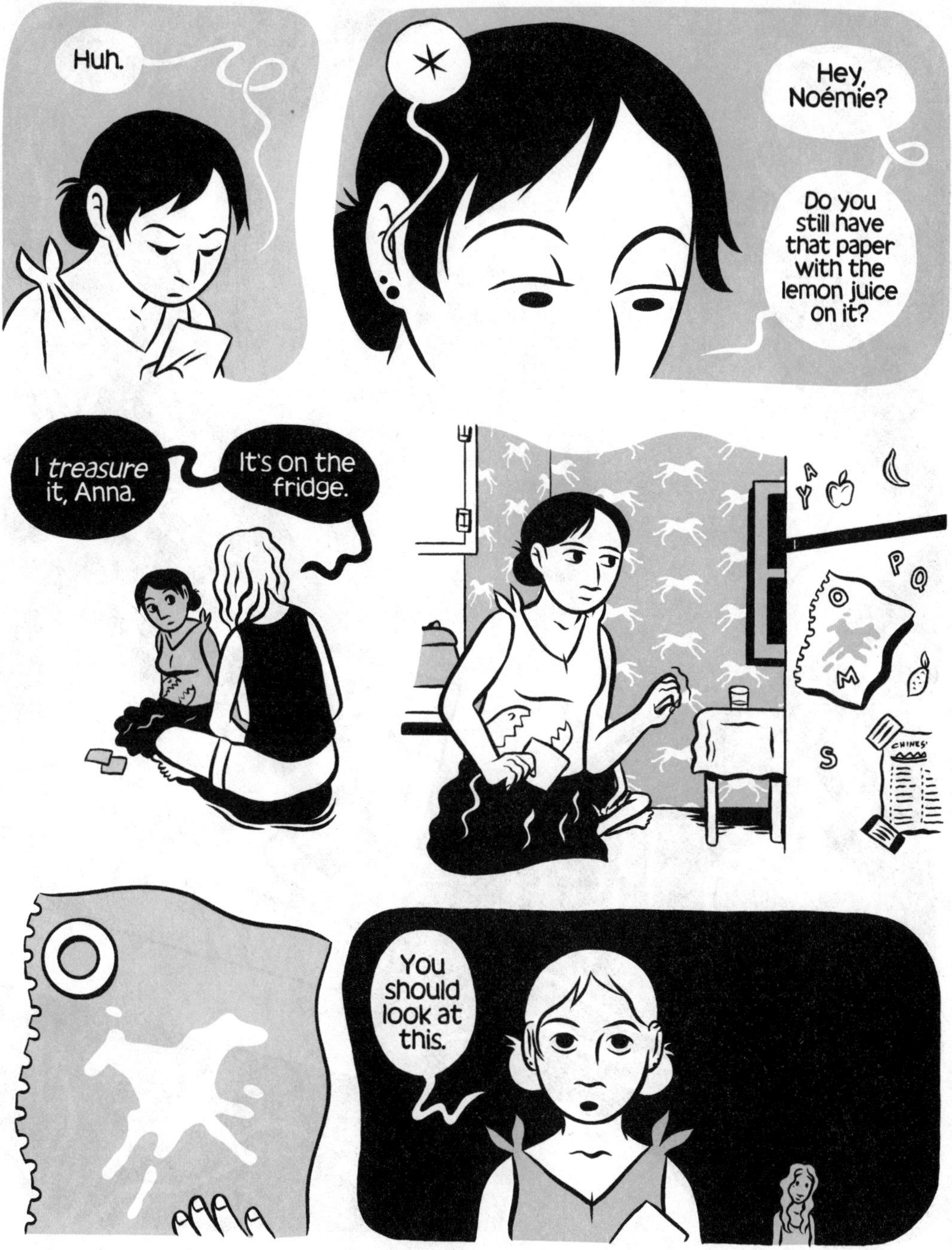
Huh.
Hey, Noémie?
Do you still have that paper with the lemon juice on it?
I *treasure* it, Anna.
It's on the fridge.
You should look at this.

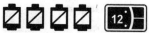

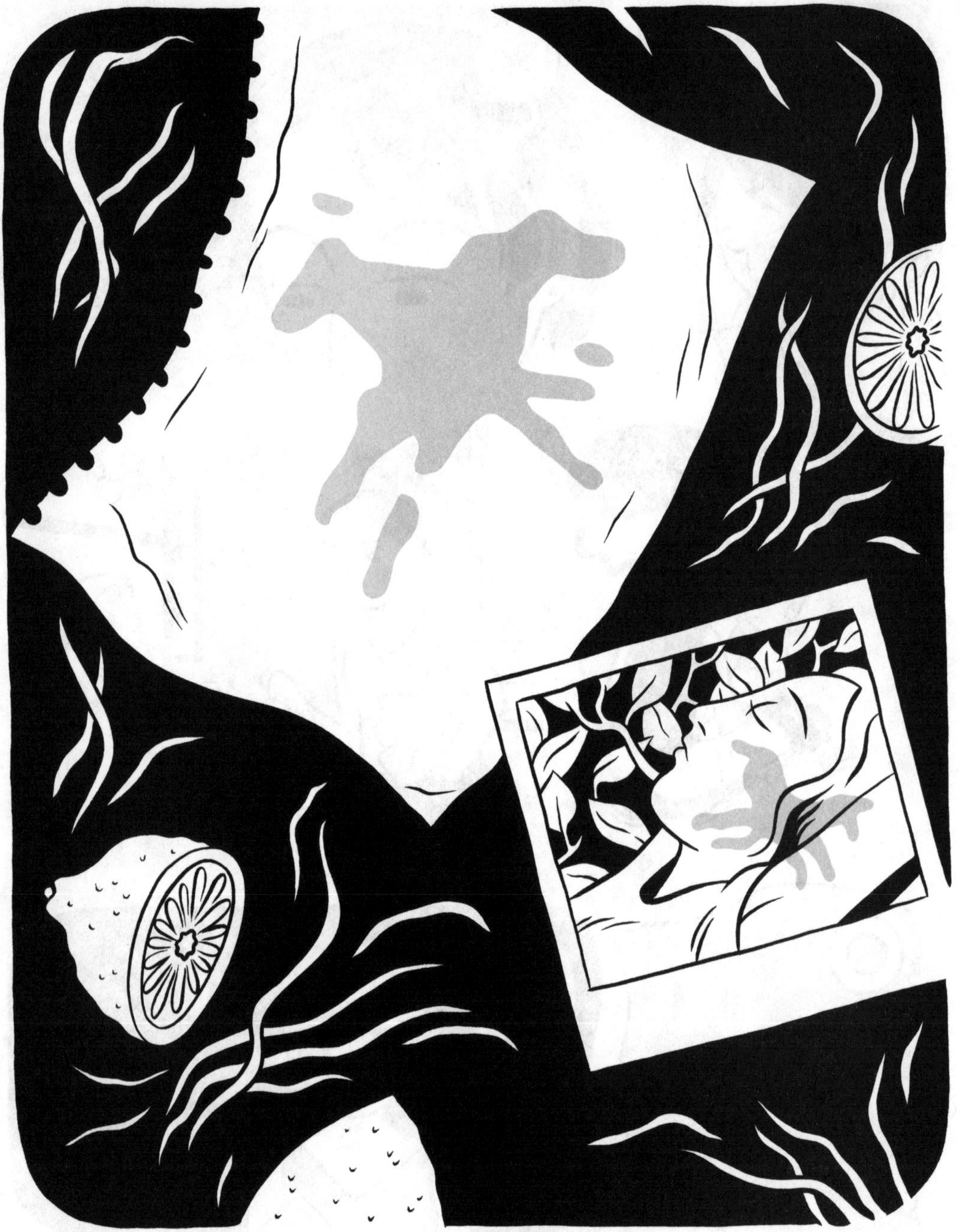

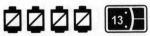

China
Han Dynasty
"Flying Horse"
China
Yuan Dynasty
Vase

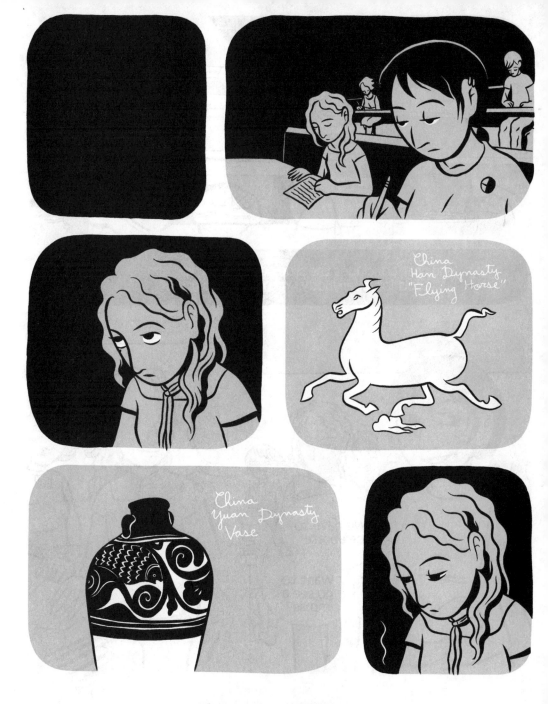

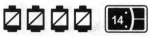

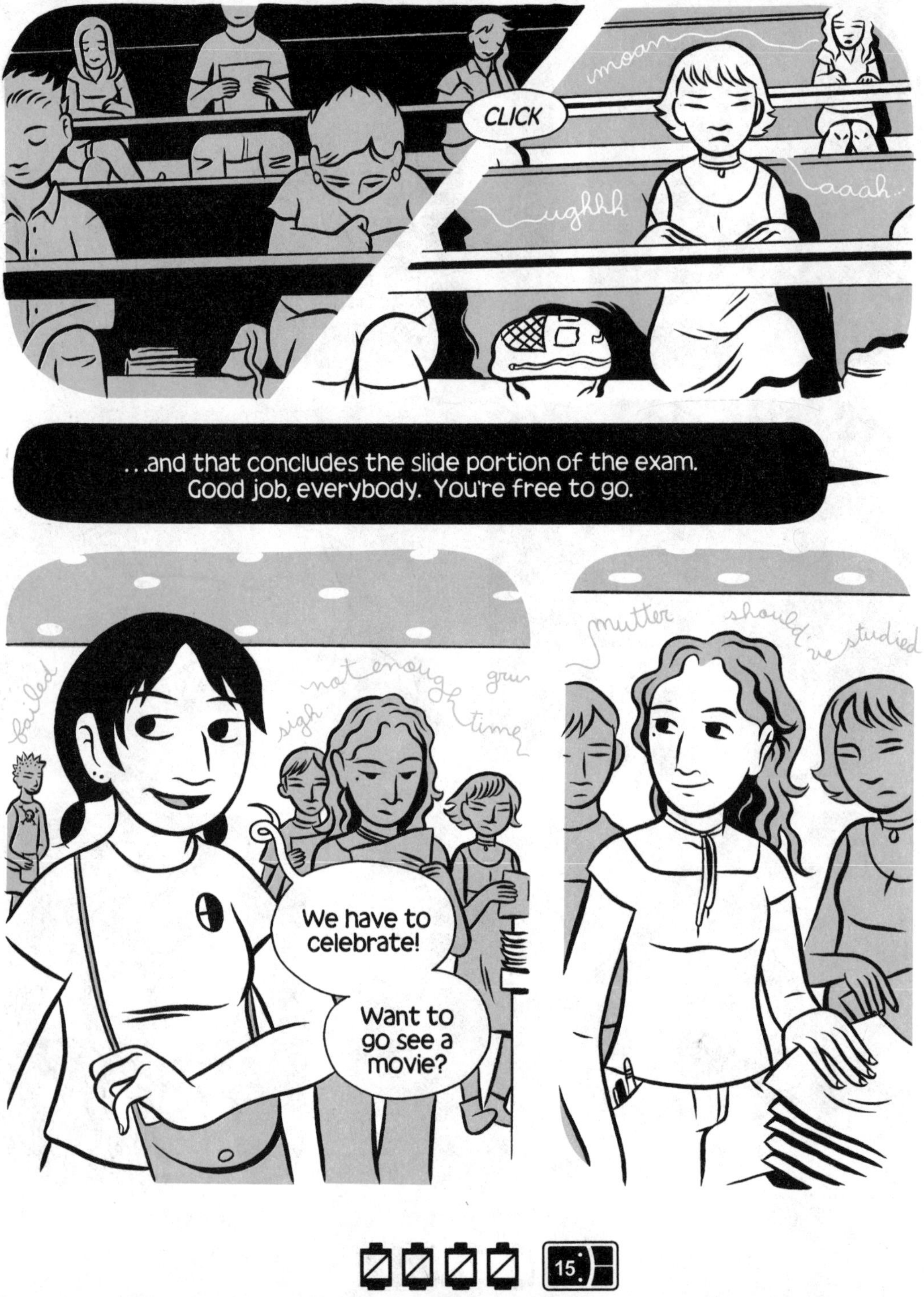
CLICK
moan
ughhh
aaah...
...and that concludes the slide portion of the exam. Good job, everybody. You're free to go.
failed
sigh
not enough time
We have to celebrate!
Want to go see a movie?
mutter
should've studied

ICBOX
wrrgh
AUUGH

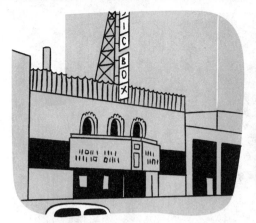

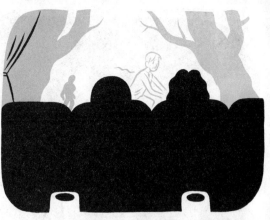

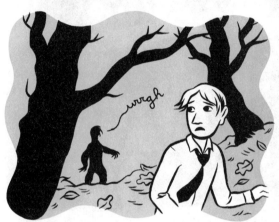

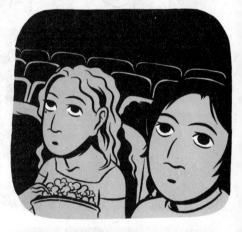

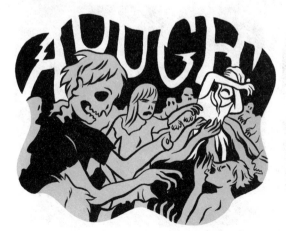

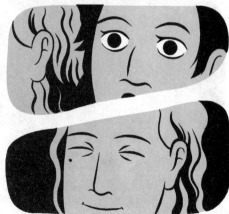

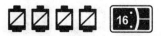

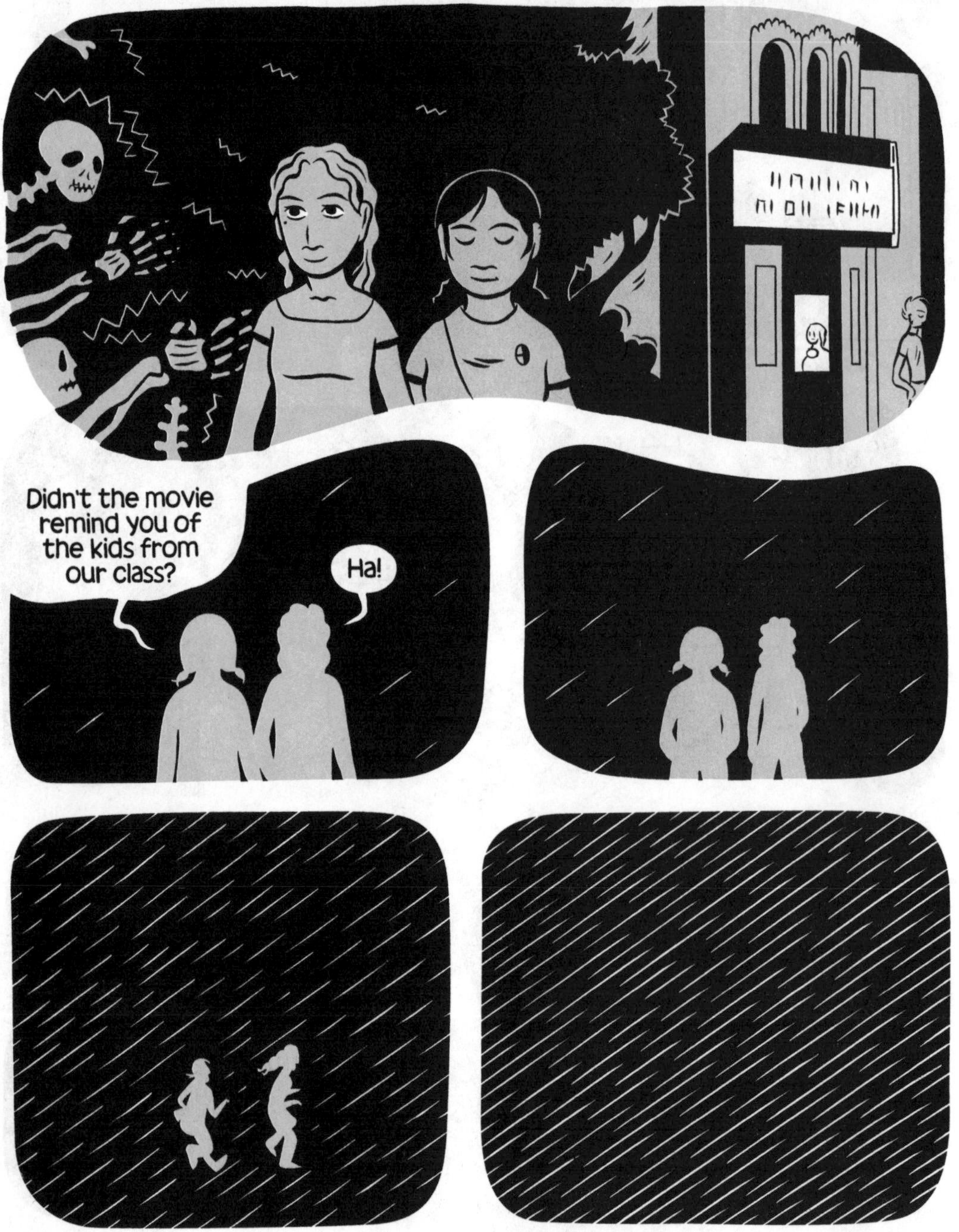
Didn't the movie remind you of the kids from our class?
Ha!

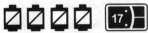

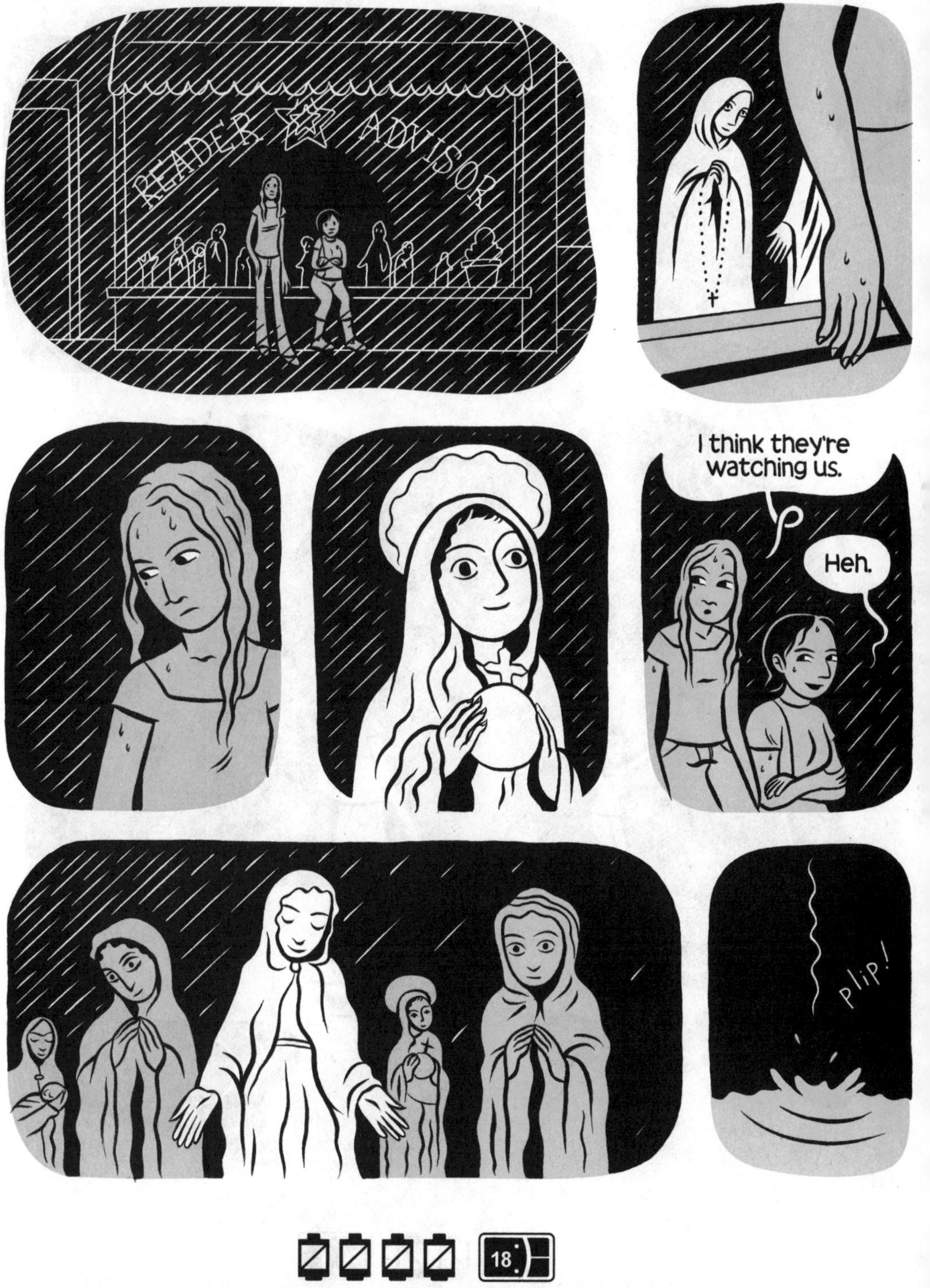
READER ADVISOR
I think they're watching us.
Heh.
plip!

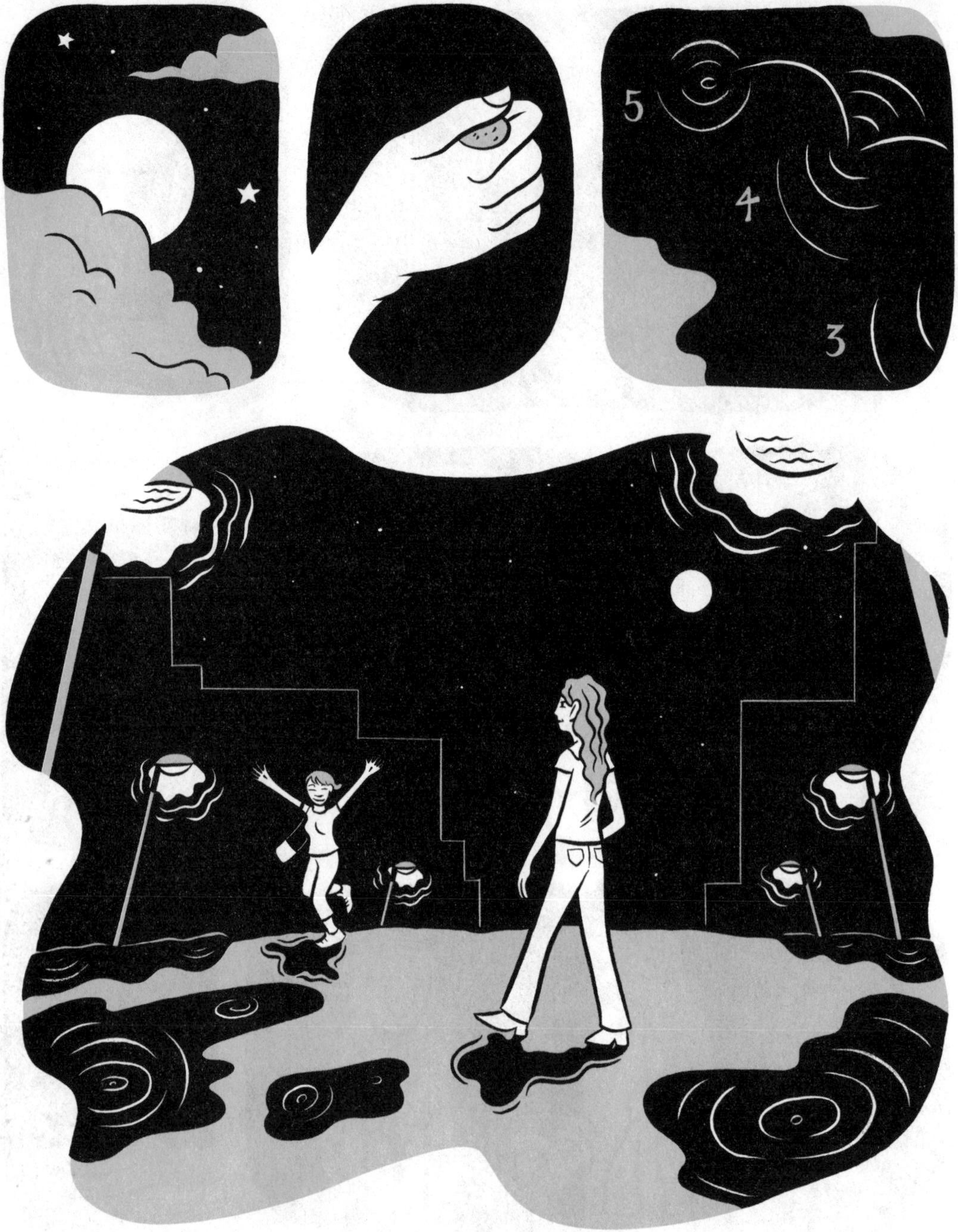
5
4
3

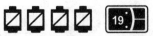

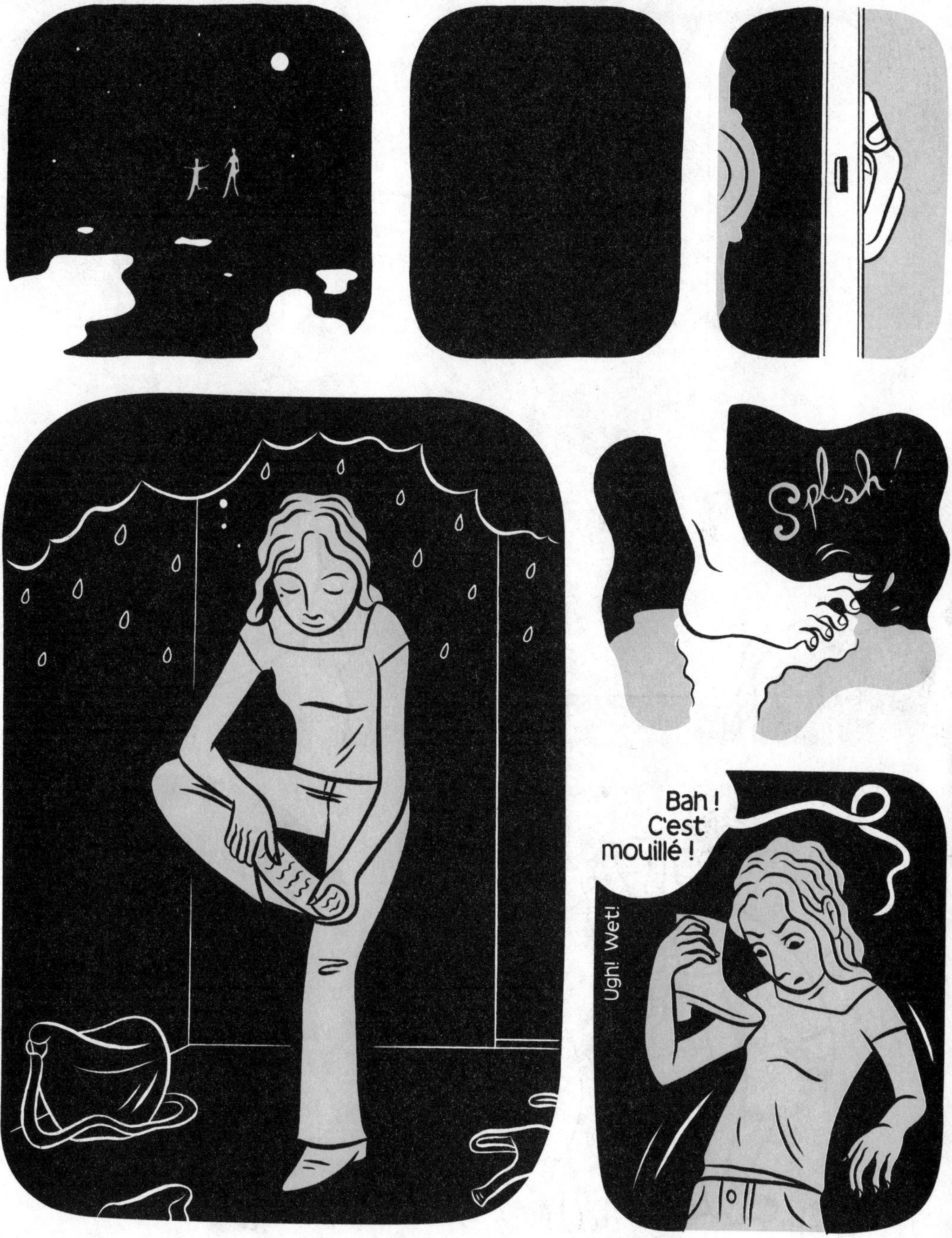
Splish!
Bah ! C'est mouillé !
Ugh! Wet!

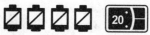

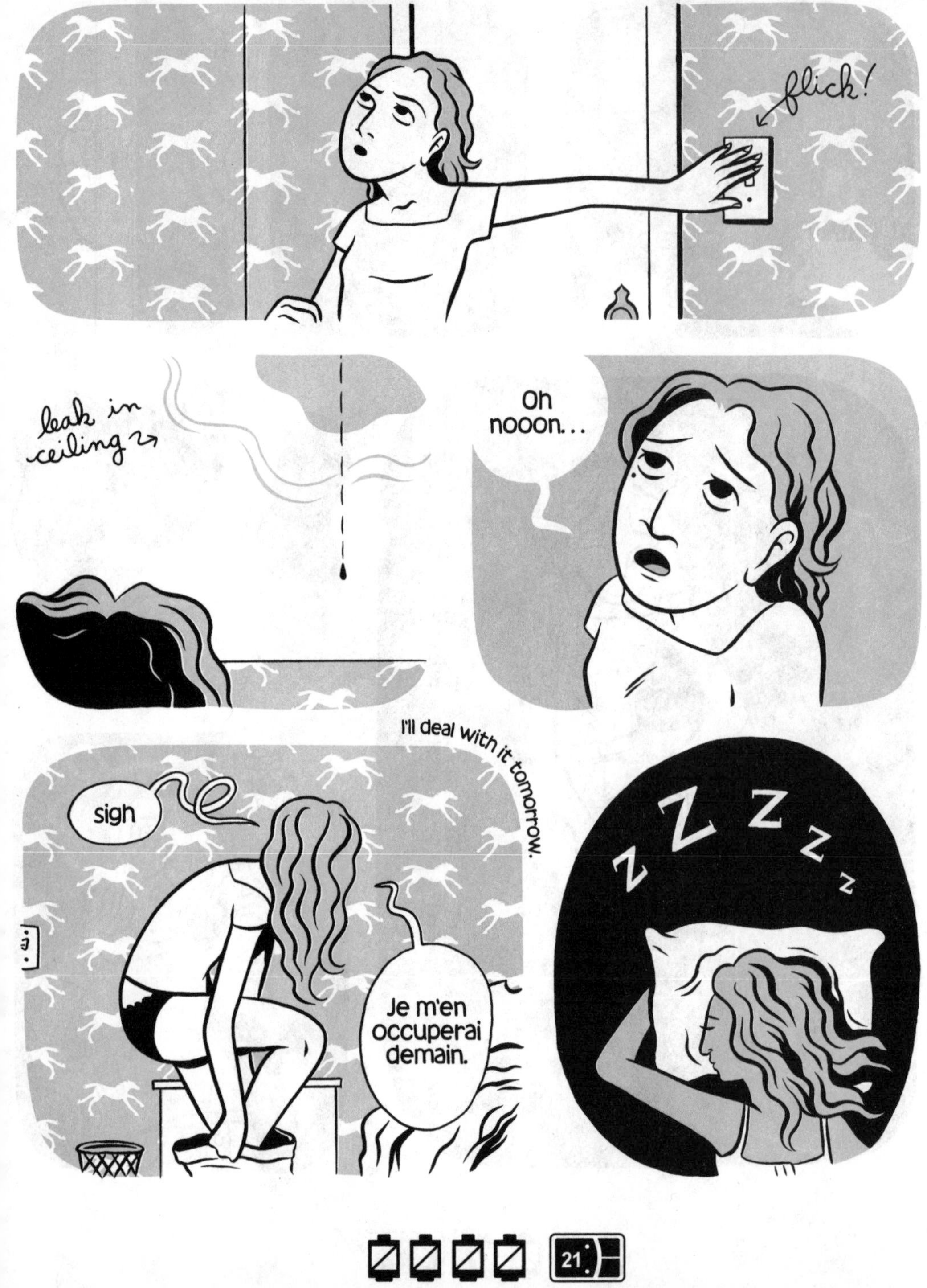

flick!
leak in ceiling
Oh nooon...
sigh
I'll deal with it tomorrow.
Je m'en occuperai demain.
Z Z Z Z Z Z

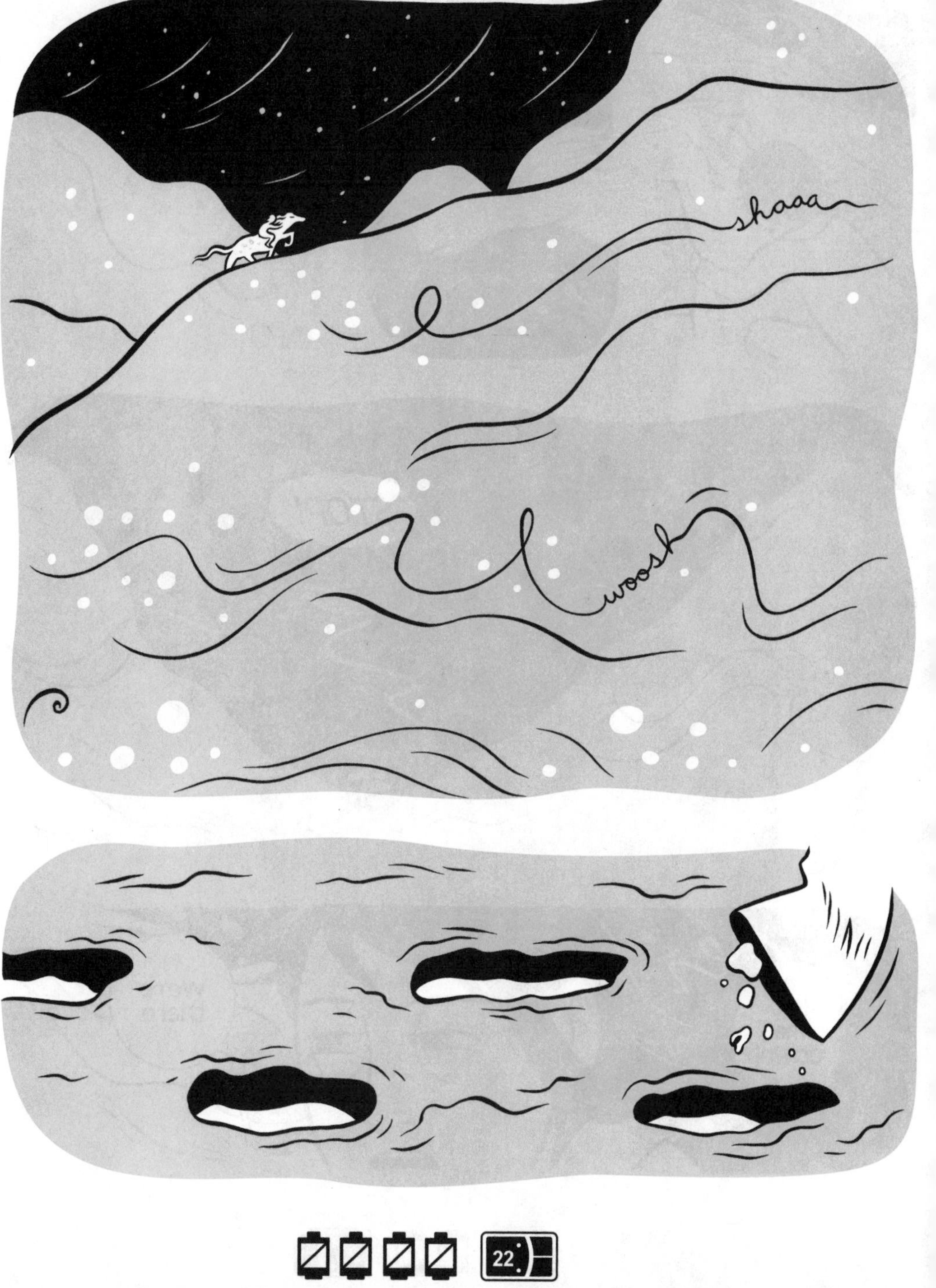
shaaa
woosh

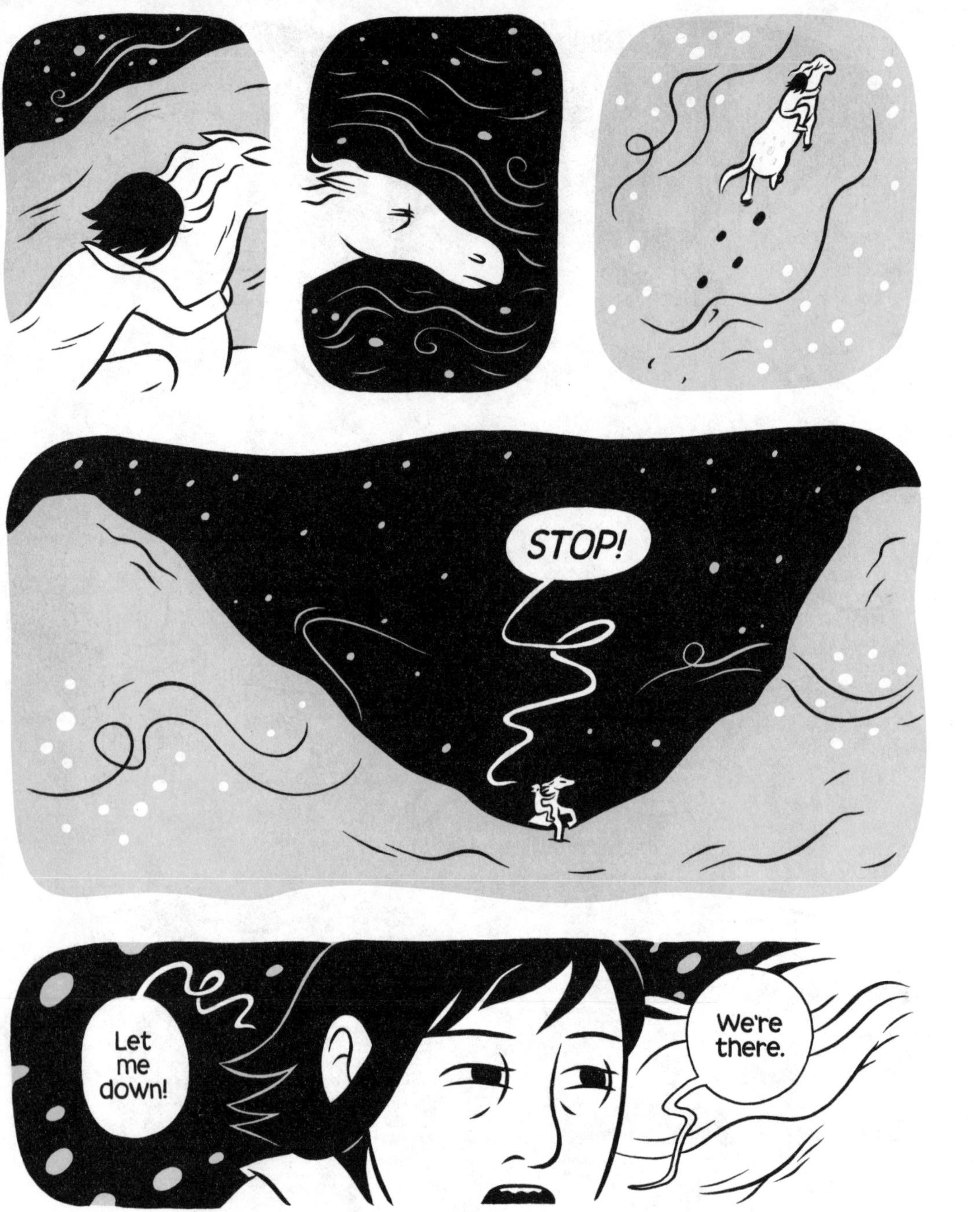
STOP!
Let me down!
We're there.

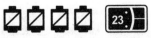

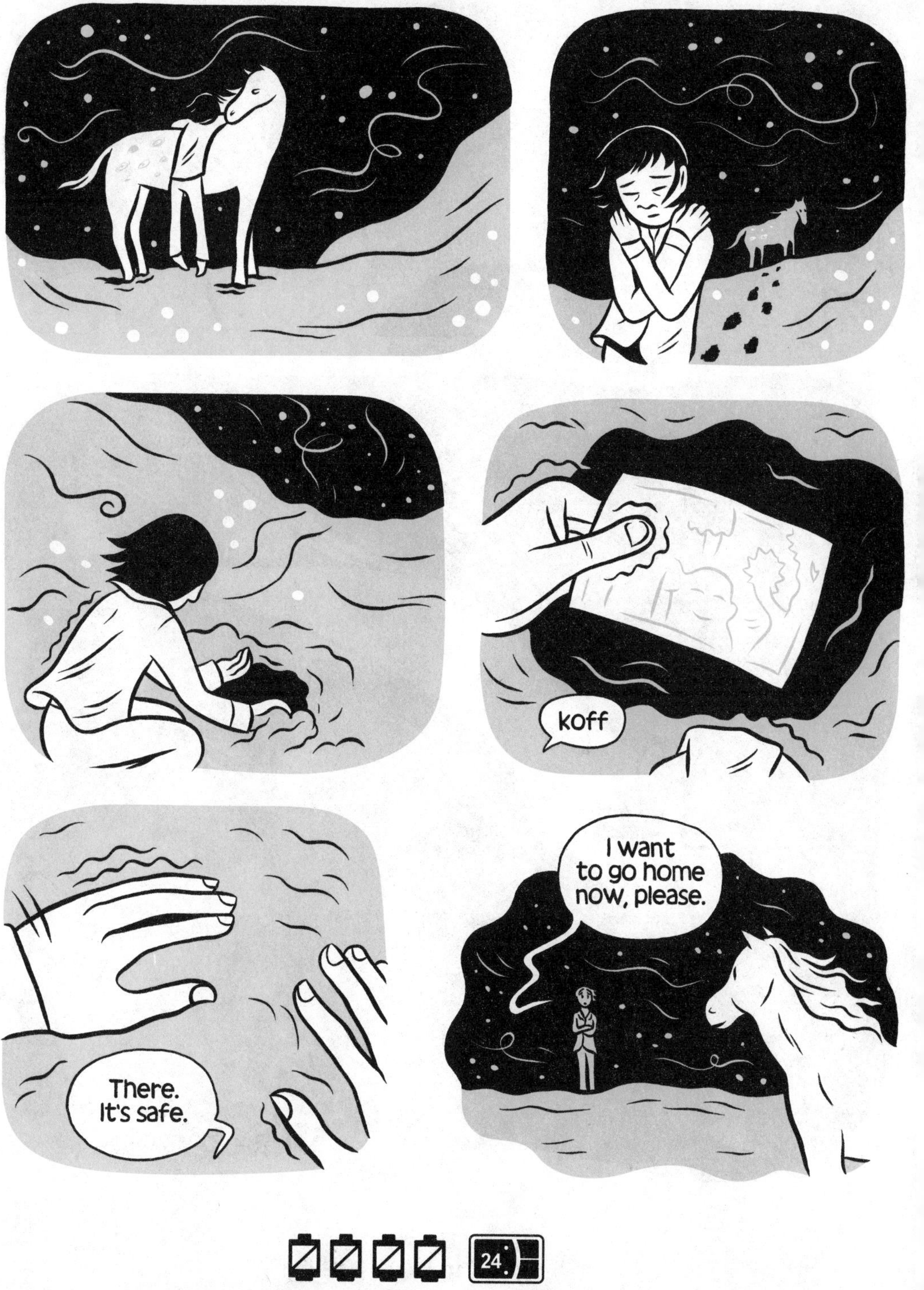
koff
There. It's safe.
I want to go home now, please.

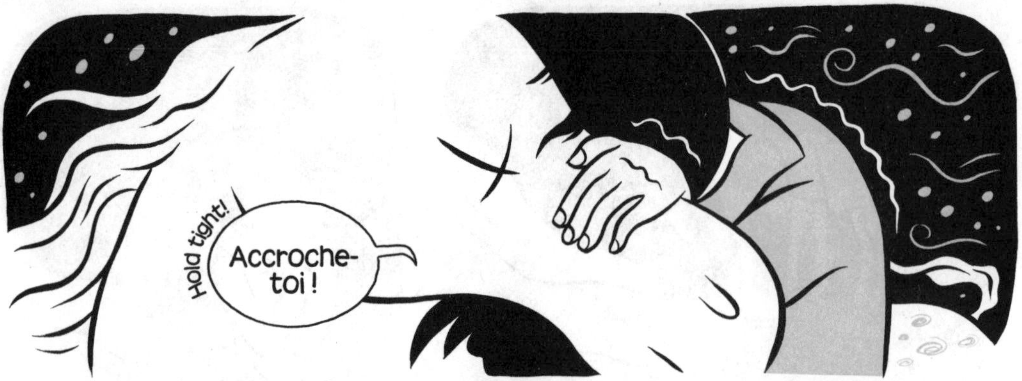
Accroche-
toi !
Hold tight!

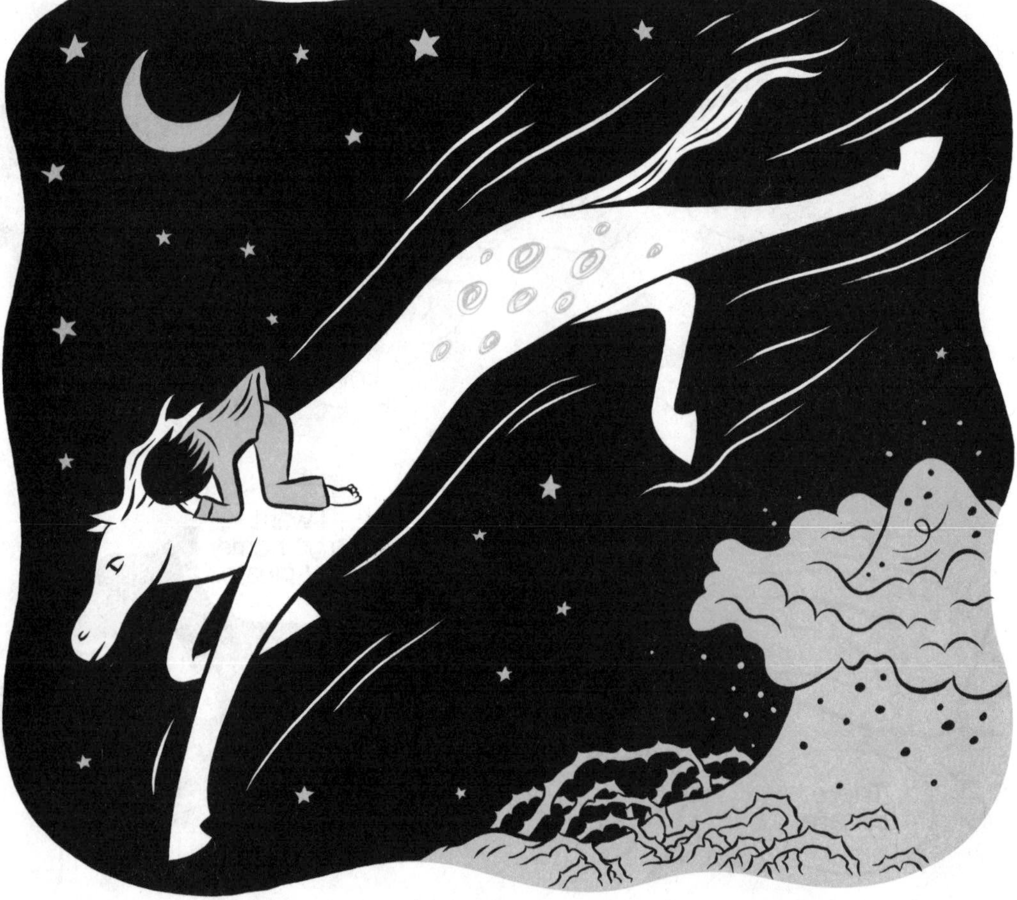

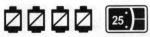

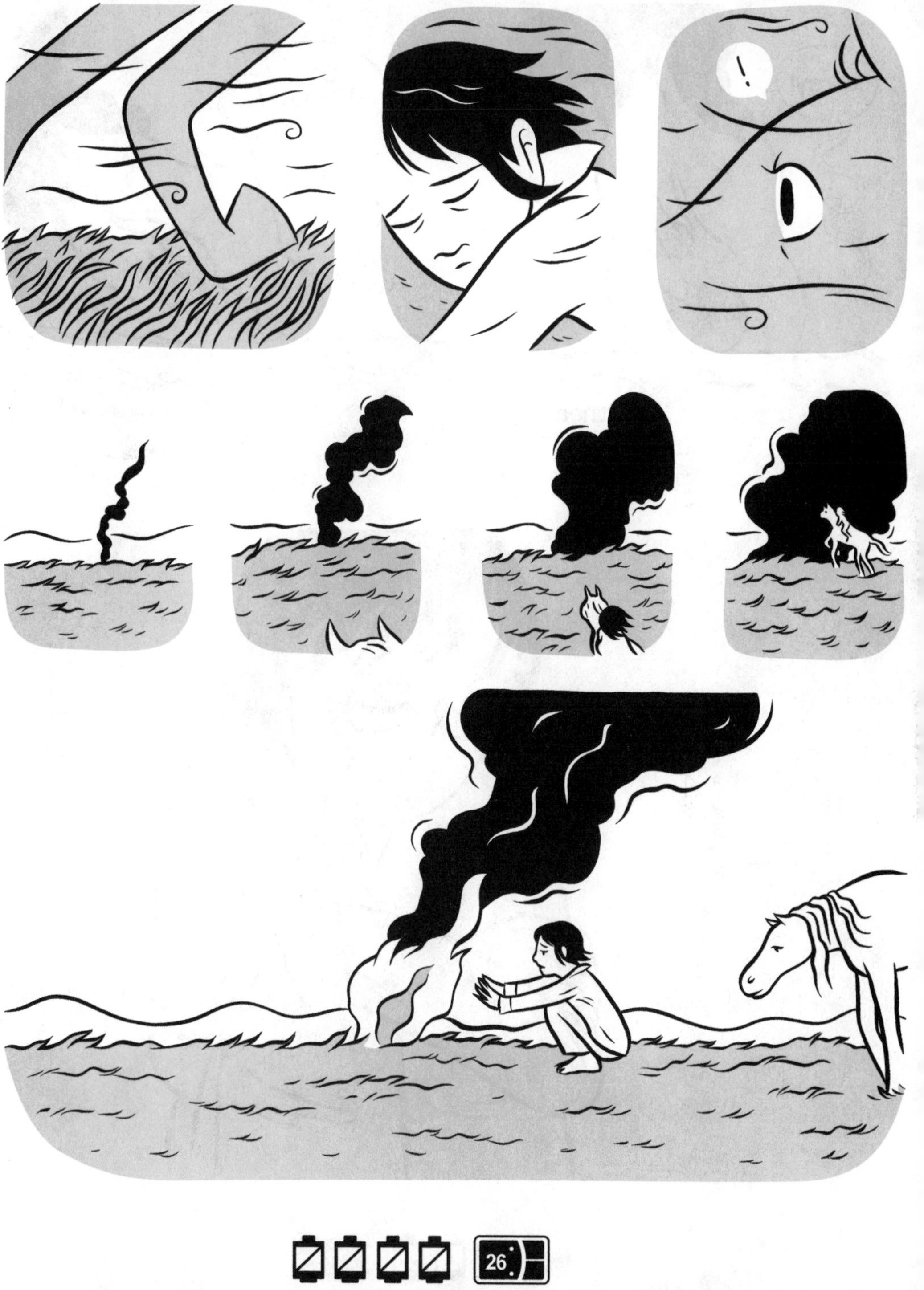
!

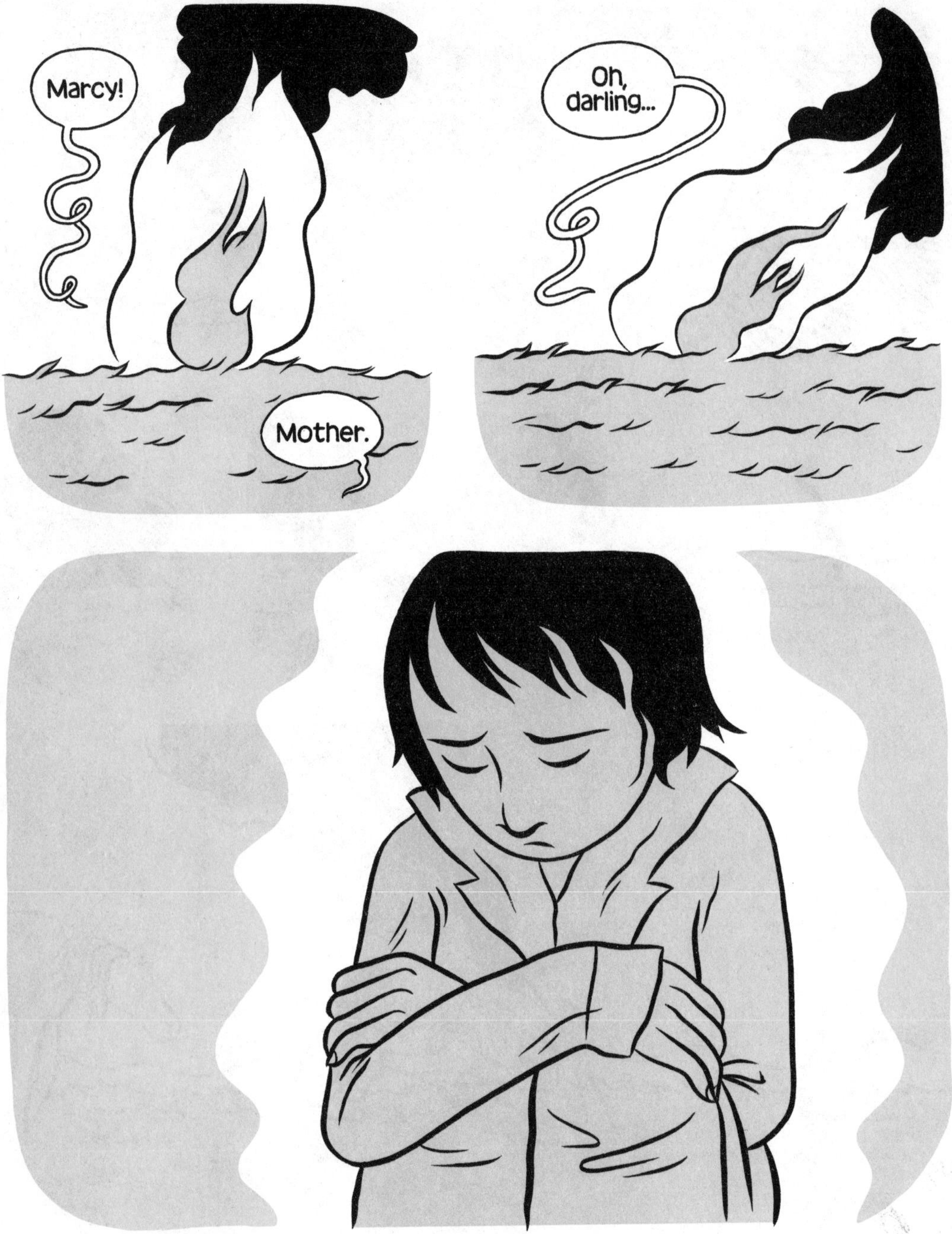
Marcy!
Mother.
Oh, darling...

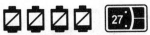

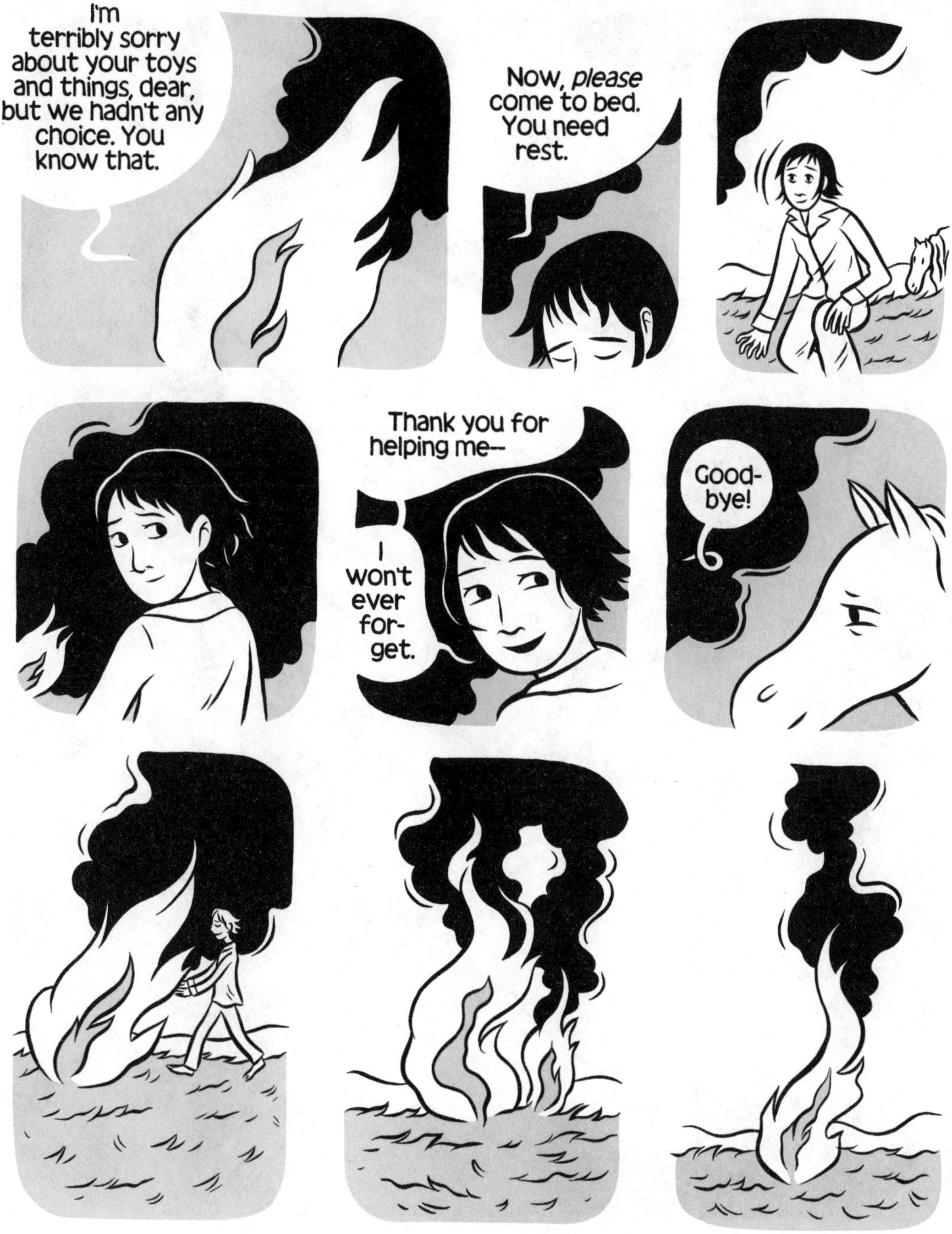
I'm terribly sorry about your toys and things, dear, but we hadn't any choice. You know that.
Now, *please* come to bed. You need rest.
Thank you for helping me--
I won't ever for-get.
Good-bye!

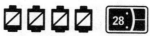

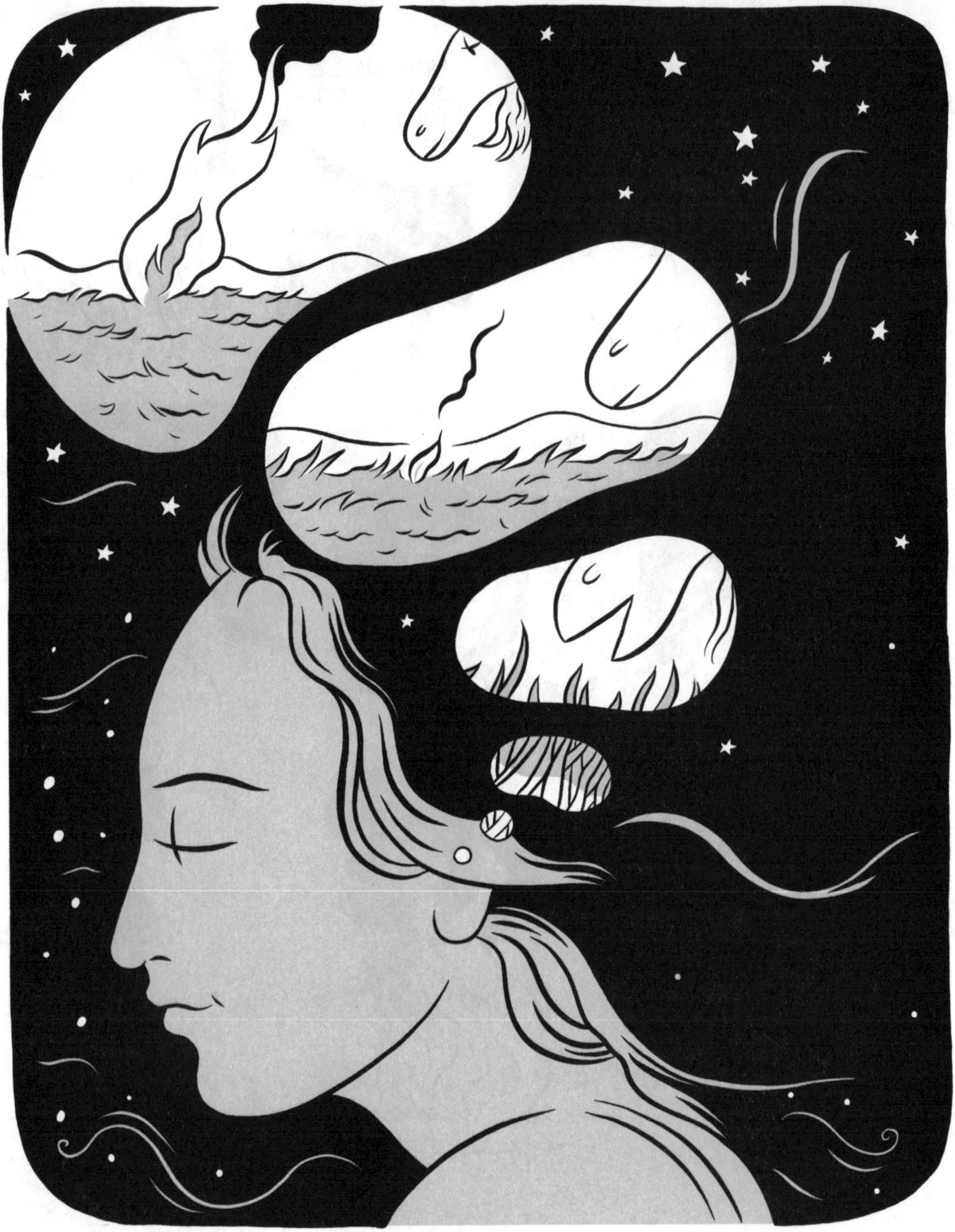

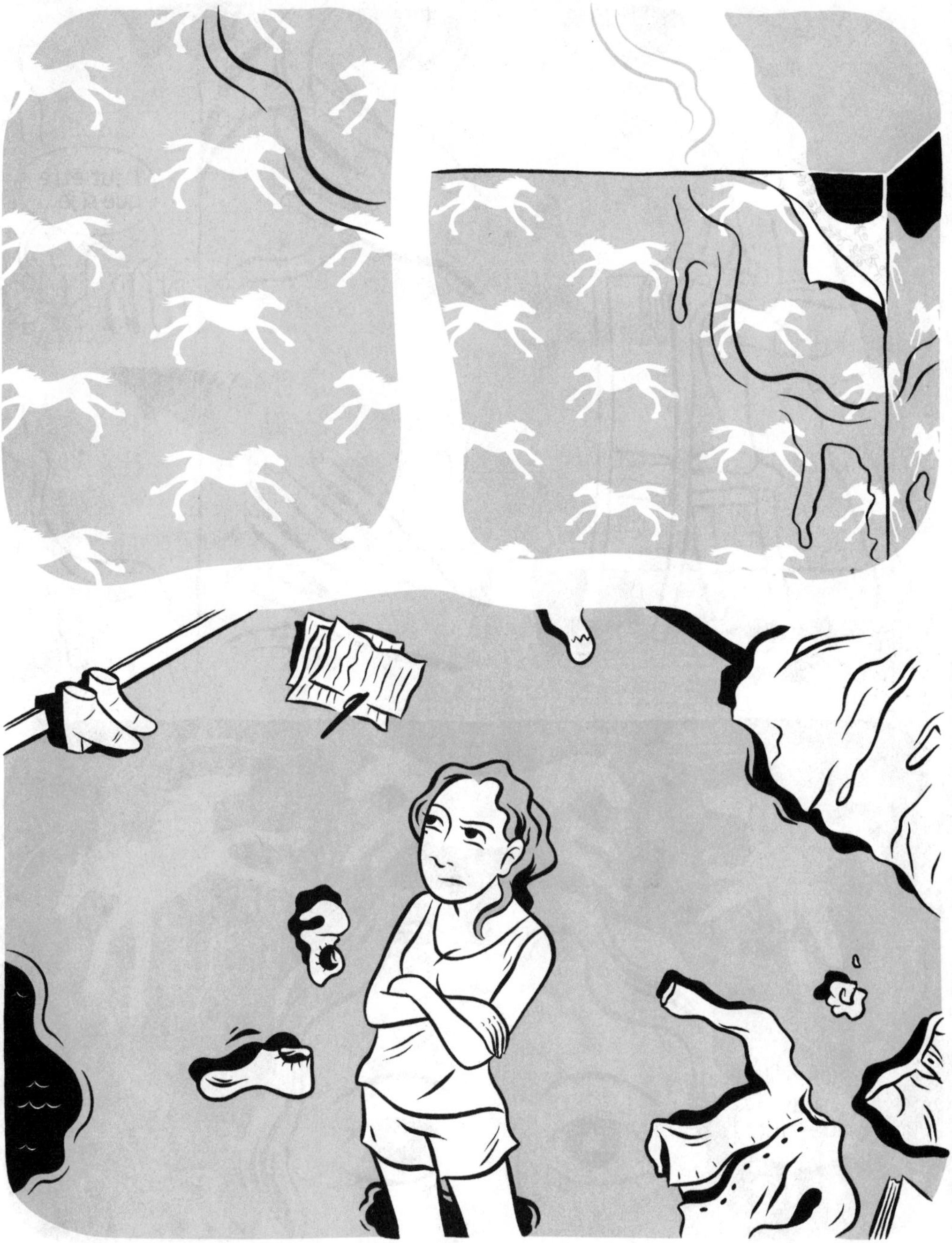

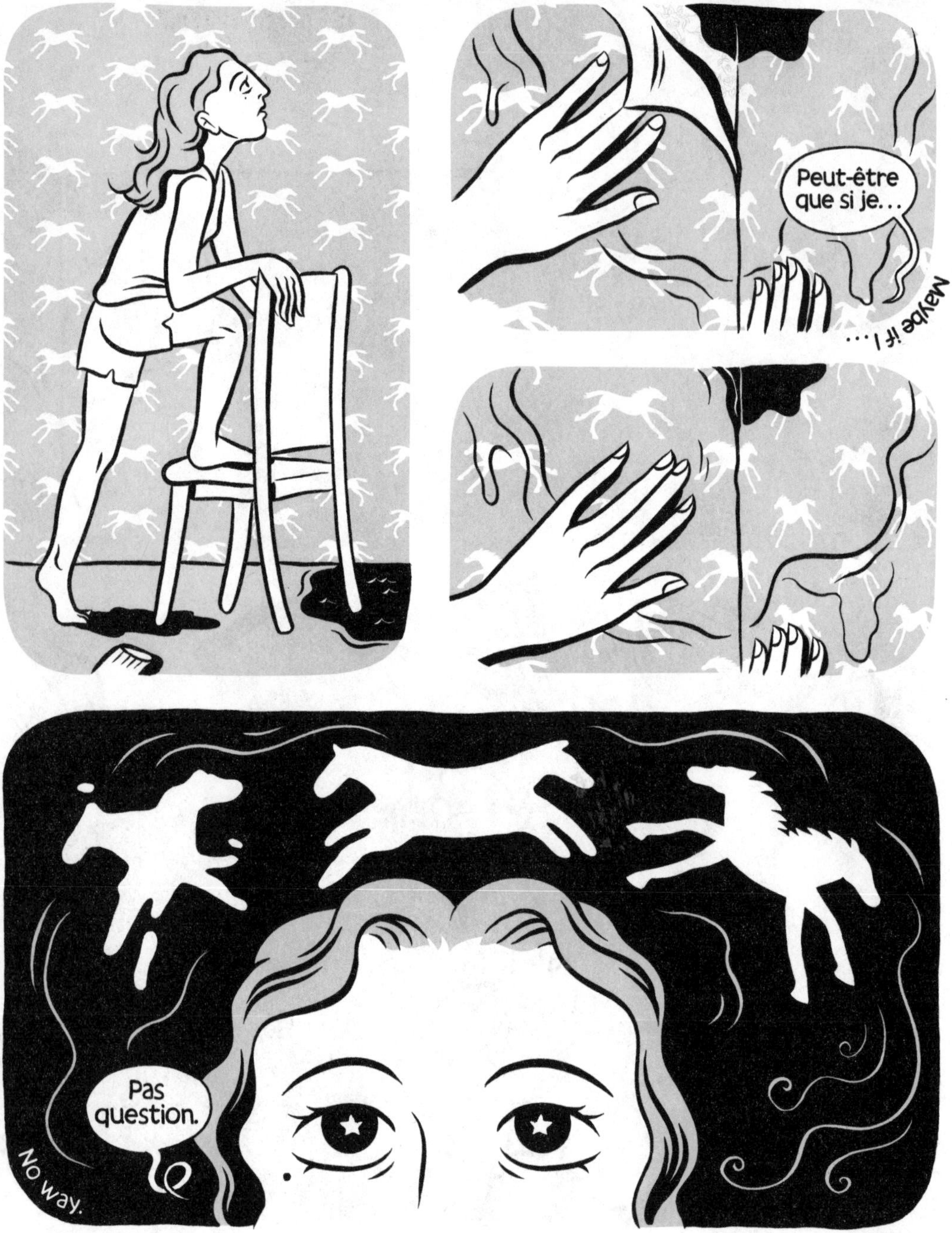
Peut-être que si je...
Maybe if I...
Pas question.
No way.

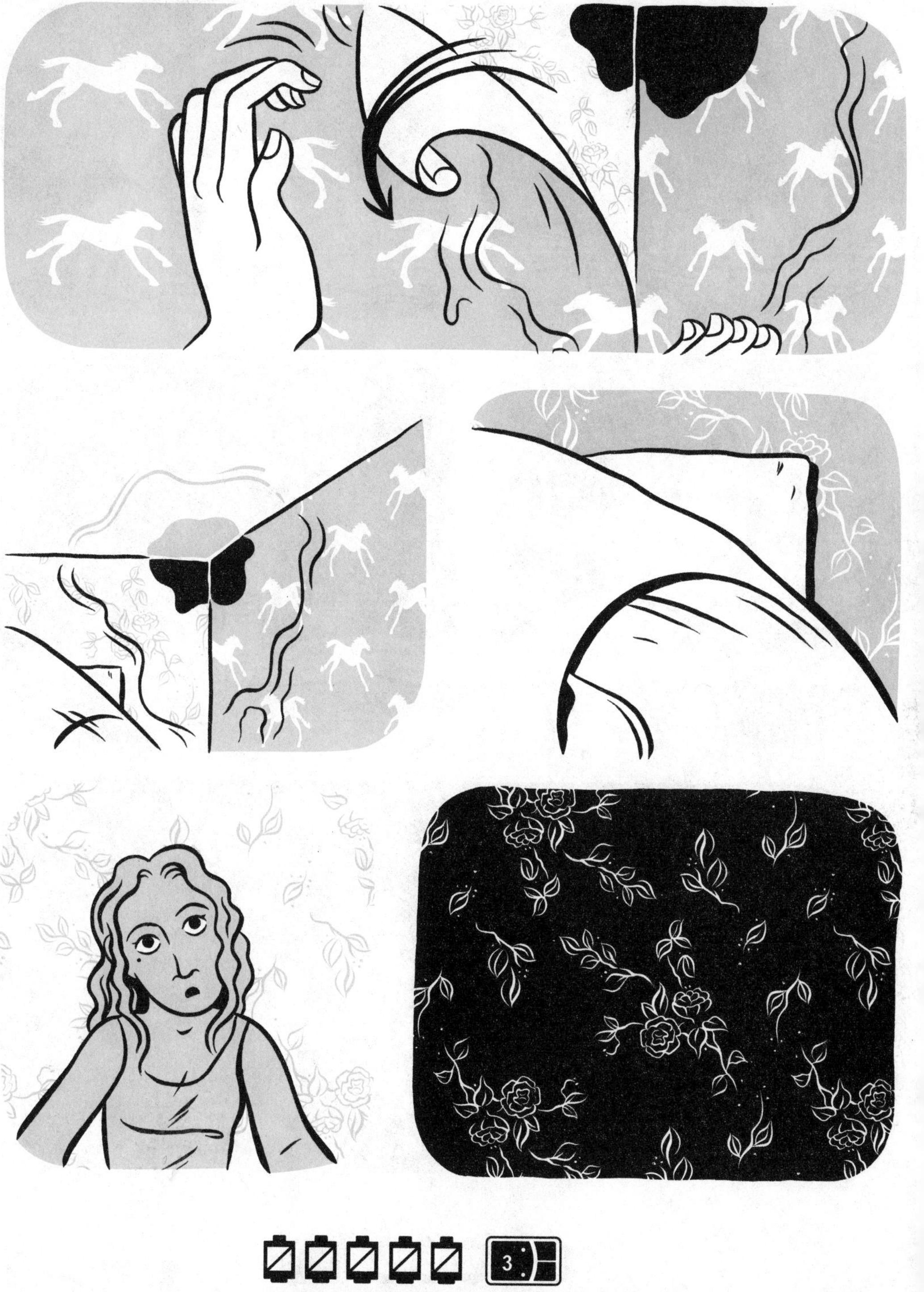

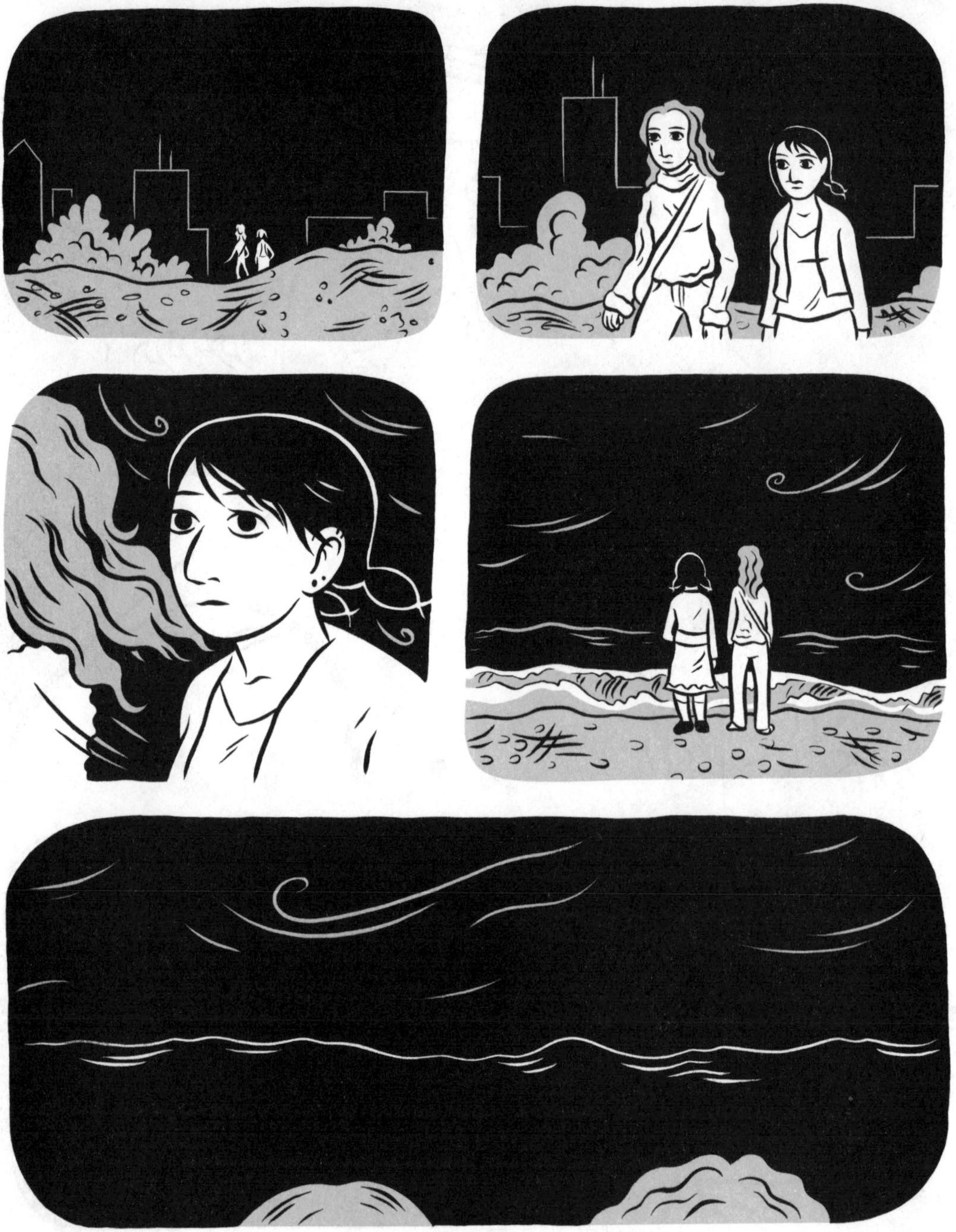

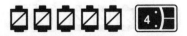

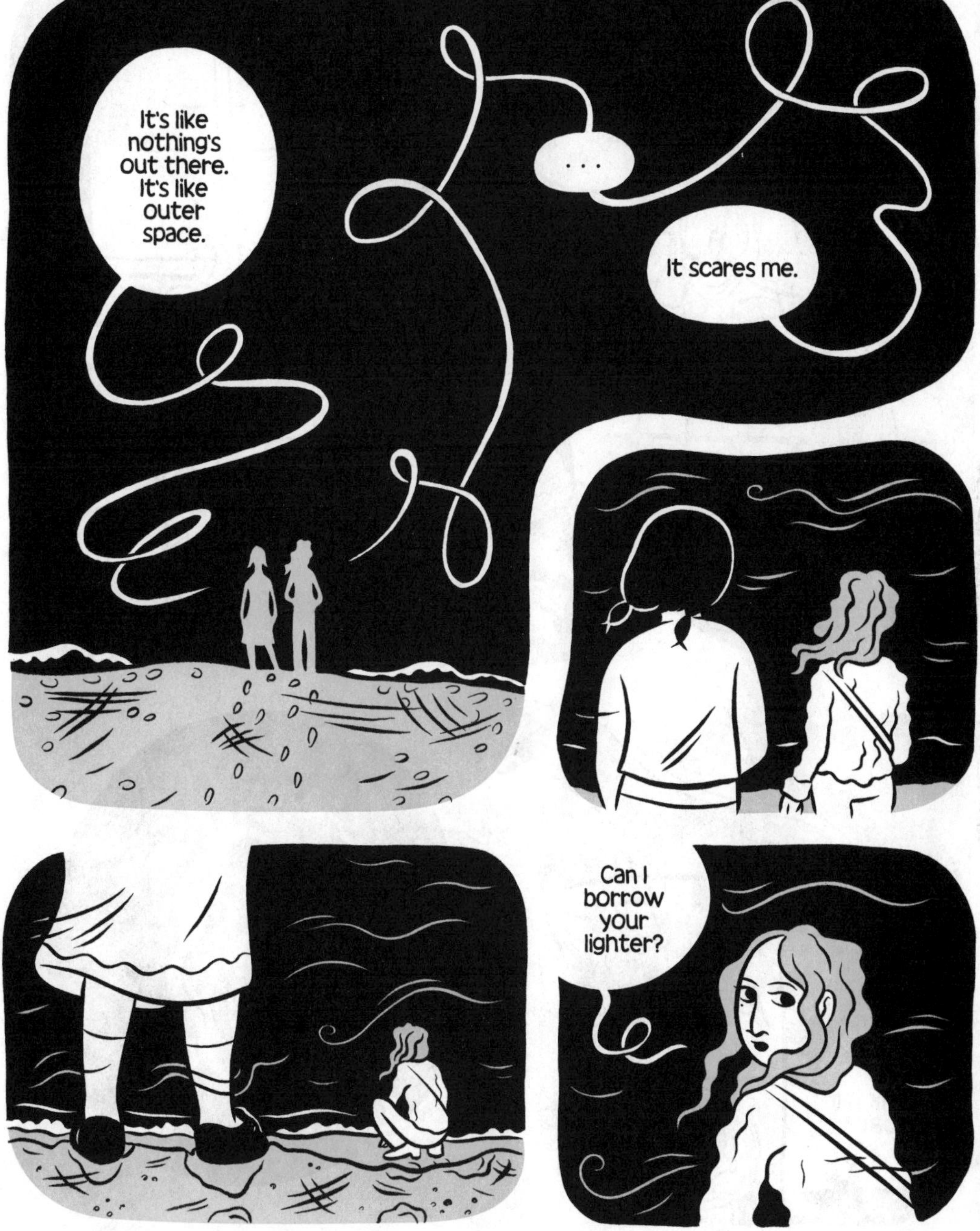
It's like nothing's out there. It's like outer space.
...
It scares me.
Can I borrow your lighter?

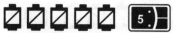

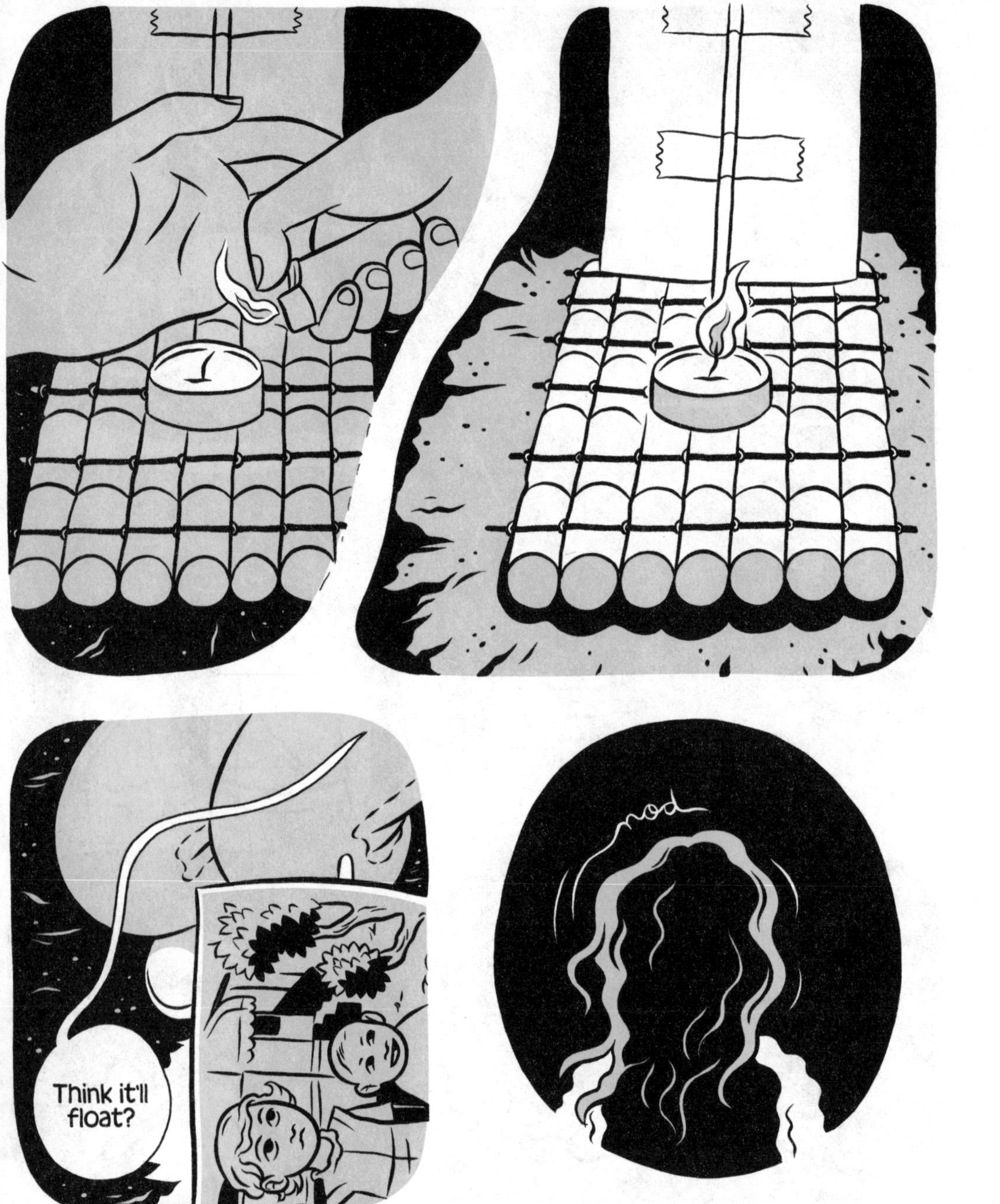
Think it'll float?
nod

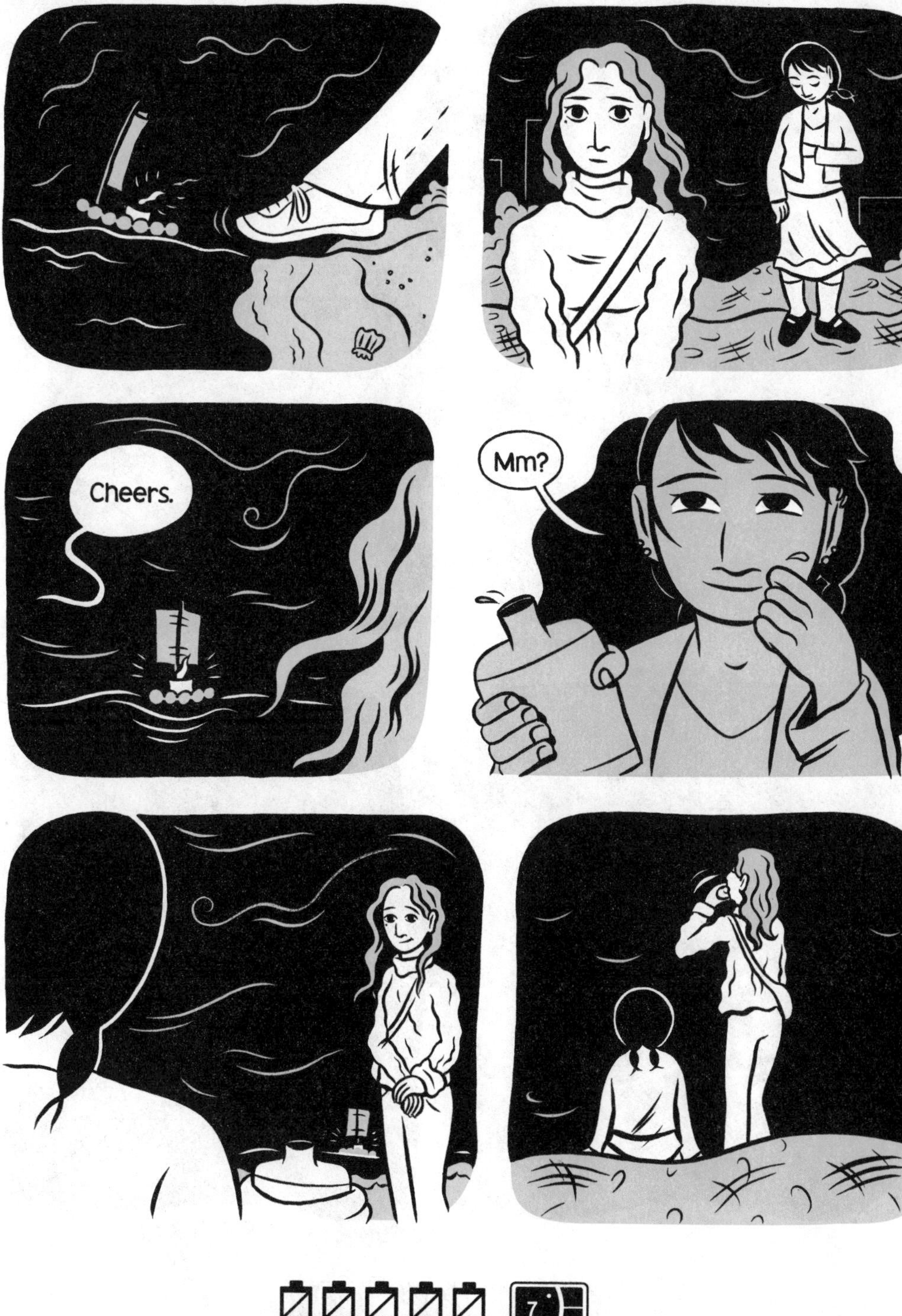
Cheers.
Mm?

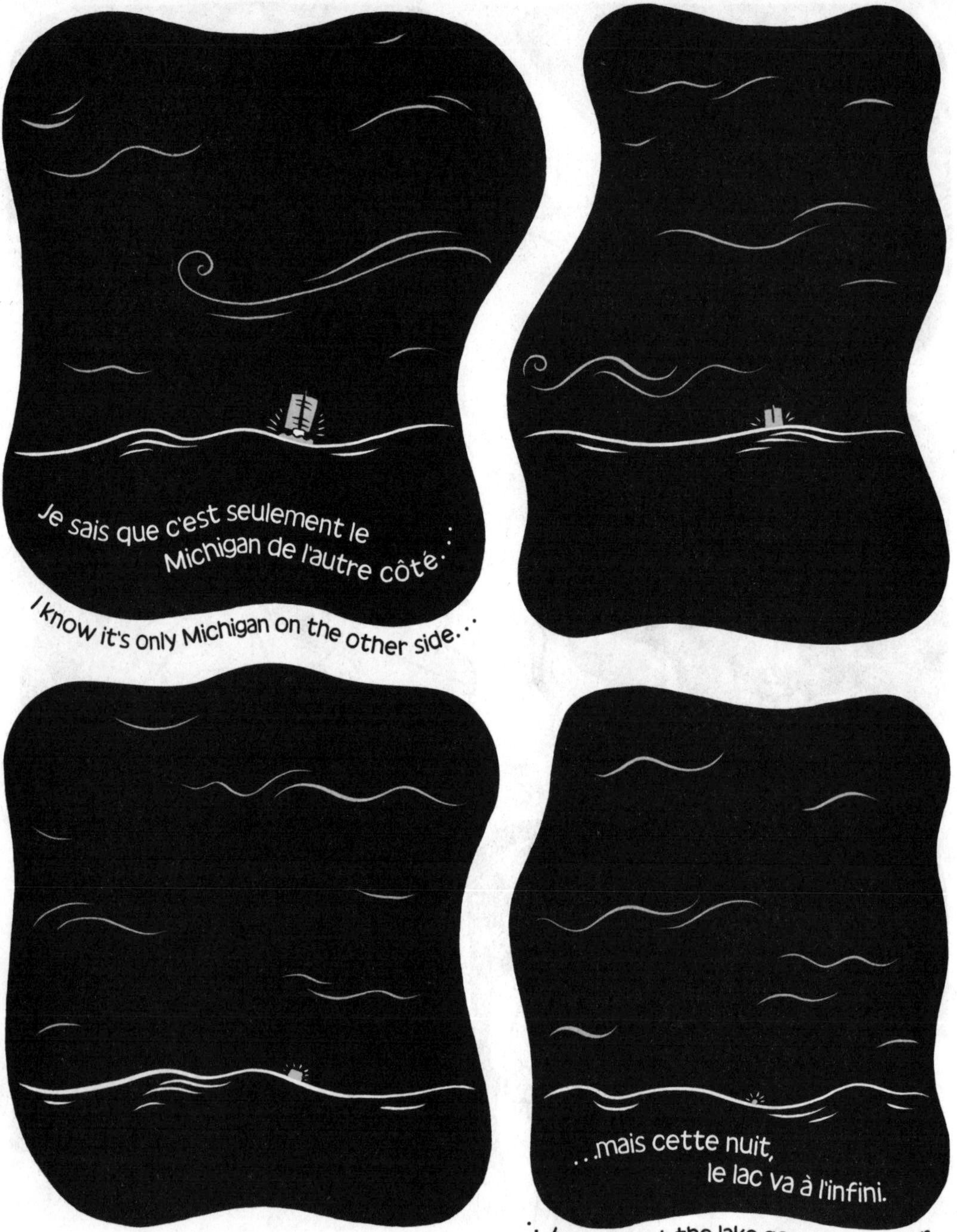
Je sais que c'est seulement le Michigan de l'autre côté. . .
I know it's only Michigan on the other side. . .
. . .mais cette nuit, le lac va à l'infini.
. . .but tonight the lake goes on forever.

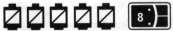

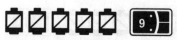

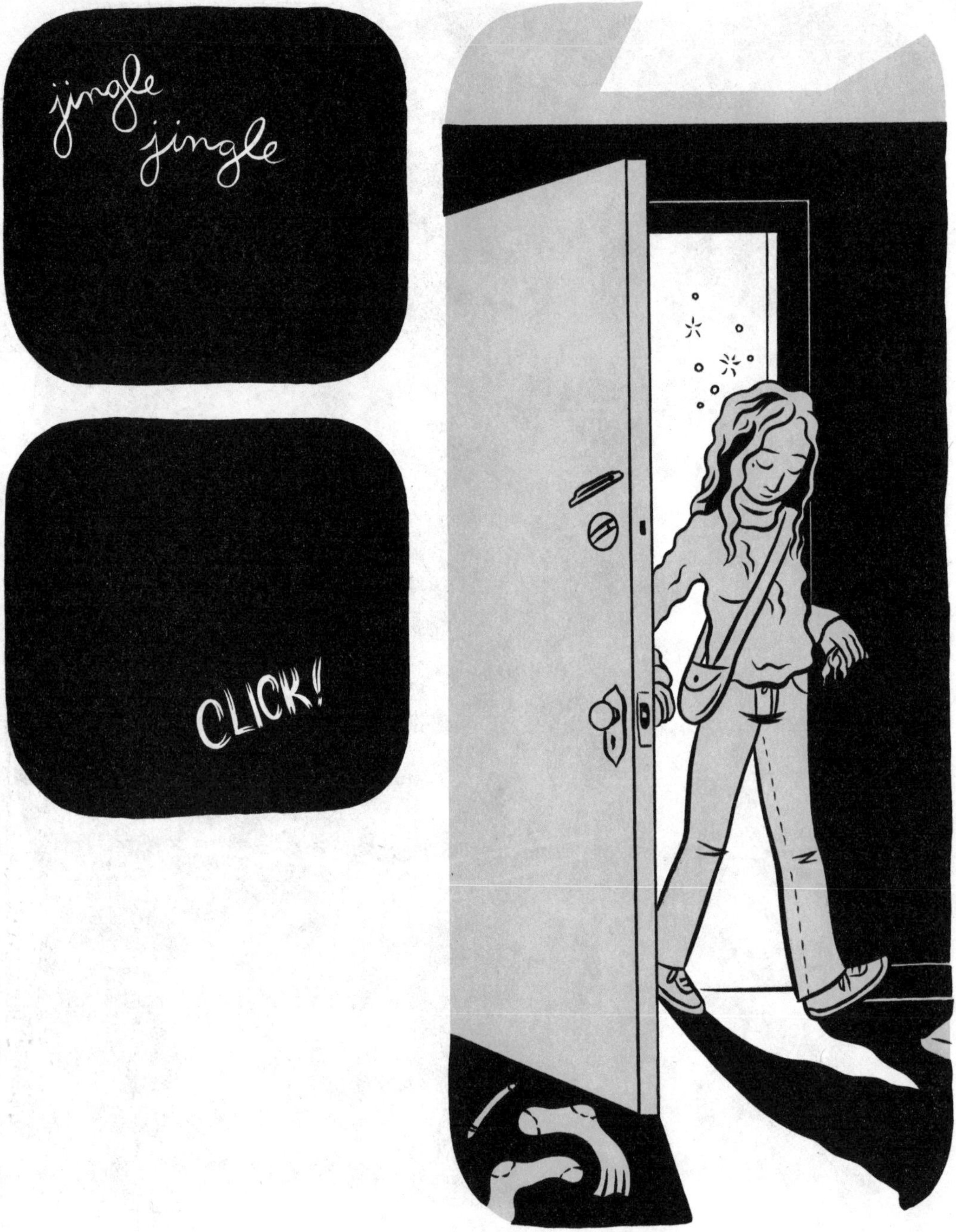
jingle
jingle
CLICK!

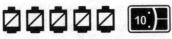

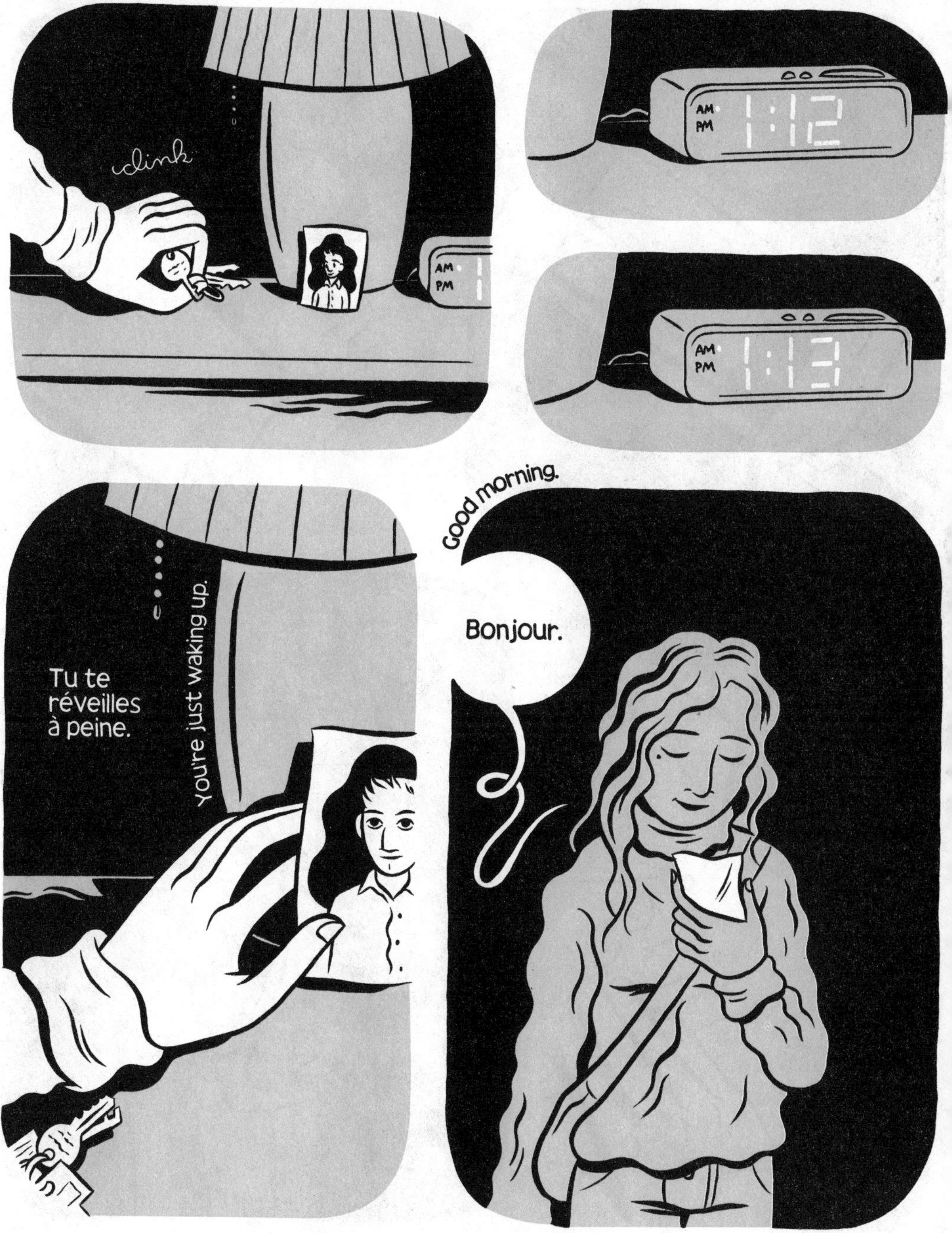
clink
AM
PM
AM
PM
1:12
AM
PM
1:13
Tu te réveilles à peine.
You're just waking up.
Good morning.
Bonjour.

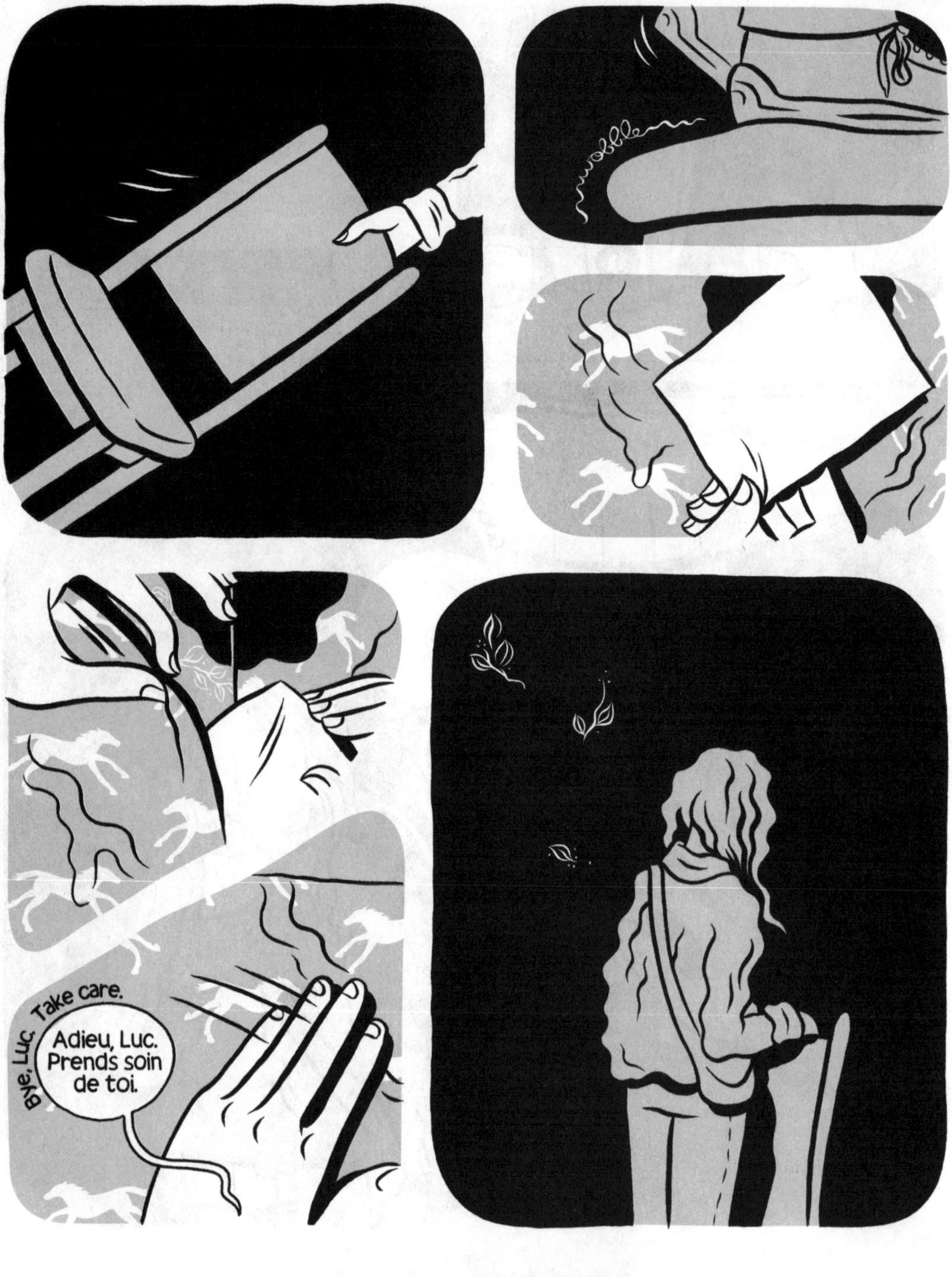
wobble
Adieu, Luc. Prends soin de toi.
Bye, Luc. Take care.

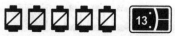

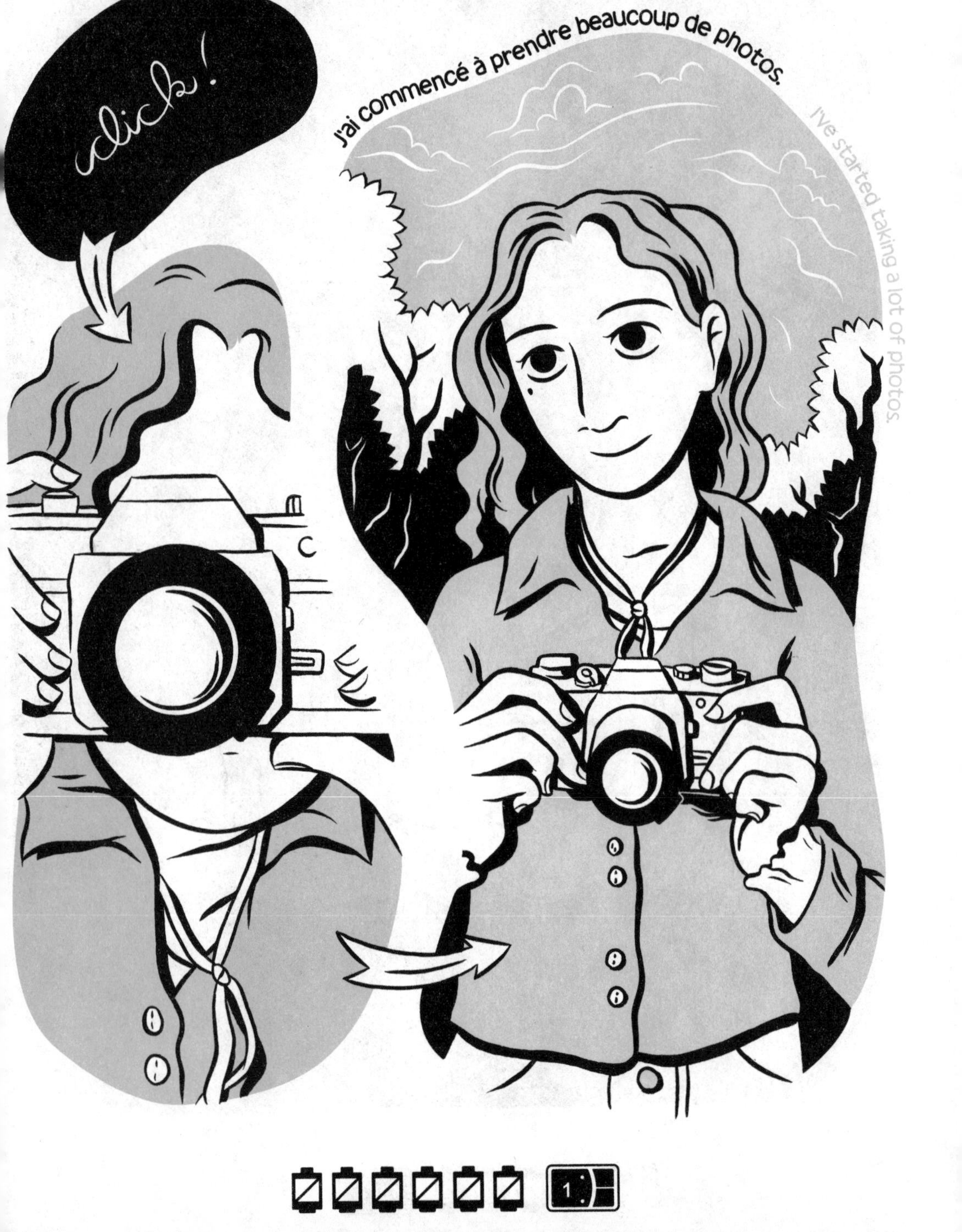
click!
j'ai commencé à prendre beaucoup de photos.
I've started taking a lot of photos.
1

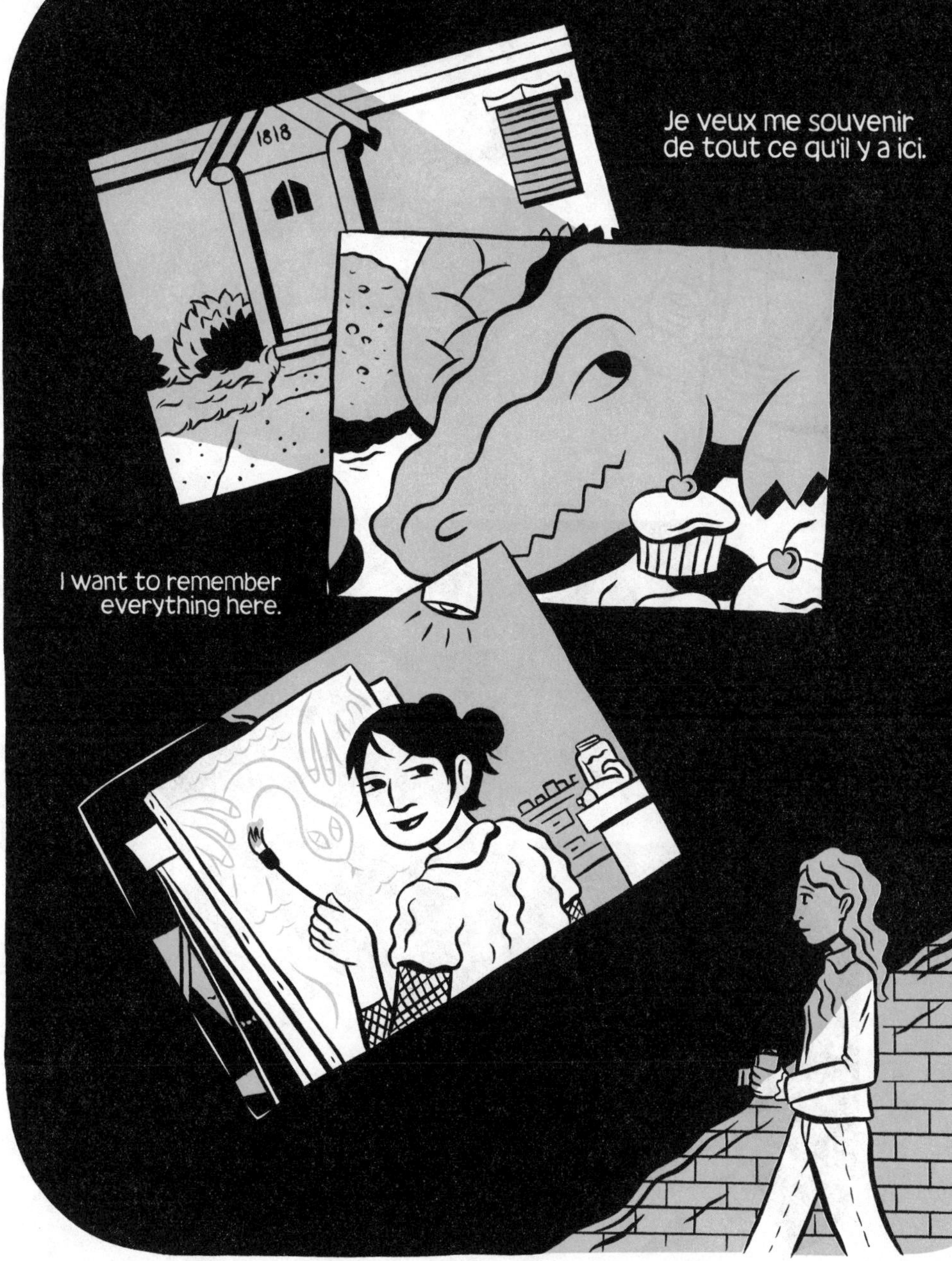
1818
Je veux me souvenir
de tout ce qu'il y a ici.
I want to remember
everything here.

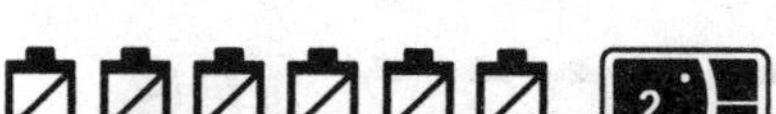
2

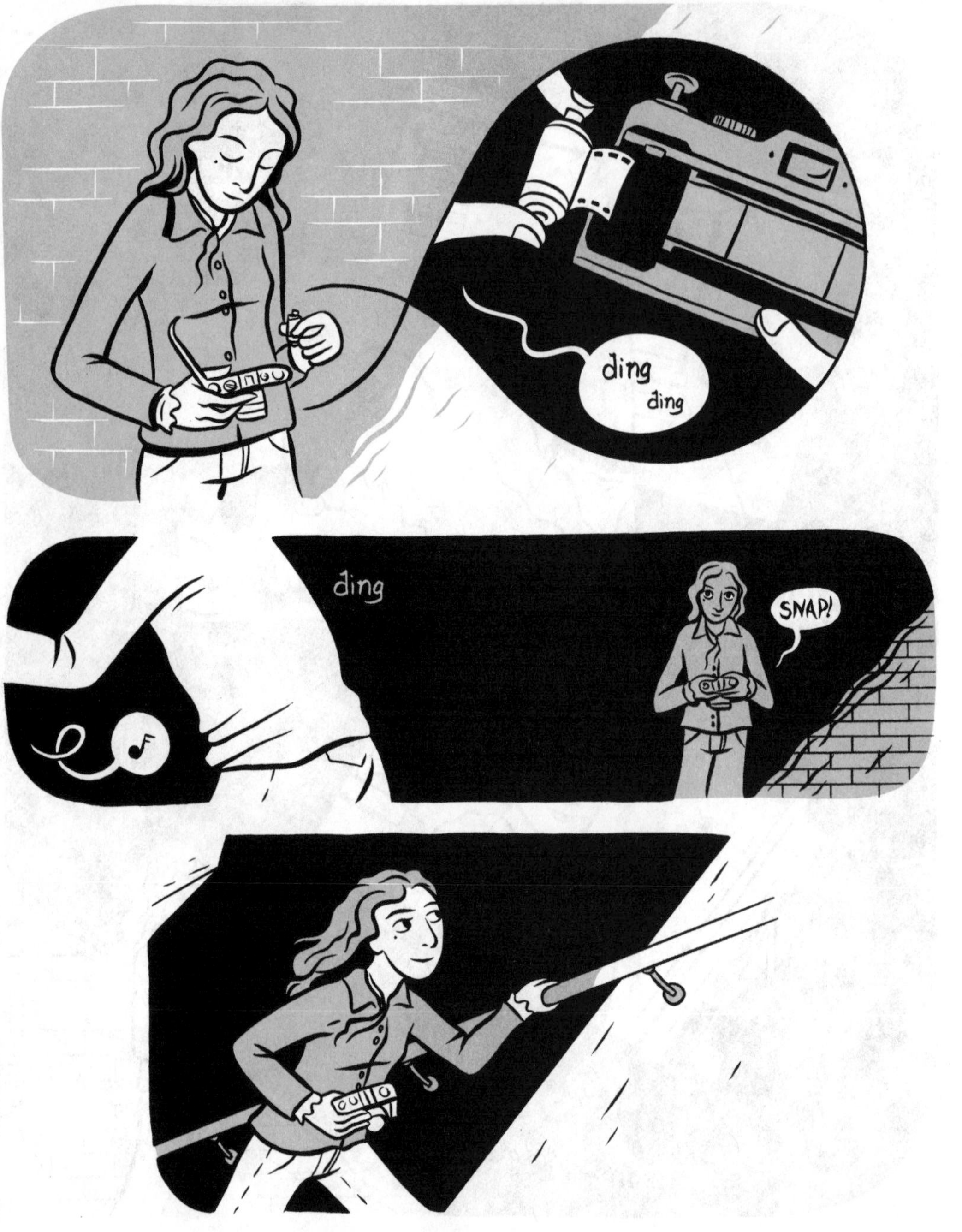
ding
ding
ding
SNAP!

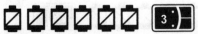

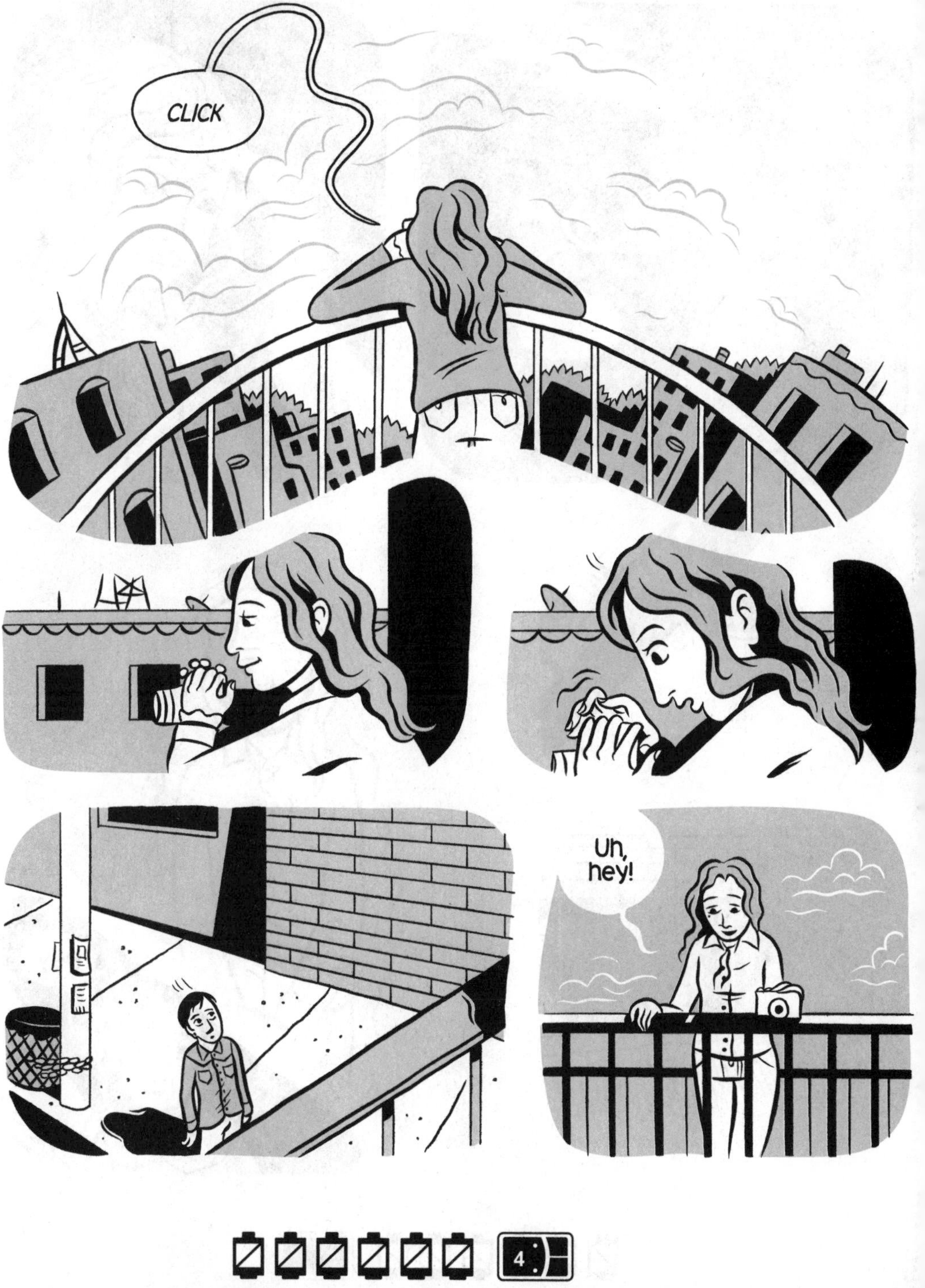
CLICK
Uh, hey!

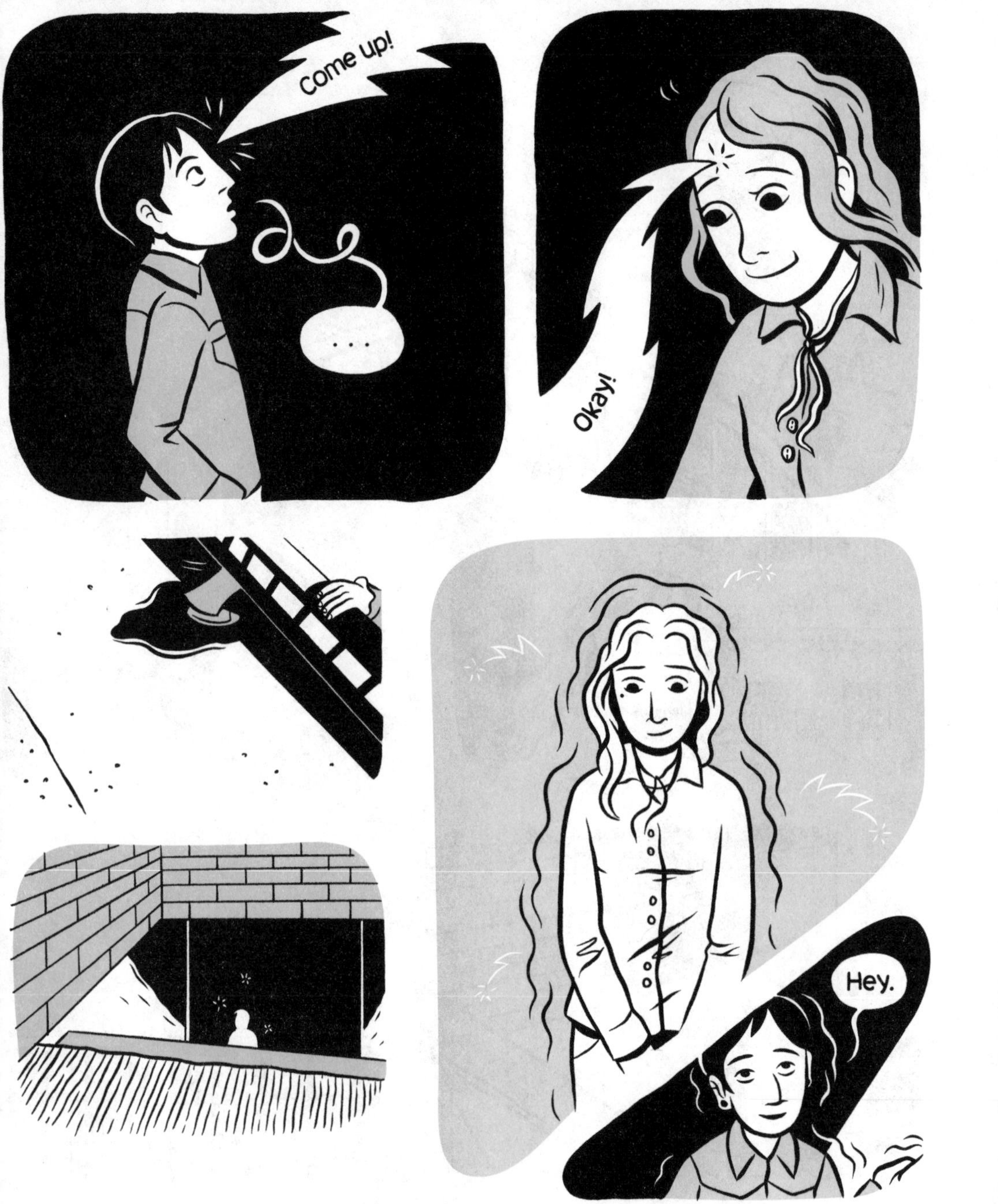
Come up!
. . . .
Okay!
Hey.

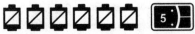

Je ne pars pas avant
un mois, mais ça me
manque déjà.

I'm not leaving for a
month, but I already
miss it.

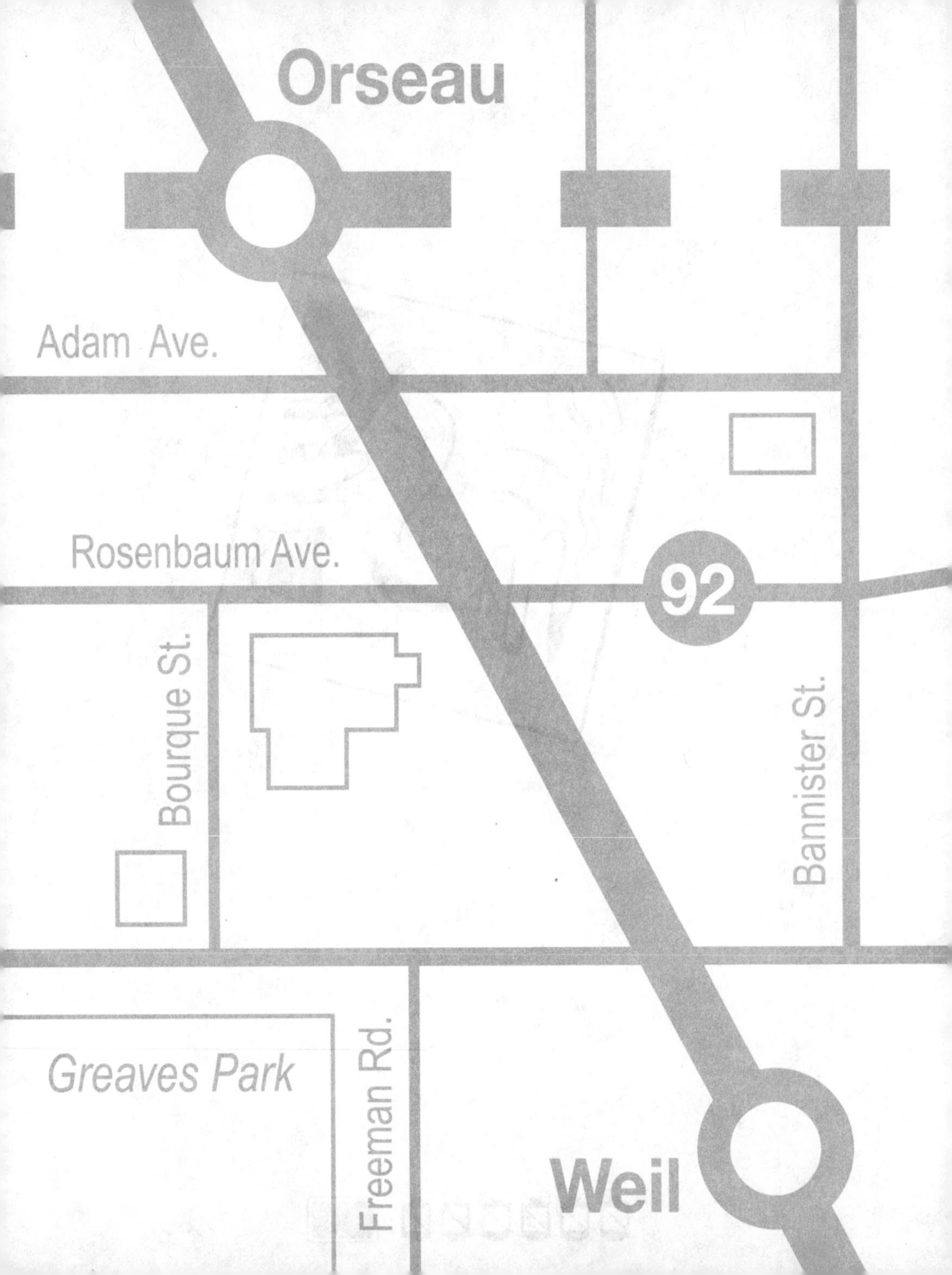
Orseau
Adam Ave.
Rosenbaum Ave.
92
Bourque St.
Bannister St.
Greaves Park
Freeman Rd.
Weil

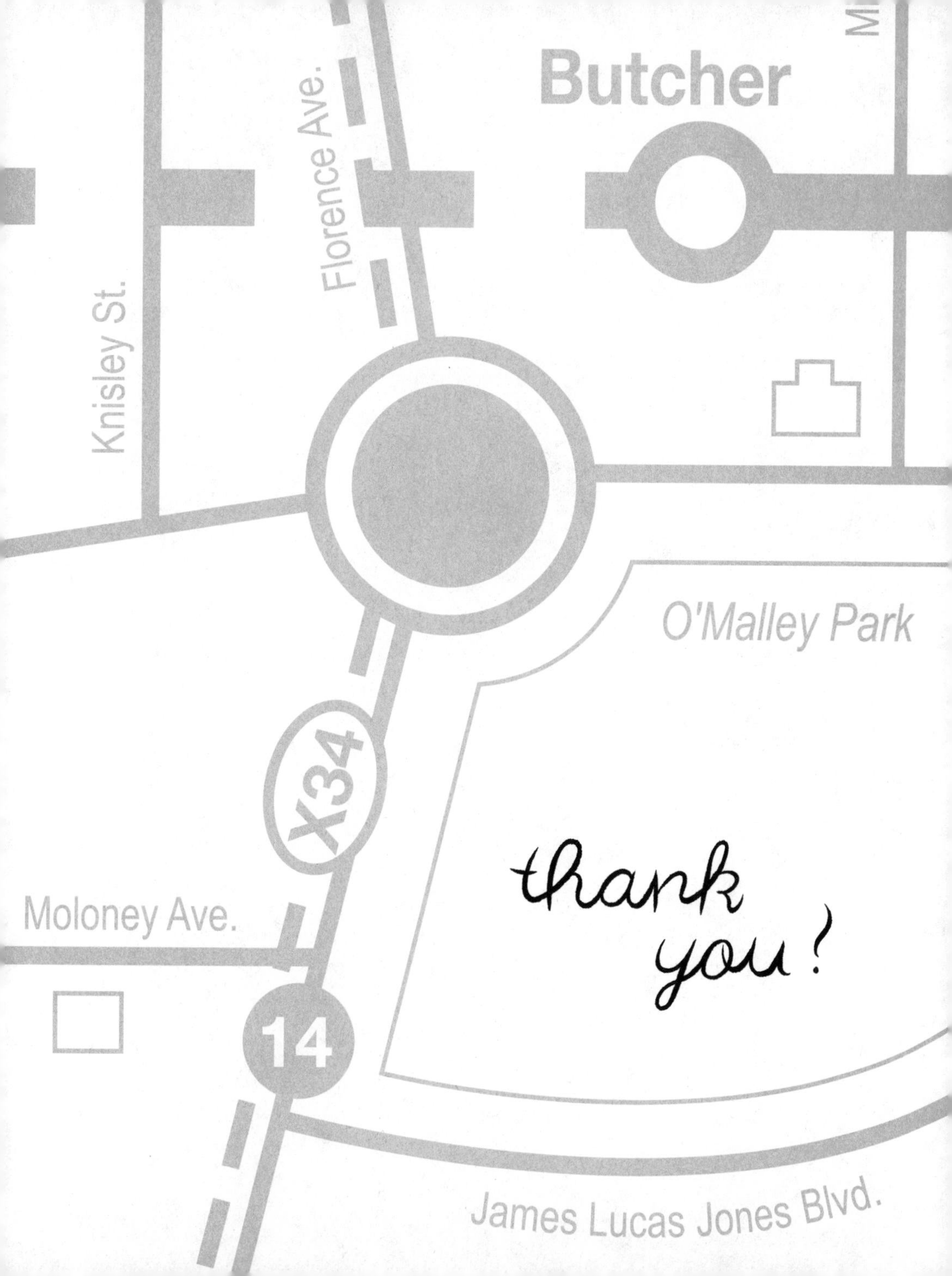
Butcher
Florence Ave.
Knisley St.
O'Malley Park
X34
Moloney Ave.
14
James Lucas Jones Blvd.
thank you!

Hope Larson grew up in Asheville, North Carolina and couldn't wait to escape north for college. She spent several years studying film and Illustration at the Rochester Institute of Technology before finding her niche in the printmaking department of the School of the Art Institute of Chicago. She graduated in 2004, moved to Toronto, and wrote her first book (Salamander Dream, AdHouse Books) while waiting to be approved as a permanent resident. She and her husband, cartoonist Bryan Lee O'Malley, now live with three cats in a little blue farmhouse near Halifax, Nova Scotia.